TRANSFORMED BY THE CLEANSING
BLOOD OF
JESUS CHRIST

TRANSFORMED BY THE CLEANSING
BLOOD OF
JESUS CHRIST
ALONE WHO IS THE GRACE OF GOD

GARFIELD CAMBRIDGE

Copyright © 2024 by Garfield Cambridge

All rights reserved. This book or any portion thereof may not be reproduced or used in any manner whatsoever without the express written permission of the publisher except for the use of brief quotation in a book review.

ISBN: 978-1-964462-25-7 Paperback
ISBN: 978-1-964462-38-7 Hardback
ISBN: 978-1-964462-26-4 Ebook

Rev. date: 06/04/2024

To my lovely wife, Natanya and to my children: Christopher, Tyana, Nathanael, and Neah. Besides God, who is in all my doings, they have been both inspirational and supportive of what God has gifted me to do in writing this book.

God has given them to me to bear out in me the characteristics of godliness. He has shown me through them His incredible forbearing love in my many experiences in this life. God has taught me through my family how to be patient, and I still have not gotten it all together yet, for God is still working with me on how to be compassionate in serving them in godly ways. I thank God so much for them.

I also dedicate this book to my mother and in the memory of my late dad, Walter F. Cambridge.

CONTENTS

Acknowledgments ix

Preface xiii

Chapter 1: The Holy Bible 1
  Understanding the Bible 4
  Prophecies that Jesus Made 15
  What God Created and Formed 17
  Principles of the Bible in Life Applications 19
  By Intelligent Design 24
  The Problem of Evolution Science 28
  What Happened? 32
  All Things Created Good by God 34
  The Bible Is a Book of Prophecies 36
  Denying the Bible Is Denying God 38

Chapter 2: Jesus: Your Savior—Who Is He? 42
  Jesus, God's Atonement for Sin 47
  Jesus, the Word Who Spoke in Creation 49
  Jesus Was Not the Result of Procreation 53
  Jesus Typed in Earthly Symbols 53
  The Godhead 54
  Christ, the Son of Man 58

Chapter 3: God, the Bible, and You 62

Chapter 4: God's Grace 67
  Type and Shadows of the Work of Christ 71

Chapter 5: God's Mercy to You...74
    Who We Are to God..93

Chapter 6: God's Forgiveness...103
    A Vessel of God's Love and Peace, Not a Vessel Bitterness and Unrest........105
    No Forgiveness, No Rest...107
    Forgiveness through Repentance....................................108
    The Love of God Forgives...113
    God Shows Us How to Forgive......................................114
    All Is Forgotten...123

Chapter 7: Faith to Believe...129
    The Palm Tree Christian..149

Chapter 8: God's Gift of Salvation..158
    We are to be watchful and stay soberminded.......................165

Chapter 9: We Are Baptized into Christ......................................172

Chapter 10: The Holy Spirit and You..180

About the Author...197

Acknowledgments

Without the help of Almighty God, I would not have had the focus and the discipline needed to write this book. It is God who has given me the opportunity to share with you who I have found Him to be. The book makes the point of who God is and the relationship between Himself and sinful mankind. My hope is that it will lead people who have not yet known the only God, the one who authored the Bible into the holy Scriptures, where they may find the truth of who they are and know that there is salvation in Jesus Christ.

This book was also written to help those of us who have already been given the gift of eternal life examine ourselves in the light of the Word of God. The hope is that God may open our spiritual eyes to see that we all need Him to help us to be more like He is. It is my hope that the reader who does not know Jesus Christ and what He can do for him or her may think seriously of the consequence of not heeding the call of God on his or her life. God wants you and everyone else to read His Holy Word so that in the Scriptures, you may find that they do testify of the Lord Jesus, who is the giver of salvation and the one who possesses eternal life, for He is the eternal God.

God has impressed upon my heart to use the gift of writing to share with you my understanding of what the Bible is talking about regarding the gospel of Jesus Christ, whose doctrine alone is taught in the Word of God. The gospel is the good news of God's remedy for sin through salvation (the covenantal relationship and interactions between God and mankind). My family has been a source of encouragement and incredibly supportive in the exercise of my faith to use this gift of writing to accomplish this book. If in everything in this life we would acknowledge God in all our ways and use the gifts we have been given in a manner that would benefit the body of Christ and glorify Him, He would direct our paths and bless our lives immensely with an Ephesians 3:20 blessing.

As a child of God, I have seen Him do many miraculous things for my family and me. He has given us His peace and has been nothing but gracious and merciful to us. When events in my life seem troubling and things seem impossible—to the point where I was consumed with worry—God was a present help in the time of my need. He can certainly be that present help in the time of your need if you would but allow Him to be your God and your Savior today.

God has made me understand that He has a better way and a better plan for my life during all the trials and tribulations that I am going through. No true child of God is ever alone in any trial, for God is with him or her unto the other side of that test. I once was blind, but God is still opening my eyes to see and behold the richness of His precious promises toward my family and me. When I was living my life recklessly, I did not hear the voice of God speaking to me, the words of forgiveness, mercy, and grace, for I was a lost person living in sin; but God, who is so rich in mercy, opened my hearing so I could hear and understand the melodies of salvation and the songs of redemption. To God be the glory for great things He has done for me and countless others, and surely He deserves our praise and worship.

Living God's way is infinitely much better than the life I had in the world. I am not saying that the new life in Christ is easy. In fact, the attacks from Satan become very intense when a person accepts Jesus Christ as their Savior and Lord. Therefore, it is challenging but not impossible to live as a true Christian because there is constant conflict from within (between the flesh with its cravings to sin and the born-again spirit that always wants to live under the whole armor of God) and from a world hostile to God. The apostle Paul, writing to the church in Galatia, says,

> I am crucified with Christ: nevertheless I live; yet not I, but Christ liveth in me: and the life which I now live in the flesh I live by the faith of the Son of God, who loved me, and gave himself for me. (Galatians 2:20)

And so life is worth living God's way, for whom the Son has set free is free indeed, and certainly that has been the true freedom I was searching for. I could not be free until the Lord called me and undid the anchors of iniquity that held me in bonds to do all manner of evil things. God has set my soul free from the chains of sin that imprisoned me in darkness. I know that in this world, my family and I will have trials, but God is greater than the adversary, Satan. He is better than any circumstance, and He is bigger than any problem that we will ever face in this life. However, He uses the difficulties of life to grow and strengthen my family's faith in Him.

We are ever leaning on God and trusting in Him for everything as we take it all to Him in prayer. God is my Creator, my Redeemer, my Sustainer, and the only one who waters me with His life-giving Word and speaks to me through His Holy Spirit. He is Alpha and Omega, the beginning and the last of all things, the only wise God, and besides Him, there is no other. Friend, let God do His perfect work in your life today.

PREFACE

The Bible, which is the Word of God, is probably the most misunderstood book on earth because of the claims it makes regarding God, who is holy, and about a wicked and sinful human race. Many people do not understand and are confused about that which is written in the Bible, including misunderstandings about who God is, the author of the Bible. Some people, when they read the Bible, find it to be contradictory, and they consider it to be out of touch with reality. The Bible is not, in any way, inconsistent, and it is every bit realistic at every level and stage of life. The misunderstandings of the Bible occur mainly because the people who consider it inconsistent and unrealistic are reading it without the Holy Spirit's leading, for it is He who must give the reader that studies the Bible the understanding of what it is saying to him or her.

There are also people in many parts of the world who think and believe that the Bible is too mysterious and that it is too hard to be understood. Yes, many things are mysterious and are hard to understand in the natural, and it is for this reason God gives those who believe and are baptized into Christ His Spirit so that He may teach them His Word that they might understand what the Bible is saying. There are others who have found the Bible to be an accurate description of who they are in the eyes of God. These people, who are some of us, have discovered, from reading the Bible, that they are indeed sinners and that they understand that they have a sin problem; and because of being confronted by God of the reality of their condition in sin, they find that there is a choice that they must make. These individuals must decide whether to seek the remedy the Bible declares is for sin or make excuses for their condition and continue in rebellion against the law of God.

Some who may have made comments about the Bible and its irrelevance to everyday life usually do not have a relationship with its author, the "I Am that I Am" God. There are also people who deny the relevance of the Word of God to all of life's issues. They reject the authority that God has over all things that exist, both on earth and the rest of the universe. If they believe that there is a god, he is not the God of the Bible but, rather, he is a concept which has been actualized with the wisdom of self or one who has been made by the hands of men.

Others may never have read the Word of God, but they make comments on the commentary others have made regarding the Bible. For the Bible-believing Christian, however, the God of the Bible is not made by men's hands but, rather, He is the Creator who made mankind, both male and female, with His own hands. God is not carried by His followers but, rather, it is He who takes His redeemed people through the courses of life in this world.

There are some people in this world who do not believe in God and creationism. They believe that all matter and all life are the results of a cosmic big bang. These people who reject the Bible's account of the history of the earth and the rest of the universe believe that complex life, as we know it, is the result of evolution occurring over millions or even billions of years.

One such person is noted molecular biologist and Nobel Prize winner Max Perutz, who said creationism is a demonstrably false theory. He concluded by saying, and I quote, "Even though we do not believe in God, we should try to live as though we did."[1] There is an apparent contradiction in this statement. One cannot advocate two opposing positions of belief without confusing oneself and his or her audience.

The Bible states this of some people in Isaiah 4:1:

> And in that day seven women shall take hold of one man, saying, we would eat our own bread, and wear our own apparel: only let us be called by thy name, to take away our reproach.

What the Bible is saying is that people will want to have the life as the children of God but then reject and deny the God of the Bible. We cannot have it both ways. It's either God or Satan whom we will serve in this life.

---

[1] Kam Patel, Perutz rubbishes Popper and Kuhn, The Times Higher Education Supplement, 25 November 1994.

Mark Twain, one of America's "great poets and humorists," was a well-known atheist who made many absurd comments regarding the Bible. One such comment he made regarding the Bible is

> The Bible has noble poetry in it; and some clever fables; and some blood-drenched history; and a wealth of obscenity; and upwards of a thousand lies.[2]

This was just one of many comments he made in his lifetime regarding God and the Bible.

Some book sales data sources estimate the Bible to be the number one best-selling book. One such source is Squidoo, which put the number of Bibles read at 3.9 billion.[3] If it is indeed the most-read book, far beyond its closest competition, Works of Mao Tse-Tung, at 890 million.[4] It seems that the power of God to rightly understand the Word of God, in which is written the testimony of Jesus Christ and all of who He is in relation to the deliverance of a spiritually dead human race from sin, is hidden from some of its readers, for they are unfamiliar with what the Bible teaches about God's relationship with mankind. This may be because many of these people read the Bible without the Holy Spirit of God leading them to understand what it says, or they read it to find points of arguments to substantiate their rebellion.

Nevertheless, there seem to be several reasons why some people do not believe the Bible for all what it says. One of the common reasons I hear people give for not believing the Bible is if God is good, why does He allow bad things to happen to innocent and to good people? The fact is some Christians, if asked this or any other questions of this type, may themselves not know the answer to such a question. They may not know because they have not studied the Bible sufficiently to be familiar with what it says about God and why bad things do happen to seemingly good or innocent people.

God is not the author of the destruction of innocent lives, but He is the Savior of anyone who calls upon the name of the Lord. Satan is the one who is responsible for the bad things that happen in this world, but God has control of all that he does; and even though terrible things

---

[2] Mark Twain, Letters from Earth.

[3] http://www.squidoo.com/mostreadbooks.

[4] http://www.squidoo.com/mostreadbooks.

happen to some of God's people, their lives are not lived in vain, and all the good works that they have done were not done in vain either. God will vindicate their innocence, and He will punish the guilty for their atrocities.

The chief architect of sin and its effects in this world is Satan, and he will be destroyed by God at the end and conclusion of this present world at the judgment of God; and according to the Bible, in Revelation 21:1, there will be a new heaven and a new earth, for the first heaven and first earth are passed away. Nothing from the first heaven and first earth will be in the new earth and the new heaven. Everything will pass away, but God's Word shall not pass away (Mark 13:31), and so I believe that will be the end of all those who were cast into the lake of fire and experience the second death. They will not exist anywhere in the universe.

Some people who identify themselves as Christians may be ignorant about who it is that's really and truly responsible for sowing problems into the lives of many people, or it may be that some of them have a wrong understanding of what the Bible teaches, and so they may share with others what they know and believe. Whatever confusion and/or unbelief people may have regarding the Bible, the fact is that it is a book that makes claims that it is the expressed revelation of God's love for a disobedient and rebellious human race. The Bible claims to be the inspired Word of God and that it is totally and absolutely true and trustworthy.

For the believer, who believes in the God of the Bible and who also believes everything that He says in it, no amount of argument and debate would cause him or her to believe otherwise about the Bible's absolute truthfulness. The Bible does declare the true nature of mankind and its relevance to the life of all men. Again, for the Bible-believing Christian, the Bible is the only reliable and trustworthy source of truth. It declares that God is the only—and I mean the only—standard bearer of what truth is. The Bible tells of the genesis of all things, and it tells of the end of this present world. It also says that every person is born, without exception, a sinner, and it talks about God's remedy for sin. The Bible is not to be feared, but it is to be read with an eye of faith, which is given by God to know the gospel of peace. God's truth can make you and your neighbor free from the prison of darkness and bring you into His marvelous light. Where there is light, there is no darkness, for God is the light of the world.

This book is written to introduce you, the reader, to the glorious gospel (good news) of peace found only in the Bible. The good news is that God

xvi

has made the only way possible for any human being to have salvation and eternal life from and in Him. The way to everlasting life with God is Jesus Christ. God did make the way to have eternal life with Himself so that mankind may not perish for their sins. It is God's will that mankind escapes His justice for sin, in the judgment, and live in eternity with Him.

> For the wages of sin is death, but the gift of God is eternal life through Jesus Christ. (Romans 6:23)

It is God in the person of the Lord Jesus Christ who took our sins upon Himself and bore the full wrath of God in His body on our behalf. Christ bore the justice of God for sin with His life instead of mankind being the ones who should have been punished, and the Bible says that He rose from the grave and became the receipt for our purchase from eternal destruction, which the law of God says must be the payment transaction for the atonement of sin.

The Bible is clear about what mankind must do to be saved (Acts 16:31–32). Just as mankind chose to disobey the commandments of God in the garden of Eden, he again must choose to accept or reject the gift of eternal life from God. Whatever his choice is, he will receive both the benefits and the rewards if he accepts salvation from God or receive the consequences of his decision if he rejects the gift of God.

God is the only source of the new life on earth. Jesus Christ is the door to eternal life with God. He is the gate through which mankind may go into the presence, beyond the veil of unbelief, to know God and have a tabernacle experience of worshiping his and her Creator. Called to be Chosen will point you to the Bible, which contains all the wonderful promises of God. Jesus Christ is the light of the world, and you can have the victory over sin in every area of your life today through Him.

You may agree with me that life has many daunting problems that many of us are unable to manage by ourselves just because they may be too difficult and too complicated. In some cases, life's problems are impossible to understand and work out on our own, and so you may be one of those people looking for answers to your questions.

You may be looking to change some things in your life, but you do not know what to do. I hope that by reading this book, you are led by the Spirit of God into the Word of God to know Christ as your Savior and Lord. I also pray that as you read the Word of God, you may find the God of the Bible to be your only source of help in the time of your need, and the greatest need that mankind has, whether they realize it or not, is to have peace with God\He is the only one who can turn your life around from where it is now to become His chosen son or daughter. I also hope that as you read the Bible, God may reveal who He is to you and that He also reveals His presence in your life so that by beholding the Word of truth, you become changed into the image of Jesus Christ.

As you read and study the Word of God, please know that there is an enemy that will seek to discourage you from seeking God and His truth, but what you must do always is to ask God to help you stand in the face of discouragement and protect you from the arsenals of Satan. God's Word continues to be my only source of the unending revelation of truth, and it has been the same to a countless number of faithful Christians.

God wants all mankind to know that He is not willing; it's not His will that any person should perish from His presence forever. The Scriptures says that God wishes that all may be saved from destruction in the final judgment. God wants every sinner to know Him as a kind and compassionate friend. God wants every person to experience the immense love He has for us. For God so loved the world that He gave His best Gift, Himself, in the person of Jesus Christ, as the atonement for the sins of mankind.

If you are skeptical about the Bible or are skeptical about Christianity because of the less-than-godly behavior of some "Christians," I invite you to taste and see for yourself if the Lord God would not be good to you.

Are you having any difficulty in your life? I am sure you are, for no one goes through life untouched by tribulations and trials. We must ask God to take us through life's difficulties. If you have a substance abuse problem or a problem with your finances, give it to God and, in faith, believe that He will make the impossible possible. If you are having problems with your health or problems with your school performance or problems in your home, read God's Word, and be encouraged. Ask Him to help you break every chain and see if He would not do it. I guarantee you—God will hear any sinner's cry for help. Just be patient for His answers, for God is also a teacher and a counselor. There is nothing too big or too difficult or too complicated for God to manage. If you put your trust in Him, He will totally take care of you.

There are many things God will teach you, and there are many life-changing lessons He will give you concerning the harsh realities of life.

He will give you counsels on how to manage the issues of life. We all have issues—but the issues do not have to have us. We must be aware of who it is that is behind the adversities of life. God is in control of everything that happens, but He is not the cause of evil and the calamities that do occur. Satan and mankind's rebellion to the Word of God are the causes of every evil act and tragedy that happens in our world.

We do not have to be fearful of the transformational work that God alone is able to do on the inside of our lives. The spirit of fear terrorizes its victims with torment, and it paralyzes them in chains of constant worry. We cannot remain dysfunctional in a chaotic environment. That is not God's best for His people. We must trust Him in everything by using the faith that He gives to everyone who diligently studies the Scriptures, and when our faith is exercised, it will lead you and me to believe that Christ is able to do exceedingly abundant, beyond what you or I or anyone else may think and ask of Him. There is nothing too hard for God to do for you and me. He will always point us to many of the Bible's examples of ordinary people who tasted the goodness of God for themselves and were changed from the inside out.

Do not be bothered about what other people may say of you. They do not know your struggles, and they do not understand your pain. They do not know that you are at your wits' end with some of life's difficulties and challenges. You may be at the bottom of everything, and the only direction left for you to go is up, but you cannot stand to run the race of faith and cross the finish line to victory because you are anchored to your problems. My friend, Jesus is the answer to all that you will ever need. Jesus Christ wants you to know Him, and He desires to undo the chains of disobedience that have kept you imprisoned in sin.

In the Bible, God invites every human being to come and reason together with Him, for thus He said,

> Come now, and let us reason together, saith the Lord: though your sins be as scarlet, they shall be as white as snow; though they be red like crimson, they shall be as wool. (Isaiah 1:18)

God has a standard that He wants us to live by, and He invites everyone to examine what He has to offer in exchange for the wages of sin. He is the only friend who will truly stay close by your side every day of your life, through thick and thin, all the way to victory on the road of life.

God is the ultimate object of perfection in the universe and beyond. He cannot be compared to anything or anyone anywhere in the universe and beyond. He is the solid rock. God is stable, unchangeable, and He is absolutely holy. There is no mark of error in Him. He is unshakable, steadfast, constant, and unmovable. God is all powerful, and He powers the universe and beyond with His power. His nature is an overflowing presence, and that is why the universe cannot contain Him, yet He is meek and lowly in heart. He is meek enough to have humbled Himself and became one of us so that He can be touched with who we are, sinners infected with the deadly virus of sin.

God is mankind's best and most dependable advocate. He is everything and more to us, way beyond whatever you and I can ever think of or ask of Him. Mankind's imagination cannot fathom the things God has in His storehouse for them. They are more than whatever this world can give you and me.

Give God your life, and see what happens. Let Him make you over into a new creature created in Christ Jesus. Watch God remake your life and see if He would not fix it better than you or anything or anyone in this world is able to do. God will totally remake you a new creation in Himself by way of a born-again spirit that is able to seek after Him, for mankind in their unsaved condition is spiritually dead and is incapable of seeking after God without His power (presence) in them. Your total makeover is from the inside out, and you are fit for His kingdom.

1

THE HOLY BIBLE

I hope that there is a reason beyond mere curiosity you may have for reading this book. Whatever the reason is that you may have for reading it, I hope that you are being led by the Holy Spirit into the Bible so that God can reveal Himself to you. You see, my friend, God already knew us way before we were born—He is our Creator—not our parents nor chance nor any other theory from the classroom of skeptical science; and so it is not that God does not know you and me, but He wants us to know who He is in the most intimate way, and when we open the shut doors of our lives and let the King of Glory come in, it will be an amazing experience of how different we will become. The change will be everlasting as long as we stick with God and don't give into the spirit of discouragement. I must also let you know this truth—that the process of transformation is not an easy one, but God's finished work in your life will be a wonder to behold, so start the journey with God and see what happens, for the life you have now has you stuck at a dead end.

It may be that God will answer the questions you may have about life and how you must live in this world. I really believe that reading this book will help you search the holy Scriptures, the Bible, for they do testify of Jesus Christ. It is also my hope that you may find, by faith, everything in the Bible to be true about you as a sinner. I hope that you may know that God so loved mankind that He was willing to come to this earth and save humanity from being destroyed forever. God came in the person of the Lord Jesus Christ to live as an example of obedience to the will of God. He came to show us how to live victoriously in every situation once we have received His salvation so that every human being might have life and have it more abundantly.

Jesus came to show mankind what true fellowship with God looks like—in that we don't have to sin and die the second death, which is total and eternal separation from God (be destroyed forever), but we can choose to have life in God and live in eternity with Him. Jesus Christ came as God's perfect sacrifice and was the atonement for sin once and for all. He bore the sins of all mankind to save sinners from the wages of sin, and therefore, whosoever may believe in Him may not perish but that they may receive salvation and have eternal life from God. Christ's purpose for coming to earth was not just to die for the sins of mankind, but His life on earth was to show humanity the way to have peace with God. Thus, there is the opportunity that is available from God to every human being to live a godly life and be at peace with his or her brother and sister. God will reveal Himself to anyone who has a sincere desire to seek Him as the Holy Spirit leads them to search Him out in the Scriptures. God will guide you and me to understand what is written in the Bible.

Many people who have read the Bible and have believed every Word, as the Spirit of God led them to truth, became the children of God, for they were washed clean from sin in the blood of Jesus Christ. It must be noted that it is not good to just believe that there is a God, the only God that is spoken of in the Bible. One must know Him by spending time searching the Scriptures daily with a sense of urgent diligence and with the spirit of patience so that the Spirit of God may guide you and me into all truth through understanding. The Bible says in Isaiah 55:6–7,

> Seek ye the Lord while he may be found, call ye upon him while he is near: Let the wicked forsake his way, and the unrighteous man his thoughts: and let him return unto the Lord, and he will have mercy upon him; and to our God, for he will abundantly pardon.

Whoever finds the Lord in His Word will have an encounter with Him that will change his or her life forever. God will let them know that the Bible has no ambivalences and that there are no contradictions in it. However, there are those who critique the Bible as having many contradictions, but it is very likely that they are reading it without the guide of the Holy Spirit of God, who is the only one that gives the understanding of the Bible to every person that asks God for His help. Some people believe that the Bible is a book of mythologies, written by the minds of creative thinkers, and so they say it is to be accepted and it is to be read as a book of fiction.

Many critics of the Bible look for discrepancies to show that the Word of God cannot be trusted. They highlight slight differences in the gospel writers' eyewitness accounts, within the four gospels of the New Testament. One of their most common arguments about the truthfulness and the reliability of the Bible is regarding the resurrection of Jesus Christ. These critics look for what they consider to be inconsistencies in the Word of God so that they may straw out a legitimate reason to reject God and His Word and reference it to be that of legendary myths.

These people do not refer to what the original Antioch, Syrian Bible manuscripts say regarding what they are critiquing. It is not that the Bible translation is not trustworthy, but it is always good to see the complete sense of what was written in the original tongues of these manuscripts. These people read the Bible with blinders on their hearts because they are not being led by the Holy Spirit. They usually are not searching the holy Scriptures to know God; however, He may lead some of them into a revelation that baffles their minds, and so they may in turn truly begin to search the Bible for more truth. The differences that these critics highlight of what they are looking at always have to do with the details these writers of the Bible paid attention to as God inspired them to write.

The Bible is a spiritual book, and it must be understood spiritually. There are things in the Bible that are to be understood spiritually. It is a book about you and the God that called you because He loves you so much, more than you will ever know and understand. I am aware that the critics of the Bible advertise their errors of what the Bible is not on the worldwide web, but pay no attention to the enemy's distractions that he uses to confuse and discourage the reader of the Bible. God will let you understand what He wants you to know if you are honestly searching for truth, but He must first kindle your spirit for the interest to occur for you to search out what the Word of God is all about.

The Bible claims to be the Word of God, and by staking this claim, the Bible simply but plainly declares that its divine authority is God Himself, who is completely infallible and who is absolutely truthful; and for the Christian, the Bible is the only book—the only source book—where anyone who is looking for truth may find it within the sacred pages of the holy Scriptures.

The Bible's authority is grounded in God Himself. We read in 1 Thessalonians 2:13,

> When ye received the Word of God which ye heard of us, ye received it not as the word of men, but as it is in truth, the Word of God, which effectually worketh also in you that believe.

What the apostle Paul is saying here is that the Bible, even though it was penned by men of God, its author is God. These men did not write the words that we read in the Bible of their own volition, but it was God who spoke to them directly into their hearts and minds what was to be written. The entire Bible was written by men who received the God-breathed Word. It is not the concoction of carnal-minded men.

Many archeological and paleontological findings have supported the Bible's account of mankind's existence in various cultural and historical settings. The Rosetta Stone is one piece of artifact that was discovered in 1978 near the Nile Delta area which described, in three types of writings, the decree of Ptolemy V, a Greek who reigned in Egypt in 196 BCE.

Another important and one of the greatest discoveries of historical and biblical significance was the Dead Sea Scrolls.

> These scrolls were found between 1947 and 1979 in eleven caves in and around the Wadi Qumran. This location is near the ruins of the ancient settlement of Khirbet Qumran, on the northwest shore of the Dead Sea, in the West Bank. The texts are of great religious and historical significance, as they include the only known surviving copies of the any Biblical documents made before 100 AD and contain preserved evidence of considerable diversity of belief, and practice of those who lived within the time period of the Second Temple in Judaism.[5]

It is amazing that God would preserve and then reveal these manuscripts of His Word in an unbelievable condition that bring to light the mysteries of ancient civilizations. Many of the archeological discoveries corroborates claims the Bible has made, of that which has been discovered, with accuracy and with details of specificity, the biblical account of mankind's existence. No other religion's holy book written has the support of archeological discoveries that supports, with accuracy, the way the Bible does.

Understanding the Bible

Understanding the Bible is not derived from the reason of mankind's mind. The Bible does not appeal to the limited and foolish reason of mankind, and it does not demand obedience because their reason sanctions its teachings.

---

[5] http://socyberty.com/history/archaeological-finds-with-great-significance-tomankind/#ixzz30iltcwls.

If it did, then notables like Stalin, Mao Tse-Tung, evolution scientists, and others who ridiculed the Bible with their sacrilegious clamor and with the spawn of Satan would have to be observed as mightier thinkers than God. The Bible's authority is God, and it is not rational to the senses of any human being although all who believe the Bible believe it to be reasonable because it is the Word of Him who is the source of all rational reasoning, wisdom, and knowledge, for God is He who said in Isaiah 1:18,

"Come now, and let us reason together," saith the Lord.

Our reason needs to be approved by the Word of God and not the Word of God to be approved by our reason.

The Bible, as it bears the standard of truth, is not derived from the church. The church, however, is the body of Christ, made up of true believers. It is God who created the church and formed it from within Himself, and its members are the true believers, who are members of the body of Jesus Christ.

People are reformed from a way of life in sin to a life of righteousness by God's hands and then are birthed in Christ, who is the Creator of all mankind. He breathes the breath of life into spiritually dead men, male and female, old and young, the blind and the deaf, the dumb, the illiterate and the learned, the wise and the foolish, the simple-minded and the profound, the rich and the poor, the haves and the have-nots. It makes no difference to God, for all men are spiritually dead without Him; and when mankind died spiritually, they were all cut off from the life-giving relationship they had with God. All the people whom God has called to be His chosen people are also made alive in Christ because of the mercy and grace of Almighty God.

The Bible does not appeal to any church denomination, and it does not demand obedience because the church decrees its teachings. Its authority is God and not the church, and thus, it's not papal. The Word of God is not subject to the will of any church. It stands alone as the only trustworthy guide for mankind to follow because it is the holy Word of truth that changes unbelievers into believers. It is God who causes the Bible to change the skeptic into a defender of the gospel and fools into wise men. The Bible speaks of the peace that God forms with people who are haters, by nature, of the Word of God. He forms relationships with them through Jesus Christ because He is the only source of the New Life that spiritually dead mankind can receive from God. No person can have the peace of God without first having peace with God.

The church needs to be approved by the Bible and not the Bible by the church. The Bible claims that the gospel of Jesus Christ is the inspiration of God, and thus, every Word of it is true, for they came forth from the infinite all-knowing mind and mouth of the Creator of the universe. Because God is truthful and cannot lie, the Bible is absolutely credible and can be trusted for what it says, and it would not mislead anyone, for we read in Galatians 1:8–9,

> But though we, or an angel from heaven, preach any other gospel unto you than that which we have preached unto you, let him be accursed. As we said before, so say I now again, "If any man preach any other gospel unto you than that ye have received, let him be accursed."

The Bible is the only religious book that says within its pages that it was written by the inspiration of God, given to holy men, forty to be exact—thirty devout but ordinary godly men in the Old Testament and ten devout but ordinary godly men in the New Testament over a period of approximately fifteen hundred years. Everyone who reads and studies the Word of God can be guided by it into answers regarding the issues of life. What we receive in a dream or in a vision or what we hear in our spirit must be consistent with what the Word of God says. Again, and as always, we must check all things out and examine every conclusion we come to with the Scriptures.

Acts 17:11 says,

> In that they received the word with all readiness of mind, and searched the scriptures daily, whether those things were so.

For if anyone speaks concerning what they have received or heard from God, what they say must be of God, and it must line up with His Word. This we read in Isaiah 8:20 and in 1 Peter 4:11.

We also read in 2 Timothy 4:16–17,

> All scripture is given by inspiration of God, and is profitable for doctrine, for reproof, for correction, for instruction in righteousness: That the man of God may be perfect, thoroughly furnished unto all good works.

That means if anyone should teach a Christian doctrine, it must be the doctrine that is outlined in the Bible and not anyone's private interpretation. The doctrine must be Holy Spirit led, and it must line up with the rest of the Word of God.

The holy Scriptures are able to comment and make criticisms on all human behaviors and lifestyles. God has explicitly written in the Bible (Deuteronomy 8, 28, and 29 for example) His law of righteousness so that everyone who obey His commandments may live, and those who reject His love for them have indeed accepted the rule of the adversary of God, Satan, to be the ruling authority over their lives. In this world—that is, in this life—we can only serve one of the two powers: God or Satan. It is either the power of righteousness or the power of lies and evil.

The law of God, which is the expressed character of God, is sufficient and is well able to point out our wrong behaviors and our sinful lifestyles. The law will point us to God, who alone is able to teach us the ways of righteousness, and it is Jesus alone who is able to deliver the unsaved from sin and save us from its wages.

The Scriptures will point every sinner, living in sin and who is in rebellion against God, to Jesus Christ. If anyone is a liar, the Bible says that he is not to lie, but he is to always tell the truth, for lying is sin (Exodus 20:16 and 1 Corinthians 6:9–10). If a person is an adulterer, the Scriptures command him or her not to commit adultery, for God says it is sin (Exodus 20:14, Matthew 5:27–28, and 1 Corinthians 6:9).

If any man has made any other thing to be an image of worship, God says that we are not to have any other gods before Him (Exodus 20:4–5). The Bible says idol worship is an abomination to God. All these examples noted are written in the law of God and were spoken by God in the hearing of Moses (Exodus 20) and were written again by the finger of God on two tablets of stone as we read in Exodus 31:18. Everything God has called sin in the Bible we are not to do, and everything He says in the Bible we are to observe and do, we are to observe and do with absolutely no exceptions.

God reveals to us in our spirit, through His written Word, by the convictions of the Holy Spirit, the knowledge of everything that is right to do and everything that is not right to do. The Bible is able to make us wise unto what salvation is, and when we do not understand what God is saying in His Word, we are to ask Him for the understanding that only He can give through the help of the Holy Spirit.

Jesus said in Luke 11:9–10,

> And I say unto you, "Ask, and it shall be given you: seek, and ye shall find; Knock, and it shall be opened unto you. For every one that asketh receiveth; and he that seeketh findeth; and to him that knocketh it shall be opened."

God will open the treasures of His Word and reveal His will for our lives to anyone who would diligently seek Him, and thus, the Scriptures were written and are given to a lost human race so that all may know, through faith, who Jesus is, for we read in John 20:31,

> But these are written, that ye might believe that Jesus is the Christ, the Son of God; and that believing ye might have life through His name.

The Bible also says in Proverbs 4 that the children of God are to hear the instructions of the Lord and attend to His voice to know understanding, for God is He who gives sound doctrine, and we are not to forsake His law. God wants us to retain His Word in our hearts and keep His commandments and live. In our pursuits, we are to get wisdom and get understanding from the Lord, and we are not to forget it, and neither are we to let the Word of God be removed from our mouth.

The children of God are not to forsake His Word, for it shall preserve them, and they are to love it, for it shall keep them from evil. When God's people embrace and exalt the Word of God, it shall promote them to be honorable and righteous among the children of men.

The Word of God shall give to the head of the righteous an ornament of grace, and a crown of glory shall the Word of God deliver to them. The Word of God shall teach the children of the Almighty to avoid evil, pass not by it, turn away from it, and pass on the other side of temptation. The instructions of the Lord are to remain in the heart of every child of God, for it is life to them.

God leaves no person in the dark with regards to his or her sin and with regards to the remedy for it. The Bible contains all that God would do for anyone who seeks Him diligently. God is holy, and He requires everyone who is called by Jesus's name to be holy in their manner of living if they are to be called by His name. God will help us to be a holy people if we would seek Him (1 Peter 1:13–17).

Living God's way through Christ will change your life forever; that is, His Spirit is He who quickens our spirit such that we are made spiritually alive in Him. God's Word will transform you by the renewing of your mind, and by beholding the righteousness of God, you become changed into the image (the attitudes and character habits) of Jesus Christ; and because of your transformation, you will have a new standard—the standard of the Word of God—to live by; and according to 1 Peter 1:13–16, we are to gird up (tighten with pure and holy thoughts) the loins of our mind, be sober, and be hopeful to the end for the grace that is to be brought unto all who are God's obedient believers at the second advent of Jesus Christ.

Because God is holy, He has commanded all who are transformed from the darkness of sin into the light and image of Jesus Christ to also be holy, for holiness is a way of life; and unless you and I turn from the truth that God has led us to know and believe to serve sin again, our soul shall be preserved until the appearing of Jesus Christ. God has not lost anyone, but instead, it is mankind who has done foolishly and separated themselves from their Creator. It is we who have sinned by disobeying the commands God gave us to do.

The Bible says in Psalms 19 that the law of the Lord is perfect, converting the soul; the testimony of the Lord is sure, making the humble to be wise. God says that His statutes are right, making the heart of the child of God rejoice, and His commandment is pure, enlightening the eyes of faithful men and women. The law of the Lord is to be desired more than that of pure gold. The servants of God are warned of sin by His law, and they that keep them, there is great reward—the reward of living right in the presence of God.

Friend, why not obey the Word of God and do good? He sees everything that we do—the good and the bad, right, and wrong. Nothing is hidden from Him; they are all naked in His presence. We cannot cover up nor disguise our thoughts, our actions, and our motives. What we do, God knows way before we do them.

So many people over the centuries, including politicians, kings, princes, philosophers, poets, the wealthy, the powerful and the influential, and the ordinary man, who oppose the Word of God, hated the truth that God has said in the Bible about the nature of all mankind. When humanity wanted to continue living immoral lives, they attack the Bible's credibility, and they attack its author. They accuse those who believe the

Word of God as being simple-minded or brainless only because the Bible contains the standard for godliness, and it opposes the sinful ways of mankind, which these people diligently sought to embrace.

In the Bible, God defines what sin is, and He commands that all men conduct themselves in godly ways. The Bible has been insulted by the scorn of nonbelievers who are ignorant of its author. The Bible has become the jest of carnal-minded men and the joke of skeptics. It has been assaulted consistently and persistently by professed atheists and has been mocked by its critics as "foolishness." Those who do not believe say that the God of the Bible is the invention of men.

Attacked by every known plan of hell, yet the Word of God has come forth untouched by every fire set against it from the host of hell. Like the three Hebrew young men, the Bible and many of its believers have been in the line of fire from the tongues of foolish men; and like these young men, the Word of God has been wonderfully preserved, and the faith of God's true children was never shaken by the powerless and cowardly words of evil men.

No evil plan and no evil work can prevail against the Holy Word of Almighty God, no matter how diligently those that oppose it may try, for God has and will continue to preserve His name and preserve the integrity of the Bible. For me and for a countless number of other Christians whose lives have been changed by the Word of God, the Bible has proven to be 100 percent accurate about the sinful nature of all mankind.

Who can know more than God regarding the true nature of mankind than the Creator Himself? Based on what the entire Bible has said about who God is, a conclusion can be made that there is no created being who has a fraction of the infinite knowledge, wisdom, and power of Almighty God. God is He who reveals the weakness and the ignorance of every human being (Job 40–41).

The fact is it is Satan who is behind the attacks on the Bible, and it is he who is the source of the charge to destroy the Word of God and to destroy the people of God; but he cannot win because he was defeated by Jesus Christ, and his end has already been determined. He is powerless, and his rulership over the true children of God ends when Christ delivers those who responds to the call of God from darkness into the brightness of His presence. Satan's influence is over those who remain in rebellion against God and are the followers of his doctrine of lies.

The Bible is not a book to be read casually. One must be immersed in the Scriptures with a persistent and consistent attitude. That person must have a hungry and a thirsty appetite for God and His Word. This can only come by setting our affections on things above, not on things on earth (Colossians 3:2). The Bible says in several places that the child of God must search and study the Scriptures diligently (Deuteronomy 11, Proverbs 6, Joshua 1, Psalms 1, Isaiah 28, to name a few). The Bible also say in 2 Timothy 2:15 to study to show oneself approved, a workman rightly dividing the Word of truth. Thus, all explanations and understanding of the Bible come by the Holy Spirit, who leads humble-minded and obedient men and women into the right meaning of Scripture. God, through His Spirit, is the only source we can go to for interpretation, and He is the only source for understanding the Bible.

Finite minds are unable to comprehend the things that are from the infinite mind of God. Human reasoning is insufficient in guiding the reader to understand the truth of God's Word, and so for those who believe the law of God that is written in the Bible is right altogether, then God is their authority of how they should live. These Christians also believe that the Bible is God's reference bearer for testing truth.

From the Word of God, we know that His truth is not relative, but it is absolute. The children of God believe that the account the Bible gives regarding the history of mankind is truthful and accurate. Many of the secular historical evidence information surrounding ancient and lost civilizations corroborates the biblical account of what once existed. Some ancient artifacts and remnants of lost and bygone eras remain intact to this day.

God has made it very clear in the Bible that He is its author and that the Bible was written by Him with the pen of His tongue and scrolled by the hands of God-fearing men. God's name and His character are in everything that He says. Mankind cannot rightly interpret the Bible; only God can correctly interpret His Word for whoever He is drawing to Himself, for He is its author, and He is the source of truth. It is God who has written the Bible so that it interprets itself, and it is God who gives understanding to the reader of His Word. The Bible does not need any source outside of itself for its interpretation, and it does not need any correction because God cannot be corrected. He is inerrant.

If mankind disagrees with the Word of God so that his and her conclusions of the Bible are always wrong, and they stand not to be corrected by the teaching of the Holy Spirit, it is evident that they are in rebellion against God and not in rebellion against the church. The church, if it believes the whole counsel of God, is to be the witness and the messenger of the gospel. It is not the source of truth. God is the only source of truth.

Everything God says has spiritual and moral application to all mankind, whether they believe it or not. We can trust God and His Word because there is no untruthfulness in Him. Everything a man does, his actions have consequences if they are wrong, or he receives the blessings of God if his actions are consistent with the commandments (Word) of God. The just are the people who God have declared righteous, and they live by faith in Him through His Word. These people live in obedience to every command of God; that is, these people do the word that they say they believe.

The walk with God is an experience in practical Christian living. If we say we have faith in God, then our works should follow after doing all that He says we are to do. If any of us is ignorant of who God is and what His Word says, the Spirit of God will lead us to hear and know the truth of how we must live.

God will not leave any human being in ignorance of who He is and what His Word teaches about sin and salvation. He has, in Matthew 28, commanded that the gospel must be preached to all men as a witness. God will not judge any man who does not yet know who He is, and He will not judge anyone who has not yet heard the gospel. However, God has said that the gospel will be preached to the entire world. People in every corner of the earth will be given the opportunity to repent of their sins and the opportunity to receive salvation through the blood of Jesus Christ.

The gospel of Christ will reach every ear and every heart because God will make sure it happens. It is only the lying lips of a dishonest heart that will seek to deny God's many attempts to save him from destruction, but God will show, when the books of heaven are open, the evidence of His diligent attempts to wrestle mankind away from the attachment they had to sin but who chose to remain in rebellion to His commandments and elected to continue in sin. We are the ones who write in the books of heaven, by our own actions, the things that we do in rebellion against God and what we do in obedience to His Word.

The Bible is very clear that no person who refuses salvation and chooses to remain wearing the garments of unrighteousness will be excused from the judgment of God. That person has deliberately refused to know the Word of God, which convicts all people of the need to be born of the Spirit of God and the water of His Word; and before God concludes this world and before His judgment begins, He has said that His gospel will be preached to all nations. When that time for God's judgment comes, no one will be able to wave the flag of ignorance regarding the contents of God's Word, the Bible, for the Bible says,

> As it is written, as the Lord lives, every knee shall bow to Him and every tongue shall confess to God and all men, that is, those with religion and those without religion, shall have to give account of themselves to God of the works they did do, that were ungodly. (Romans 14:11–12)

The true people of God believe that every claim in the Bible can absolutely be trusted for its accuracy and its truthfulness. They believe that some things are to be understood literally, and some other things are to be understood figuratively, but it is God who makes the distinction between literal and figurative applications through the teaching and revelations of the Holy Spirit. It is He that gives us the understanding of all that He wants us to know and in what way, literal or figurative, the things in the Bible are to be understood.

The children of God believe what the Bible says about its author, that He is the God that cannot lie. God is not the author of confusion (1 Corinthians 14:33). The Bible states in Numbers 23:19 that

> God is not a man, that he should lie; neither the son of man that he should repent: hath he said, and shall he not do it? Or hath he spoken, and shall he not make it good?

The Word of God is to be studied and must be rightly divided by its reader (2 Timothy 2:15). The Holy Spirit, whom we will talk about in a later chapter, is given to help us understand the Word of God. He is our teacher, and it is He who will bring back to our memory everything He Himself has taught us from the Word of God.

To you, the reader, if Jesus Christ is not your Savior and Lord or if you have not yet known who He is, I invite you to ask God to guide you into seeking who He is through the reading of His Word, the Bible. I pray that you will find out who Jesus Christ is as you read the Scriptures and that by the will of God, you come to know the truth about the sinful condition of mankind; and with knowing the revealed truth, it is God's will, according to the Scriptures, that you receive salvation through Jesus Christ.

Why should you or anyone else trust the Bible? Well, for one thing, its author is God, the only true, all-wise, and all-knowing Creator, who is truthful and trustworthy. He will not mislead you about the facts regarding Himself as Creator nor will He mislead you about His creation; and so for the Christian, the Bible—that is, the Old and New Testament—is the only book known that chronicles, with details of specificity, how all things came into existence.

God is responsible for designing and creating all matter and substances into existence. The Bible emphatically states that God is the Creator of the heavens and the earth. His actions are seen in Genesis 1, in Job 37 and 38, Psalm 137 and Colossians 1, and throughout the rest of the Bible. God reminds the reader who studies the Scriptures that He is the Creator of all their details. Nothing was started by God and then left to evolve. We will talk about the theories of evolution later and where this concept came from.

There are other books that may be as old as the Bible that do give expositional poetic works of literature of polytheism, belief in more than one god. One example of such writings is the Epic of Gilgamesh. It gives sketches of a global flood occurring around the time of Noah and the Bible flood. For the Christian, however, the Bible is the only truthful and dependable God-inspired holy book in which its account of earth's history is accurate, for it is written by the mind and mouth of the all-knowing and eternal God.

The Bible is a book whose information remains unchangeable, and its truths remain relevant in every age, whether it was the time of the Old and New Testament or today. The Bible is never out of touch with reality, for there is nothing new under the sun regarding man's sin condition and the problems of this world.

The interactions between God and mankind have always been the same throughout the ages. God has not changed, nor has He altered His Word to suit any generation of people. Instead, it is mankind who has made attempts to water down and modify the sacred Word of God to suit himself, but for this, the unsaved people will have to give an account to God, and they will be judged by Him for their acts of rebellion throughout their lifetime.

Every choice that we make in our lifetime, we will have to give an account to God in the judgment; but because there are some people who refuse to believe the Word of God with regards to what it says who God is in the universe and beyond, the true origin and complete history of mankind and all other living things, the history of the earth and the universe are big question marks in their minds. These individuals unapologetically reject the Bible and the revelation God gives regarding who He is; and therefore, they remain confused intellectuals.

Prophecies that Jesus Made

The Bible makes many predictions about future events, and some have been fulfilled already. The Bible has boldly predicted and declared the rise and fall of many governments, empires, and kingdoms, and some have come to pass already (Daniel 2:32–44).

In Matthew 24, Jesus stated predictions of wars and rumors of wars, but He reassured the saints not to be troubled, for these things must come to pass. He continues to say that nations shall make war with other nations and kingdom against kingdom and that there will be famines and pestilences and earthquakes in various places. Christ also says that His people shall be delivered up to be afflicted and to be killed—yes, killed. We see that today in our time. He said that many false prophets shall rise up, and they shall deceive many, and we also see that today.

There seems to be an increase in the proliferation of many false religions that are teaching the doctrines of Satan, the father of lies. Also, there is a startling rise in the types of evil and heinous acts committed by both men and women, including the youngest among us; and according to Isaiah 59:7 and stated again in Romans 3:15, wicked men and women, without a drop of conscience in their being, will be bent on committing evil acts and swiftly rush to shed innocent blood because their thoughts are thoughts of iniquity, and destruction is always in their minds.

The Bible talks of the brutal behavior mankind had committed against his and her brother and sister, beginning with Cain who killed his brother, Abel, out of envy, jealousy, and anger. These acts of barbarism continue to happen in our time, thousands of years later; and so the Bible is very relevant to today's events because the nature of mankind never changed, for no one but God can change the hearts of a sinful human race, but mankind has to respond to God's call to repent from a life of unrighteousness to receive a life of righteousness through Jesus Christ.

The Bible states in Matthew 24:11 that there will be many false prophets who shall arise and deceive many people in the last days. These people will be deceived because these individuals never had any real root in them to anchor the Word of God that was sown in their hearts. These are people who did allow themselves to be deceived by Satan's seeds of lying doctrines. The doctrine of lies is planted by Satan when negative and discouraging thoughts enter people's mind. These lies only become effective when individuals believe in their hearts that the gospel of Jesus Christ is not true.

The Bible also states that there would be people in the church who will be offended or ashamed of the gospel of Jesus Christ and shall turn away from the faith because of tribulation and persecution, and because of that, they will give heed to the seductions of seducing spirits and the doctrines of devils (Matthew 13:21 and 1 Timothy 4). Many people in the church also will betray one another because they never had a faith relationship of trust and obedience to Christ. The Word of God, therefore, did not profit these individuals anything, for it never had a chance to grow when it was sown in them. Well, you may say the betrayal of others in the church cannot happen, but God knows the future and the past at the same time. He is all-knowing, and everything in the universe He knows about, and He is in control of every single event that happens including those that are yet to be fulfilled but will come to pass.

Jesus continues to say that iniquity shall abound, and we see that happening today, right before our eyes, but this is only the beginning of what is to come. People will do every evil thing imaginable, and because of that, the love of many for God and His Word shall become cold. After all this, Jesus says, there shall come a time of great tribulation, which would be very immense in both scope and in intensity, such that there was not anything like it seen since the beginning of the world nor will there be any after it; and except those days are shortened by God, there shall be no one saved; but for God's elects' sake, He said that He would shorten the time of the tribulation. These are just some of the predictions God makes in the Bible regarding future events, and they are the dire calamities that He forecasted will come upon the earth; but for the true people of God, their faith is in Jesus Christ, who is their only hope beyond this world into eternity with Him.

God is the same yesterday, the same today, and the same forever. Friend, God does not want to destroy anyone. That was not His plan—to create mankind and then destroy them—that was the hope and plan of Satan, for the Bible says that he came to steal, kill, and destroy mankind. God wants to save you and all mankind from the wages of sin. Would you accept Jesus Christ today to be your Savior and your Lord? If your answer is yes, then confess and repent of your sins to God, and receive His gift of salvation now. You can have peace with Him and have an abundant life on earth and eternal life with Jesus Christ. After you have done that, please stay in the Word of God, and ask Him to direct you to a Bible truth-teaching church.

The Bible does not only describe the works of God's hands, but it also shows that He has absolute control of this endless universe. God is self-existent, and He is self-sufficient, needing nothing and needing no help. Isaiah 42:5 says,

> Thus saith God the Lord, he that created the heavens, and stretched them out; he that spread forth the earth, and that which cometh out of it; he that giveth breath unto the people upon it, and spirit to them that walk therein.

There was never a time when God became a being. The Bible states that He has no end, but this world has a beginning and an end. God's power is limitless. He creates and recreates, and He makes new again that which was broken by sin. He will resurrect any spiritually dead person to live again, in a godly way, by being connected to Him; and again, according to the Bible, God does the work of salvation alone. Angels or other created beings did not created the universe with God. It is God alone who can recreate any person to become the new creature in Christ. Thus, we read in Isaiah 44:24,

> I am the Lord that maketh all things; that stretcheth forth the heavens alone; that spreadeth abroad the earth by myself.

What God Created and Formed

The Bible is a spiritual book that teaches us about the nature of mankind and the nature of God as it relates to His holiness and His remedy for sin. It also has within it the accounts of the creation of all life including mankind.

As is recorded in Genesis 1, God created plant life of every type. He created fish and other water creatures of every kind. He created birds of every type. God created four-footed animals and other crawling land animals of every kind. All these things that God created were made to multiply in and replenish the earth.

Since Christians, in general, believe that God is responsible for the existence of all life because He created and formed every one of them for His pleasure, for some Christians don't believe such, then they should believe that He is able to sustain everything in the universe and beyond. He is in absolute control of all that He has made. Some people who say that they are Christians say that they believe that God has some control but not absolute control of everything in the universe. They say God is not sovereign. Everything, living and nonliving, in the heavens and on earth is under the control of the God of the Bible, so when we study the life of all living things in biology, we can't help but give God praise and give Him glory, for all life is very complex and was wonderfully made by an infinitely intelligent Creator.

According to the Bible, mankind is of particular importance to God because we were created in His image and formed after His likeness. We read in Isaiah 44:24 that it is God who forms us in the womb. He created us with all the equipment and the abilities to procreate, and He put into every life the engine of life, the organs and the organelles, the body's systems and subsystems, and the breath of life for it to function in harmony with the sustaining power of its Creator. Every human life that is born, God knows everything about it.

The life that was being formed but did not come to full fruition, I am of the belief that God's love abides over the unborn. I have heard some Christians speculate and debate about how God would judge the unborn. I believe it is unwise to make conjectures about things we know nothing about, for the Bible is silent in this area. What the Bible says of every soul is that it is God's (Ezekiel 18:4); and because all souls are His, then it is for God to be the judge of that life, not us. We waste time in useless discussions about things God may never have intended for us to deliberate. Such conversations do not benefit us from anything, and they have nothing to do with our salvation and the salvation of others. What we need to think about is how we would be judged by God in the light of what has been revealed to us by Him in the Bible. It is none of our business to know those things that are of God's right to know. We need to be concerned about ourselves and how we are living in His presence and how we treat our fellow man.

Principles of the Bible in Life Applications

In Genesis 2:21–23, God did something extraordinary, which is used as a pattern and copy in medicine today, and the Bible says,

> And the Lord God caused a deep sleep to fall upon Adam, and he slept: and he took one of his ribs, and closed up the flesh instead thereof; And the rib which the Lord God had taken from man, made he a woman, and brought her unto the Man, and Adam said, This is now bone of my bones and flesh of my flesh and she shall be called Woman, because she was taken out of Man.

Here we see God performing the first surgical-like procedure on mankind with His own hands.

This procedure that God performed on Adam was done after he was completely formed and was fully functional with no mark of sin in him. It is interesting to see, from reading this Scripture, that God caused Adam to go into a deep sleep before He operated on him, as it were, for this was major surgery; and while Adam was in a deep sleep, his life was sustained by God Himself. It is His power that sustains all living things. It is the same principle that occurs during all complicated surgical procedures—that a person is placed under anesthesia, and his or her life is sustained by a complex set of machines. We do know it is God who sustains all life in any given situation.

Has anything changed in modern surgical procedures from what God did in the garden of Eden? This is a patterned method that modern medicine follows today, whether we realize it or not. In Leviticus 17:11, we also read, "For the life of the flesh is in the blood." We know that the blood of all living things carries nutrients and other biochemical substances, including oxygen, necessary to sustain health and maintain life to all body cells and tissues.

In Genesis 1:11–12, 21, and 25, we see the Bible describing the genesis of plant and animal life. God spoke all plant and animal life into existence, and He put in them the specific ability to reproduce, each after their own kind. God is not the maker of the mess and confusion that we see coming out of research labs today. We get into all sorts of trouble when science crosses the line to do foolishly with that which God had made good. There have been some successful attempts made to change God's creation into something strange. An example of such is the fluorescent pigmentation cat that glows in the dark. This use of time and valuable resources to manipulate nature into producing useless things—things that are not favorable and beneficial to nature itself—make no logical sense as to their value and benefit to mankind.

God created mankind with the gifts and talents to be creative so that he can produce beneficial products using the tools of honest science and technology that honors and glorifies his Creator.

We can look around and see hundreds of millions of marvelous inventions that have affected the way mankind lives. There are bridges, roads, automobiles, marine, land, and air. Just look around your home, your place of work, your community and see the technology that are there. The radio, the telephone, the computer, the Internet, and others like them are products useful to mankind. In medicine and in the field of engineering science, we see many parts of the apex of scientific breakthroughs with many incredible life-saving apparatuses.

The problem arises when some human beings try to play God and go beyond where they should not be and invent things that are useless and/or destructive to nature, and so they believe that God is either incompetent or is irrelevant if they indistinctly believe He exists anyway. Thus, these people think that they are in charge of nature and that they know more than the God they do not believe in, and they do their best to reject His existence. Now the mess they have made from their own corrupt thinking is now next to impossible to have a fix, and so humanity has to suffer the consequences of some people's destructive actions.

In Genesis 2:7, the Bible says God formed mankind of the dust of the ground and He breathes into his nostrils the breath of life and man became a living soul. God, as it were, performed pulmonary ventilation therapy to a lifeless body. Modern medicine today has performed this type of therapy by cardiopulmonary resuscitation (CPR) and using artificial airway ventilation such as in tracheostomies and in mechanical ventilation therapy in life-saving situations. Mankind cannot create life; only God can. It is Satan who is behind the efforts to create life, but God has given us the knowledge to, whenever possible, medically treat and save biological life. Today we know from medical and biological sciences that one of the vital signs of life is breathing, measured as respirations in breaths per minute.

The Bible uses the principles of mathematics in numbering the generations of the Israelites (Numbers 1). Mathematics was also utilized in the building of structures God commanded the Israelites to build using patterns of measurements He gave them. We read in Genesis 6 that God instructed Noah to build the ark using specific mathematical measurements, then in Exodus 26, God gave Moses the pattern for the building of the tabernacle using specific measurements. In 1 Kings 6:2–10, we read about the construction of the house that Solomon built in which the principles of mathematics were used.

In the Bible, we also find references to names of planets and solar systems given by God. We read in Job 38:31–33 that God asked Job questions about the bands of Orion and Pleiades. The Bible also talks about a literal seven-day week of creation (Genesis 1), and the Bible talks about months in the year, Abib, Exodus 13:4; Nisan, Nehemiah 2:2; Nehemiah 6:15 is the month E'lul; and the month Zif, 1 Kings 6:1.

With regards to physics, the Bible in Genesis 1:3–5 records God creating light by speaking it into existence. Verse 3 said God saw it and said it was good. Everything that we know and don't know about light was created by God. The Bible says in Job 38:24,

> By what way is the light parted, which scattereth the east wind upon the earth?

The scientific observations and discoveries that have been made give us some understanding of the characteristics of light. The insights into these findings have led us to understand the electromagnetic spectrum that is visible to the naked eye. Mankind has also discovered light-intensity wavelengths and light-wave-particle physics that are very complex, and it is only an intelligent Creator who could have created and formed light with multiple levels of complexities, some of which mankind may never discover and never understand in this life.

In the Genesis creation, God created the natural laws of physics that hold everything in its place; hence, the reason why we see order and stability in the physical world. We do not see disorder and chaos anywhere where humanity has looked. All gasses, the inert and the very volatile, were created by God in the right mixture and concentration into the earth's atmosphere to support the livability of life.

As stated before, the Bible is also a book of history because God is the author of the history of mankind and of the universe. In Genesis 1, we read the creation account of all things. In Genesis 3, the Bible tells us where, when, and how sin began on earth, and who was the agent that caused it to happen? Sin did not begin with God—it began with Satan—and so in Genesis 6, the Bible tells us about the building of an ark, and we read the Bible's record of a worldwide flood (Genesis 7).

The Bible also talks about the destruction of Sodom and Gomorrah by the judgment of God (Genesis 19) and the destruction of Jerusalem (2 Chronicles 36). These are just some of the historical accounts that are recorded in the Bible, some of which are corroborated by archaeological discoveries. More archaeological discoveries regarding other significant Bible historical accounts are being made. It must be understood that we may never discover everything the Bible says happened in the past, but that does not mean that the Bible is not the true source of the history of humanity.

The Bible references us to the subject of economics as we read in Leviticus 25:14–15. We also read more about the principles of economics in the Bible in Deuteronomy 2:6, and we read in Acts 1:1–3.

God owns everything, but He gives mankind the opportunity to manage what He has put into our care (Psalm 50:10–12). In Genesis 1:28, God gave mankind the responsibility to care for the earth, with everything in it; and thus, we read in this scriptural reference that God gave Adam dominion over everything. He had rulership over all life in the sea and the fowl of the air and dominion over every other living thing that moved on the earth, but because man sinned by disobeying God's commandments, the territory and the power that God had given them were handed over to Satan. He became the ruler of unsaved humanity.

In Luke 19:23, we read that we are to manage what God has entrusted to us, and thus we read,

> Wherefore then gavest not thou my money into the bank, that at my coming I might have required mine own with usury?

God is teaching His children to invest that which He has given them—that is, our time, our talent and gifts, and our money are to be managed in a God-fearing and soberly manner. We are admonished not just to invest, but we are to do so wisely as God impresses us how to so do.

Many of us need our minds to be transformed by God from that of a consumer consumption appetite to a mindset of temperance. We need to have a mindset of being a financial investor and an investor of our time, of our gifts, and our talents, for if we invest and manage wisely what God has given us to care for, our children and our children's children would have an example and a legacy to follow.

The Bible also says in Proverbs 3:9–10,

> Honour the Lord with thy substance, and with the first fruits of all thine increase: So shall thy barns be filled with plenty, and thy presses shall burst out with new wine.

God is clearly admonishing us to put Him first with the first portion of all our possessions. It is from Him we have received what we have if what we possess was gotten by godly means. It is God who has given us the power to obtain wealth (Deuteronomy 8:18). If we say we trust God and then say we have faith in Him, why wouldn't we want to trust Him with our possessions? We trust the banks with our money, and they make a fortune from us when they lend to us what we collectively have deposited into their barns.

So many of us Christians struggle financially because we hold back from God what belongs to Him, for we lack the discipline of practical money management, and we lack the faith to let God be our investment banker. God will give it back to us anyway, many times over, for He is our provider. It was from Him that we did indeed receive what we do have, and that's everything.

Many of us give grudgingly, stingily, and sparingly to God, and some of us don't give anything at all because we don't believe that we are going to receive anything back from Him. It is He who freely gave us what we have in the first place. It is God who had promised us, and His promises are sure in that He will open the windows of heaven and pour us out a blessing that we may not have room enough to receive all that He will give us (Malachi 3).

Give God His portion first, and He will multiply a return unto us far exceeding our giving so that we receive manifold increased blessings in every area of our lives. God, in His Word, instructs His children on the attitude of their giving; and so we are not to give stingily to God, but we are to give to Him with a pure heart and a clear conscience, not grudgingly or of necessity, for God loves a cheerful giver (2 Corinthians 9:7).

If we sow bountifully with the Lord, we shall reap bountifully from Him; and if you and I sow sparingly into the treasury of God, we will also reap sparingly. If we did not sow anything at all, then we will not have a harvest. We cannot invest stingily and expect a bountiful harvest. We should learn wise investment strategies from other God-fearing people so that we do not invest carelessly with a reckless mindset and with the "2:00 a.m. get-you-rich-quick investment scam disasters."

By Intelligent Design

We will not debate and deliberate in this book whether creation or evolution is true. What we will see, however, from the Bible is that all things that exist, the visible and the invisible, do have a Creator.

For starters, just think for a moment about the fact that your body and mine, with all its complex systems, work extremely well as one synergistic operation with its external environment. It continually monitors itself and adjusts for changes in internal and external equilibrium. Every cell, every tissue, every organ, every organ system, and all biochemical substances found in the body were perfectly designed by God in just the right size and in the right quantities for their particular locations within the body.

All biochemical substances are distributed throughout the body in the right proportions based on the need for the functionality of a specific body part or system. The body uses the system of metabolism to break down what we eat to its useful forms, and the body uses the process of biosynthesis to manufacture other biochemical substances. An example of bioprocessing is cell and tissue repair. This is a process by which substances that are derived from the food we eat and are broken down by the body's biochemical machine system to simplified and usable forms so that the body's cells can do their work. Another example of bioprocessing is energy production made from carbohydrates and fats that are also from the foods we eat. All human body systems are the same, and they operate no different from the human body that lived thousands of years ago.

All human beings today are the same as the male and the female bodies that existed thousands of years ago. Nothing has changed; nothing has evolved. We are genetically linked to one another as human beings even though we may vary in phenotype—that is, the observed properties or expressions of the physical makeup of human beings—for example, height and hair texture.

These morphological differences are explained through the heredity information we have in our genotype, the genetic makeup determined in our DNA. The genetic makeup and physical expressions of living things also explain why we have different types of plant and animal life.

Different varieties of plants and animal life within the same species exist the way they are because God had designed their genetic makeup to have differences. Some trees that exist today are thousands of years old, showing us that God is also the Creator of unique things. One example is the old Tjikko tree of Sweden, which is dated to be approximately 9,550 years old.[6]

Mankind is still begetting their own kind with no evolving features and parts evident in their offsprings. Plants still manufacture their own food through photosynthetic means as they did when God made them. There is no shred of evidence anywhere that points to plants evolving when we examine the genetic information of plants thousands of years ago and those that we have today. Even if the changes that evolutionists talk about take incrementally millions of years to occur, we still do not find any evidence of meaningful evolutionary stepwise changes in any life form. The apple tree still only bears apples, the great white shark still begets great white sharks, and so on.

There were adjustments made in our bodies that were allowed by God to accommodate what the consequences of sin had done as the consequences affected the internal environments of our bodies and external natural environment of nature, and so there was disharmony between mankind and his environment.

We were created by God to consume only a plant-based diet for meat (Genesis 1:29). God, however, allowed mankind to kill and eat selected group animals for meat, which He explains in Leviticus 11; but meat consumption, if one must eat flesh, I believe, should be in moderation or as little as possible to lessen or prevent cardiovascular complications and different types of cancers from occurring.

Some Christians believe that God never changed the prohibition in the New Testament of the types of animal (clean) meats mankind may eat while other Christians interpret and believe the vision God gave to Peter, as recorded in Acts chapters 10 and 11, to mean that God intended that mankind may now eat the meats of unclean animals in addition to the meats of clean animals.

What God was showing Peter was that the preaching of the gospel is also for the Gentiles. God knew that the Jews considered the Gentiles unclean because they were uncircumcised and were not of the Abrahamic

---

[6] Karl Brodowsky, July 19, 2011.

covenant, and thus, they ate anything and everything, the clean and the unclean meats. I must add that it is God who designates what's clean and unclean as we read in Leviticus 11 and Deuteronomy 14. No creature is clean and unclean unless God says it is. If a person regards anything to be unclean, he or she should not eat it according to Romans 14:14; to him or her, it is unclean.

In 1 Timothy 4:4–5, what the apostle Paul is saying in regard to every creature of God is good and nothing to be refused, if it is received with thanksgiving, it is sanctified (set apart for godly use or is consecrated) by the Word of God; and so I, as a Christian, don't believe that God was just speaking to the Jews about certain dietary practices that were shadows of things to come, but we also are to see these prohibitions as part of a health message from God for our lives. It has been established by many in the medical and healthcare community that what we eat affects our health one way or the other; and so why add to the complicated environmental issues that affects our health? I am not saying that what we eat affects our salvation, but what we eat to nourish our bodies affects our health; and therefore, we should do the things that God wants us to do so that our bodies thrive and be in good health. People will be making up stories, saying God has said when He has not said.

First Timothy 4:4–5 is a prophecy that will come to pass and is being fulfilled in our day, and with everything that we receive from God as His provision, including divine revelation, we are to always give thanks through prayer. The Bible is clear about the spiritual condition of some in the church of God—that they would depart from the faith to practice apostasy. So God used what Peter was knowledgeable of, as in clean and unclean meats, to teach him lessons to accept and to treat every human being like his brother and his sister without regard to who they were and who they were not, for their Maker and Creator is God, for the Bible says in Galatians 3:28 that all are one in Christ. There is neither Jew nor Gentile, male nor female; there is neither bond nor free, but all are made to be partakers of Christ through the covenant God made with Abraham.

Animal meat has its disadvantages, even though God permitted mankind to kill and eat, for these types of animal meat deposit large amounts of complex carbon chain compounds, known as triglycerides and cholesterol, into our bodies; and if left unchecked, these substances can contribute to significant cardiovascular diseases and other body system maladies. Vitamin B12 is a very important vitamin that is essential for red blood cell production and nerve cell function, to name a few. It can only be derived from animal meat sources and from soil bacteria. It is also fortified into vegetarian meals, soy products, and cereals.

The restrictions that were placed on what types of animal meat mankind can eat were given to protect us from consuming the contaminants that are found in the animals which were designated by God to be unclean. This was important for our good regarding our health and was also significant for what the unclean meats represented spiritually.

The contaminants found in animals designated by God to be unclean can cause serious complications in our bodies resulting in serious illnesses and even death. God has also instructed mankind to abstain from the blood and the fat of the clean animal that they were permitted to eat so that they may not suffer the ailments of the diseases that are associated with eating these parts of these animals (Leviticus 17). Blood is the vehicle for transporting nutrients, including oxygen, but it also carries metabolic body waste; and when the animal is sick, blood transports the disease-causing microbes to all parts of its body as it does ours; and if any clean animal is sick, we are not to kill and eat its flesh according to the Bible.

The Bible says that the life of living things is in the blood (Leviticus 17:11). This fact is significant for spiritual reasons because the blood of the clean animal was a shadow and a picture in the Old Testament of the blood of Christ and what it will do for mankind's sin. Blood is a covenant sign made by God to remit man's sin through the shedding of the blood of Jesus.

The unclean animals that God listed in the book of Leviticus are scavengers which clean up the earth's environment wastes. These scavengers contain very high levels of environmental toxins such as lead, mercury, phosphates, deadly disease-causing microorganisms, and other micro-element toxins found in the ground and in the earth's water. These scavengers also contain extremely high sodium levels.

Many of the toxins found in these creatures are carcinogens, meaning they can cause cancer. Some of these substances are deadly when ingested even in tiny amounts, while others cause serious damage to our bodies and lead to debilitating diseases. That's the reason there are so many types of cancers and many other types of killer diseases. These toxins trigger susceptible genes in our bodies and cause healthy cells to become unregulated to form many disease types, and so the susceptibility factors in our bodies and the environmental toxin triggers increases our vulnerability to biohazard harm. The Bible gives us a template for healthier living, for

God knows what's best for our bodies since He is our Creator and our Maker. Please read Leviticus 11 if your diet includes meat.

The Problem of Evolution Science

Many scientific theories and postulations change over time. There are no absolutes in evolution science in and of itself with regards to life on earth and with regards to the origin of a very complex and vast universe. The level of complexity that we see in nature says a lot about who God is, who is infinitely wiser and is far beyond intelligent than any of His creation. If evolution science had answered the question of how life began and when it began, then there would not be any further need to continually debate the subject of the origin of life and the origin of the universe. Evolution science creates more questions than it is able and capable of providing answers to the questions it asks. It uses controversial methods for dating the fossil artifacts of nature to time stamp the age of the earth and life that is found in it.

Some modern scientists who are materialists believe that physical matter is the ultimate reality. They suppose that everything in the cosmos, including life, can be explained in terms of interacting matter.[7] Materialists do not accept the biblical record regarding the origin of life and the origin of the universe. They believe that life is purely materialistic in origin and that they can replicate it in the laboratory. There are many problems with such a concept. For starters, whatever principle one can come up with must have order. When we are building anything—a house, for example—we build according to an architectural plan and design. In the construction of the house, the foundation must be laid first, then all the complex and intricate details are added until the building is completed.

Nothing that mankind makes can be built without a creator or a designer. It takes an intelligent designer and creator to create life and to create the universe, and that intelligent designer and creator is the God of the Bible. Mankind or chance cannot create life. All living organisms can procreate, but nothing outside of God can create life. There is no evidence nor is there any logic that can show how chance can cause life to come into existence. It is only God who can create into existence whatever is in His mind using only His Word to do so. When God speaks, good things happen, so let God create a new heart and renew a right spirit in you by letting Him speak into your life right now.

---

[7] Paul S. Taylor, Films for Christ.

When we look at human growth and development, we see the specific order in the union of two gametes, the male sperm cell and a female egg, progress in specific logical sequences into the full development of the offspring. The DNA of every living thing is a remarkable molecule that is very complicated. Evolution cannot produce such a complicated chemical structure that is found in all living things. Any change in the sequential operational steps in bio-life development can alter the normal life functions of that offspring, showing us how God designed every detail to be precise enough to maintain the typical livability of life. Even though Christian creationists may accept and believe what the Bible says about God and His creation, we are still awestruck and are left with a sense of bewilderment to the beauty of nature. We marvel about how all living and nonliving things came to be and how all living things operate as God has made them to function. Everything in nature has usefulness, which mankind may or may not understand.

Some scientists have used an approach to try to create life called spontaneous generation, in which matter in its simplest form, and in some cases, it was hypothesized that dead, decaying matter, or nonliving substances could spontaneously organize themselves to produce life. For the life of me, I cannot fathom how learned men and women could have assumed that life would have appeared by such illogical methods; but it's obvious that people thought it was possible, not that anything pointed them in that direction other than their intentions may have been to disprove the Bible and, thus, deny the existence of God.

The probability or odds for the simplest life form, such as a one-cell organism, which would produce a more complex organism by the method of spontaneous generation is extraordinarily astronomical, making it totally impossible for such an event to occur, but evolutionists still pursue these and other illogical pathways as they try to explain the origin of life and the origin of the universe occurring outside of an infinitely intelligent Creator. The simple fact is this: we can believe that a car has a designer and a maker, a watch has a designer and a maker, a house has an architect and a builder, and so on; but we find it impossible to accept that there is a God who created everything, and He is Elohim Adonai, the one God who is master over all things in the universe and beyond. The things that men build do not just randomly appear. They are designed, and then they are made to be what they were designed to be.

No watchmaker, no house builder, or a car maker put the materials needed to build their product in one place to see what will happen. Someone has to take the materials and actually make the product. The products did not just happen into existence by random assortment. These are products of invention, produced with a plan and by design. It was an idea and a concept that was given to individuals by God to make and produce a product. Many times, an invention is the result of several painstaking attempts to get the right design and the right science for that thing to work safely, correctly, and as efficiently as possible.

God uses the natural things in nature and the things people make to let us know and understand that He is the all-intelligent Designer-Creator. God wants us to know that He is the Creator of all things and not the theories of chance and evolution that are responsible for the origin of all life, matter, and substance. He created all things, both in the heavens and on earth, for His pleasure and by His power, and that's the record of the Bible.

We do not see macro changes occurring in living things, and if any changes do occur, they are small changes, occurring from time to time, because of genetic mutations. Such mutations do not produce a new variant of the same species or produce a genetically and physically different living organism. The DNA in monkeys has and will forever remain the same. Any similarities between man and monkeys that originally have been thought to exist have been refuted by evolutionists themselves.[8]

Of all the research that has been done on the DNA molecule among several classes of animals, including humans, there was never found a switch mechanism in the DNA molecule that is responsible for the evolving of simple life forms to become other types of living things, from simple to complex. If such a mechanism were ever discovered, the question would be how do we intelligently explain its mechanism of action—that is, how does it work? There is just no such thing that exists.

I believe that the relentless efforts spent to find something that does not exist is fruitless and is a complete waste of valuable time—time that could be used meaningfully to help our fellow human beings in desolate situations and in deplorable conditions around the world. The most common type of genetic mutations that occurs in nature from time to time is point mutations, which usually does not provide any benefits to the organism; but

---

[8] Originally published in Journal of Creation 17(1):8–10, April 2003.

rather, these mutations have undesirable outcomes.[9] Some examples of such mutations that occur in humans are sickle cell anemia, cystic fibrosis, and muscular dystrophy. If we all were to accept the Bible's claim that all things were created by an intelligent Creator, then we may have more answers than questions regarding the origin of life and the origin of the universe.

The Christian creationist believes that nothing about God is evolutionary, and nothing He created evolved. For the Christian creationist, no logical argument can be used to substantiate and validate the counter position that says there is no God and that the Bible is not true and reliable. Christians who believe that the Word of God is inerrant and believe that God is the Creator of all things do so as a matter of their faith in the Word of God. The Bible says that all things, both the visible and the invisible, were created by God the Son (Colossians 1:16), and when He made anything, it was good (Genesis 1); and so, the Christian who believes that the Bible is absolutely true also believes it would take a tremendously greater amount of faith to believe the ever-changing theories of evolution. The ever-changing theories in evolution science are the evidence that its arguments are based on suppositions and assumptions.

Evolutionists use their arguments, which they identify as facts, to promote their points of view as the game-changing truth of how life began. Some evolutionists have also used their conclusions to suggest that the origin of the universe and the beginning of all life came about by random and obscure chance, and others have added that the universe and life came about exclusively by the big bang theory. Their theories suggest that certain forces magically sought out all the chemicals necessary to support life on some distant planet and were transported to Earth by cosmic dust.

Their science cannot prove that the origins of evolution occurred on planet Earth, so they continue to search for evidence elsewhere to support their theory. Such postulations boggle the mind of any rational thinker as to where and how evolutionists came up with this type of science.

Theories of evolution science are all over the place. It says one thing today and something else the next day. God does not change. His Word has not changed, and His message of salvation has not changed either. Who are we going to believe, unstable evolution science or the unchangeable Word of God? For many other Bible-believing Christians and me, the answer is clear—it's the Word of God—and in addition to the truthfulness of the

---

[9] National Human Genome Research Institute.

Bible, the record that it gives for the origin of all things, in the heavens and on the earth, remains the same. There are never any adjustments to the truth. It does not evolve. It stays the same. The record of the Bible is unchangeable because God is immutable. Jesus said in Matthew 24:35,

> Heaven and earth shall pass away, but my words shall not pass away.

When God created anything good, it meant that there were no imperfections in that thing when it was created; but because sin altered all that was made well, everything in nature became affected by the curses that sin brought. Mankind's perfect relationship with God was severed by sin when the spirit of mankind died. The artery of life between God and mankind was cut by the scissors of disobedience. Sinful man, in his sin condition, could no longer have communion with a perfect and holy God; and so mankind went from total rest in their Creator, where God provided all his needs, to a state of total unrest.

What fellowship has righteousness with unrighteousness? What relationship does the living have with the dead? And what fellowship has darkness with light? The unrighteous man does not understand the righteousness of God, neither does darkness comprehend the light. The dead knows nothing, neither does it have any knowledge of the Almighty. It is God who brings spiritually dead men and women back to life so that they can know Him in an intimate way by way of salvation.

What Happened?

In Genesis 3, the Bible says that God cursed the ground for mankind's sake, meaning that if God did not curse the ground, Adam as a sinner would have had access to the benefits of God's provision without bearing any consequence for transgressing the law of God. The fact is God knew that mankind needed to work to produce his own food after he had sinned, for idle hands would have made mankind very useful to Satan. What mankind needed to physically live was now to be found on the earth.

Mankind now had to toil in sweat to eat bread. Through work, mankind is also able to exercise his gifts and talents that God had created him with so that he may glorify Him; but because man is also very sinful, his hands are also capable of committing the most egregious of offenses toward his fellow man in the presence of a holy and righteous God.

Evil men slaughter their brothers and their sisters without any regard for the life God did create. He kills his fellow man as if he were a wild beast. We read in history, and we see in the news of today the many heinous and barbaric criminal acts that are committed by men toward their fellow men. Since the day when Cain slew his brother Abel, the bloodthirstiness of mankind, at every age, against his brother has been profound.

So Adam and his wife were driven out from the presence of God to find work outside the garden of Eden. The fact is God did this because He is absolutely righteous and holy, and a holy and righteous God cannot behold sin. God cannot permit sin to exist in His presence. Just as God had to cast Satan out of heaven when he sinned, He had to drive Adam and Eve out from the garden of Eden after they had sinned to keep them from the way of the tree of life (Genesis 3:24). They could not eat from the tree of life and live forever in sin, and so one may conclude that Satan would have had a charge against God that he should live forever if, indeed, Adam and Eve were allowed to live in sin without bearing any of the consequences of their rebellion against God.

So it may be safe to say that sin would have existed forever by the permission of God and the Godhead would have been in shambles and chaos in the universe would have existed forever, but God is absolutely holy and perfect, for He was and is always in control of all things, and so we see the goodness of God removing the hand of sin before it could get to the tree of life. It is God who foresees all things way before they happen and provides the perfect solution for any problem before they occur. How great and marvelous is our God, and how just are all His ways.

At times it appears that we live in a world that is in complete chaos, and Satan seems to have gotten the upper hand in every society and community in our world. Many disturbing brutal acts of evil are being committed every day, but God is still in control of every event that happens. He will have the last say about the actions of humanity. God has to let sin run its course until the fullness of time, and when that time comes, then will all sin and rebellion be dealt with severely in His judgment.

No human being has an inkling as to the severity and the terror of the judgment of God. God is He, the only one, who can and will destroy both body and soul of the rebellious, unrepentant sinner in the lake of fire. It is not God's will to destroy anyone, but He has to in order to purify the heavens and the earth from the damage that sin caused and restore purity and order to His creation. The Bible does say that God will shorten those days for His true children's sake because evil and wickedness will abound, and Satan's deceptions will be at their strongest.

According to the Bible, Satan, together with those who follow him, will be completely destroyed by God in the unquenchable flames of the lake of fire. I do believe that there will be no trace nor memory of anything that God will destroy in the judgment anywhere in the universe and beyond. Those who committed acts of barbarism, including those who falsely believe their actions are pleasing to God, will be destroyed. These workers of iniquity are the servants of Satan and are not the servants of God. The Bible is clear in Psalm 37:38, 2 Peter 3:7–9, and elsewhere what will be the end of every evil person who remains a servant of Satan. God is not slack concerning His promise, as some people count slackness, but He is long-suffering to all humanity. He is not willing that any sinner should be destroyed for his or her sins (2 Peter 3:9). It is God's plan for mankind to have eternal life, but it is mankind's choice whether to accept or reject salvation and receive eternal life from Jesus Christ; and so in the judgment, God will repay every person according to his and her deeds that they have done in their lifetime.

Those who terrorize others with their satanic acts of brutality have absolutely no idea what the judgment of God is going to be like. If anyone believes that the judgment of God that did occur as recorded in Genesis 7 and 19, regarding the worldwide flood and the destruction of Sodom and Gomorrah, were terrifying or that they are Bible myths, they are in for a shock and a serious surprise of what shall befall this world on the last day in the judgment; and even though the Bible talks a lot about the judgment of God, mankind does not have an inkling of what the final judgment is going to look like. No one can really understand what the judgment and the destruction of this present world are going to be like, for it will be nothing we have ever seen or could have ever imagined. God is loving, and He is kind, but He is also just and righteous and is very serious about the destruction of sin wherever it is found. The judgment of God will be talked about in volume 2 of the book Called to be Chosen.

All Things Created Good by God

An all-powerful, all-wise, and all-knowing God can only create good things. If the things God created were less than good, then it would indicate that God may not be all-powerful, that He may not be all-wise, and that He may not be all-knowing. Whatever is made by God was in His mind in eternity past. We read in Romans 11:33–36,

O the depth of the riches both of the wisdom and knowledge of God! how unsearchable are his judgments and his ways past finding out! For who hath known the mind of the Lord? Or who hath been his counselor? Or who hath first given to him and it shall be recompensed unto him again? For of him, and through him, and to him, are all things: to whom be glory for ever. Amen.

According to Genesis 1, all things, including the earth and all things on the earth, were created good by God. However, everything changed from that state of being good to one of death and decay. These drastic changes were because of mankind's disobedience to the commandments of God. As it is in the natural world, where every action we make has a corresponding reaction, so is it also in the spiritual. Disobedience to God's commandments is sin, which has built-in consequences.

The Bible says in Psalm 19:1,

The heavens declare the glory of God; and the firmament sheweth his handy work.

Mankind is still learning about the wonders of our planet and the wonders of the universe even though some are attributing its wonders to that of chance or the result of a big bang theory. In Psalm 33:4–7, we read,

For the word of the Lord is right: and all his works are done in truth. By the word of the Lord were the heavens made; and all the host of them by the breath of his mouth. He gathereth the waters of the sea together as a heap: he layeth up the depth in a storehouse. For he spoke, and it was done; he commanded, and it stood fast.

We do not need to see God to believe He exists even though Christ was the very declaration of who God is. The evidence of His existence is in His creation, and His Word declares that He is the Creator of all things. Thus, the Bible says,

Hast thou not known? Hast thou not heard that the everlasting God, the Lord, the Creator of the ends of the earth, fainteth not, neither is weary? There is no searching of his understanding. (Isaiah 40:28)

Psalm 19:1 says,

> The heaven declare the glory of God; and the firmament shows His handiwork.

The Bible Is a Book of Prophecies

Many of the prophecies of the Bible that were given by God have been accurately fulfilled at their appointed time. Other prophecies about events occurring at the end of time have not yet been fulfilled. Some are being fulfilled in our day as we speak. Everything the Bible had predicted to occur at a specified time, for those things that have been fulfilled already, happened precisely as predicted in the Bible by God, who spoke it. When God speaks, things happen according to His will and His purpose.

Several prophecies are recorded in the Old Testament that were fulfilled in the New Testament regarding the birth and crucifixion of a Savior. Isaiah 9:6–7 says,

> For unto us a child is born, unto us a son is given: and the government shall be upon his shoulder: and his name shall be called Wonderful, Counsellor, The mighty God, The everlasting Father, The Prince of Peace. Of the increase of his government and peace there shall be no end, upon the throne of David, and upon his kingdom, to order it, and to establish it with judgment and with justice from henceforth even for ever. The zeal of the Lord of hosts will perform this.

In Isaiah 7:14, we read,

> Therefore the Lord Himself shall give you a sign; Behold, a virgin shall conceive, and bear a son, and shall call his name Immanuel.

In Isaiah 53, the Word of God tells us Christ's purpose for His incarnation and what things He must suffer as the Savior of mankind. We also read in Malachi 3:1,

> Behold, I will send my messenger, and he shall prepare the way before me: and the Lord, whom ye seek shall suddenly come to his temple, even the messenger of the covenant, whom ye delight in: behold he shall come saith the Lord of hosts.

These prophecies were fulfilled in the New Testament books of the Bible (Matthew 1:21–23 and in Mark 1:1 and throughout the rest of the New Testament). In Daniel 9:24–27, we read the prophecy of the seventy weeks that was given to Daniel by God. This prophecy was fulfilled with Jesus being crucified at three and a half years into His earthly ministry, exactly in the timeline of the seventy weeks as the prophecy had predicted.

To test prophesy to see whether it is from God or if it is from some other source, we need the Bible to do that for us. It gives the test of a true prophet and the test of a false prophet. There are many people today who are calling themselves prophets, and they need to be carefully checked out against the Word of God to see who they really are and to know what they are teaching.

The true child of God should not be in the classroom of untruths and outright lies and listen to the doctrine of devils. Thus, says the Bible in 2 Peter 1:21,

> For the prophecy came not in old time by the will of man: but holy men of God spake as they were moved by the Holy Ghost.

We also read in Isaiah 8:20,

> To the law and to the testimony: if they speak not according to this Word, it is because there is no light in them.

"This Word" means all that God has written in the Bible. The true prophet must say what God has said in His Word, and it must come to pass.

All prophecies must relate to that which is written in the Bible. A true prophet must declare that Jesus is Lord. He must testify that Jesus was crucified, was buried, and rose from the dead on the third day. The prophet must also declare that Jesus ascended into heaven and is seated at the right hand of God the Father, as it is written in the Bible.

A true prophet will not indulge in any sinful practices, as it should be of all believers. The prophet must live a pure and godly life that is consecrated unto God. These were the marks of the Bible prophets and of every other Christian. The prophecy to destroy Nineveh did not come to pass only because the people feared (reverenced) God, repented of their sins, and God forgave them.

The Old Testament prophets did not testify about Jesus Christ, but many Christians believe what the Bible says about the faith of the Old Testament saints. They are certain that these prophets and the other saints of old looked forward to and expected that God would indeed send one after the throne of David, the Messiah, Jesus Christ, who would bring salvation to all mankind and would be the Savior of the whole world. Abraham, Moses, and Elijah and other like-minded believers were given a picture of Christ in types and shadows, as was declared in the tabernacle God had made Israel build. These believers trusted God that He was in all the ceremonial laws and activities He had instructed the Israelites to observe.

These shadows and types pointed to a better covenant, which Jesus made by His sacrifice on the cross at Calvary. Hebrews 11 declares the faith the Old Testament saints had toward the promises that God had revealed to them in their heart.

Denying the Bible Is Denying God

The Bible states in Romans 1:18–22 why the wrath of God is against the wicked who refused to acknowledge the Bible and its author, God. These people have been shown the evidence of the existence of God by God Himself in the physical visible things that He had made. He has opened their understanding to know enough truth that there is a true and living God, but these individuals made every effort to substantiate their reasons not to believe the truth that was revealed to them by God. They do this by refusing to acknowledge Him and denying the evidence that He has shown them.

Many ask the question—if there is a God and if the Bible is true, why is there so much suffering in the world? "And if He exist why doesn't He stop it." They also ask, "Why does God allow so much evil to happen right under His nose?" Some of these individuals make those statements not to get the Word of God to answer their questions, but sometimes these questions are asked with the intent to raise doubt in the minds of Christians about the reliability and trustworthiness of the Bible. These unbelievers want to win the argument as to why they should not believe in God nor believe the Word of God. They want to satisfy their appetite with the pleasures of sin that seeks to disobey the commandments of God by indulging in a sinful lifestyle.

The redeemed of God do not get any credit for what He has done in their lives. Before the gospel came to us and God made it so that we should believe, we were all like the unsaved peoples of the world; for thus, we read in Ephesians 2:4–5,

But God, who is rich in mercy, for his great love wherewith he loved us, Even when we were dead in sins, hath quickened us together with Christ [by grace ye are saved].

And verses 8 and 9 says,

For by grace are ye saved through faith; and that not of yourselves: it is the gift of God: Not of works, lest any man should boast.

How sad and foolish it is that mankind would go to extreme lengths to deny the many evidence of the Bible that clearly show that there is a God. It is God who puts into the heart of those that believe the knowledge that there is an eternal, immutable, and infallible Creator, who is self-existent and self-sufficient, and it is He who is to be worshiped.

No man is to worship the creature that God created nor is he to worship the work of his hands including the gifts and talents he did receive from the Almighty. Rather, he is to worship the Creator, the giver of life and the Creator of all things, both the visible and the invisible; but because mankind is in such rebellion against the commandments of God, they are determined to remain defiant in his opposition to the Word of God such that these people find pleasure in living sinful lives.

The issue with mankind's ignorance and his defiance toward knowing who God is is that he is caged in in his prison of foolishness. He refuses to acknowledge the only all-knowing and all-intelligent God, who has the key that can unlock him from the chains of sin to freedom in Christ Jesus. There is no other way to know God, my friend, other than for Him to remove the scales of unbelief from your heart.

My friend, the physical evidence we see all around us, whose design and operation points to the existence of a Creator, also points to the fact that the Bible can be trusted because God is absolutely truthful and trustworthy. The natural man, one who thinks carnally, does not want to hear the truth of what the Bible has to say about the way he or she lives. He or she does not see that what he or she does is sinful, and to add to his defiance toward God, he or she finds pleasure in committing the most abominable sins. The Bible says this of all mankind in Jeremiah 17:9:

The heart is deceitful above all things, and desperately wicked: who can know it.

So every person that is born by the will of the flesh is wicked by nature, and their actions are evil. Every person who is born of the Holy Spirit is of God.

It is amazing to know that the Bible, which has been universally attacked, could survive, and retain its place of distinction, eloquently testifying to its supernatural origin. People of every social stripe have slanderously attacked the Bible in fruitless attempts to discredit its truth and to silence its believers. However, despite the attacks the Bible has received, countless numbers of new believers are being added to the body of Christ every day, some under the threat of death to themselves while others face certain death to them and to their families for declaring that Jehovah God is their Lord. The Bible, thus, for all its believers, is their only guide to truth, and every word in the Word of God is to be heeded.

The Bible says in Revelation 22:18–19 that if anyone adds to the Word of God, He will add unto him or her the plagues that are written in the Bible; and if anyone shall take away from the words of the prophecy, God shall take away their part in the book of life and out of the holy city. What God is saying is that there will be people who will try to change His Word to say things He did not say. To substantiate their audacity to tamper with the Bible, they may claim God had said when He did not say, so it becomes more important that the children of God know the Word of God from the inside out. It is also important for the people of God to be aware of false teachers. If we know the truth, which is the Word of God, we shall know what Satan's lies look like.

It takes faith to believe that there is one true and living God. It takes faith to believe that the Bible is God's only Word and that every Word of it is true, and it takes faith for anyone to absolutely trust God and His Word. The Bible says in Romans 10:17 that faith comes to the reader through hearing and hearing the Word of God. So then, faith gives the unrepentant heart of a person access to diligently seek God out and to know Him in the pages of the Bible.

I believe that it is the Spirit of God that touches spiritually dead mankind (in trespasses and sin) in their minds by sending them thoughts about their sinful condition as they hear the gospel. Faith then is the all-encompassing instrument through which people come to believe what they are reading in the Bible is undeniably true and trustworthy about who mankind is by nature. It is at this point when you and I are convinced about who the Bible says God is, that we are convicted in our hearts by the

Spirit of God about the sin condition of our lives. We must then choose whom we will follow—God or continue with Satan. The choice that is before us that we will have to make is either eternal life with God through confession and repentance of every sin or eternal separation from Him through the destruction of body and soul in hell when it is cast into the lake of fire. God forgives us of every sin and gives us eternal life in Jesus Christ when we receive Him into our lives, and so, as the true children of God persistently continue to read, study, meditate, and live the Word of God, He reveals more and more of Himself to them. Romans 1:17 says, "The just shall live by faith."

2

JESUS: YOUR SAVIOR— WHO IS HE?

Before we proceed any further into the book, we will discuss a little bit about the Lord God and Jesus Christ. Are they one and the same, or are they two separate Gods—one for the Christians and one for the Old Testament believers, the Jews? There is a lack of understanding in the minds and hearts of some people, which is rooted in unbelief and rebellion, that God, who spoke throughout the Old Testament, and Jesus Christ are the same. God the Son, the Lord Jesus Christ, is the same nature as God the Father and the Holy Spirit. They make up the Godhead: the three co-eternal persons of God, having no beginning or ending.

The Godhead spoke and were active throughout the Bible—the Old and New Testaments—and so God in three persons who spoke to Abraham, Moses, David, and all the other prophets in the Old Testament also spoke to all the writers in the New Testament. He is the same active supreme Holy Power spoken of in the Bible who is and will always be powering and running the universe and beyond. There is one God, not two different Gods: one for the Old Testament Israelites and another for the New Testament church.

Non-Christians of other religions do not believe that Jesus, the Christ, is indeed the second person of the Godhead or that He is God, for that matter, revealed and declared in the likeness of mankind, for the Bible says in Colossians 1 that He, speaking of the Lord Jesus Christ, is before all things, and in Him all things consist. All things were created by and for Him. Read 1 Timothy 6:14–16 to also see another evidence from the Bible of who Jesus Christ is. Please also read Titus 2:13.

God is not simple. His nature is very complex, way beyond the understanding of any of His creatures in the universe, and so His nature and existence cannot be reasoned out nor be understood in the minds of mankind nor by angels. It is only by faith, which is given by God Himself, that any of us may believe what the Bible declares who God is. The Godhead will be discussed later in more detail.

Non-Christians also do not believe that Jesus Christ is the atonement for the sins of the whole world and He is the Savior of sinners who believe that He is the only way, the truth, and the life. Anyone who comes to God must believe that He is and that He is the rewarder of them that diligently seek Him. So why do people not believe or refuse to believe that Jesus Christ is the all-powerful and all-knowing Creator God? It is because we are all born spiritually dead individuals. No spiritually dead person has any relationship with the living God. He or she cannot understand God, for the things of God are foolishness to every unbeliever.

Some of the Old Testament chosen people of God have so far refused to acknowledge and to accept Jesus Christ as the Messiah. Jesus is indeed the fulfillment of the animal sacrificial system that God had them use as the atonement type or shadow for all their sins. Some of these old covenant believers still deny the deity of Jesus Christ, and they deny that the prophecies of the Old Testament spoke of Him. These nonbelievers also deny the fulfillment of those prophecies in the New Testament, and they dismiss the evidence the Bible gives regarding the life of Christ and what He said regarding Himself of who He is and the great miracles that He did. They reject the facts the Bible gives concerning His crucifixion and deny His resurrection. However, there are an increasing number of new Jewish believers who believe that Jesus Christ is Messiah God, and they also believe and accept the entire gospel message.

As Christians, many of us believe that God has not forsaken the people with whom He had made a covenant to redeem them unto salvation. God did promise to save them, through their faith, using the sacrificial types and the feast-time ceremonies as signs that pointed to Himself in the person of the Lord Jesus Christ. He was the true sacrifice and the fulfillment of the feast times, who was to come and did come at the appointed time; and God did make a new and better covenant with all mankind so that whosoever will believe in Him, that He is the only deliverer of mankind from a life of sin, shall not perish but shall have eternal life.

So many people have not yet received the Lord Jesus to be the true and only Savior sent from God the Father to redeem mankind from their sins. Only He has the power to give to anyone the opportunity to become a true child of God. It was revealed to those who worshiped God, by faith, under the old covenant, that Christ is He that was the promised atonement for all the sins of every believing sinner. Jesus Christ is He that was spoken about by the Bible prophets. It is He who was seen in the types and the shadows by the true Old Testament believers. The feast times and the animal sacrifices, which were of the old covenant, were all nailed to His cross at Christ's crucifixion (Colossians 2). God forsakes no one, but rather, it is mankind who has forsaken Him.

There are others who belong to other faiths that believe Jesus is a God, created and is separate from God the Father and the Holy Spirit, which is the Spirit of God. It may be impossible to find a non-Christian who believes in the three-person nature of God. The Godhead description of who God is must be accepted by faith alone. The Word of God, the Bible, says that every human being has sinned, and all have fallen short of the glory of God. Those who have accepted Jesus as their Savior and Lord have also accepted the Bible to be the only Word of God. Christians are not superior to non-Christians, but rather, they that receive salvation from Jesus Christ are saved by the grace and mercy of God alone.

No one can earn merits into heaven nor can anyone do anything to earn the favor of God for a place in heaven. God does the saving. The whole deal, if you will, is done by Jesus Christ and by Him alone. Christians are not right about everything. We are ever learning from the Word of God. Our brothers and sisters, the Jews, are not right about everything either. God is the only one who is always and is absolutely right about everything, for He is the author of truth. The Bible is the only holy book that says Jesus is God. No other religion's writings speak of Jesus as God, for if any other religion's writings do talk about the problems of mankind, they do not tell the whole story. No one knows the whole story but God Himself, and thus, no one has any real solution(s) to man's problems except that the Bible tells us everything we need to know about sin and God's remedy for it.

According to the Bible, sin is the root of all mankind's problems. The Bible says that the solution to mankind's predicament is Jesus Christ (Romans 5). That's one of the differences that set the Bible apart from every other religion's writings. The Bible is about Jesus Christ and His love for all mankind. The Bible is also about the righteousness of God, and it lets us know that salvation is through Jesus Christ alone and no one else.

We will see from the Bible more evidence, in addition to the ones already stated, that Jesus is indeed eternal God, the same "I Am" of the Old Testament. Christ is the first begotten from the dead, the first fruit. He is the faithful and true witness as He is written about in the New Testament and prophesied about in the Old Testament. Jesus Christ is the fairest of all. He is the fountain of living waters, and He is the former of all things. He is the fortress of salvation and the foundation that no one else can lay.

Christ is the anointed one, author, and finisher of our faith. He is Alpha and Omega, the beginning and the last; no one is before Him, and there shall be no one after Him. It is impossible for anyone to precede or succeed Jesus Christ, for He is from everlasting to everlasting. He is the arm of the Lord. He is the Horn of Israel. He is the Advocate of the redeemed. He and the Ancient of Days are one. He is the Everlasting Father. He is the Prince of Peace. He is the Revelation of God, and He is the Bread of Life. He is the end of the law to them that believe and who are begotten of Him. He is the gate through which we must enter to know God, and He is the giver of salvation. He is the gift of God for the wages of sin. Christ is the faithful high priest, and He is the Holy One of Israel.

He is head of the true church—His body. He is the image of the invisible God. He is the head of all principalities and powers. He is our only hope for redemption. He is Lord of lords, and He is King of kings. Christ is the only wise God. He is the maker of a better covenant. He is the Passover Lamb. Christ is the Resurrection and the Life. He is the way, the truth, and the life. He is the Chief Corner Stone, which the builders rejected. He is the bright and morning star. He is just. He is the purifier's fire. He is light unapproachable. He is holy, and He is Jehovah, the one who is self-existent. He is the Tabernacle of God that is with men, and He is the Son of Man.

He is Jehovah Rapha, the Lord who heals. He is Jehovah Jireh, the Lord who provides. He is Jehovah Rohi, the Lord is my shepherd. Christ is Jehovah Tsidkenu, the Lord is righteousness. He is Jehovah Nissi, the Lord is my banner, and that banner is His agape love over all of them that believe. He is Jehovah Shalom, the Lord is peace, and He is El Shaddai, the all-sufficient one. Jesus Christ is the Word that spoke in the beginning at Creation.

Jesus is He who spoke to Noah about building the ark. It is Jesus who sent Moses to deliver the children of Israel out of Egypt. It was He who spoke to Moses and gave him the Ten Commandments on Mount Sinai, and it is He who spoke to the prophets in the Old Testament. It was Jesus who wrestled with Jacob and changed his name to Israel. To the Israelites, Jesus was the pillar of cloud by day and a pillar of fire by night. He was the Israelites' covering and their protector as they journeyed from Egypt, and it was Jesus whom King David prayed to and sought counsel and guidance for all his battles. It was Jesus that fought all Israel's battles, and it is He who gave them victory over their enemies. It was Jesus Christ who divided the Red Sea and made all Israel to walk on dry ground over to the other side. It was Jesus who took Enoch alive into heaven, and it was He who also took Elijah in a chariot of fire into heaven. It was Christ who gave Moses the instructions to build the tabernacle of God. It was He that smote Sodom and Gomorrah with the flames of His judgment, and it is He who will judge both the living and the dead in the coming judgment. He is the all-knowing God, and He is eternal.

In the book of Matthew 1:23, we read,

> Behold, a virgin shall be with child, and shall bring forth a son, and they shall call his name Emmanuel, which being interpreted is, God with us.

God took on flesh and became human, yet He did not sin. We also read in verse 21 of Matthew chapter 1,

> And she shall bring forth a son, and thou shall call his name JESUS: for he shall save his people from their sins.

He is called the Christ because He is the anointed of God. Jesus is the great high priest of God, who is touched with the feelings of our infirmities in that He was tempted in all points like as we are, yet He sinned not (Hebrews 4:14–15).

Jesus, God's Atonement for Sin

According to the Bible, it was absolutely necessary for the Lord Jesus Christ to come into the world. His coming was important only because without a Savior, all of humanity would be lost from God, in sin, forever. Christ was the Lamb of God promised to all men, to the Jew first and also to the Gentiles. God made it so because there was no other way that the sins of men could have been atoned for. Animal sacrifices were insufficient in that their blood was limited in power to totally atone for man's sins once and for all, and so these sacrifices had to be done daily and yearly for the atonement of the sins of every sinner in Israel. It was the system for the redemption of the Israelites that foreshadowed the atoning work of Christ, and as stated before, all animal sacrifices pointed to Jesus Christ, God's perfect sacrifice for the atonement of the sins of all who would believe in Him. This atonement, of which Christ is, was perfect, for Christ is perfect.

The Bible says that Christ was without sin, totally sinless before God (2 Corinthians 5:21). Because Adam no longer had dominion over what God had given him, Jesus Christ was the only perfect and sinless person that did qualify to redeem that which was lost when mankind fell into the corrupt hands of Satan. Thus, it is understood that all of humanity are lost from the presence of God because we have the nature of sin in us.

In Matthew 4 and Luke 4, it is recorded that Satan tempted Jesus to sin; but the temptations did not work, for Jesus resisted the lies of the chief devil. He did this by speaking the Word of God to Satan starting with "It is written" to all his temptations. Jesus relied on the presence of God the Father in Him and spoke only what was written in the Bible, and so what Jesus's responses were to the temptations of Satan is the example for all Christian believers to follow when faced with temptations.

Christ was obedient to the whole law of God. He never wavered at Satan's temptations. Had Jesus sinned, His dominion over the universe would have been handed over to Satan, and God would have become Satan's subject. You can just imagine the consequences of such a defeat of God, but thanks be unto God, just for who He is, for His works are just and righteous altogether.

Satan must have thought that since Christ emptied Himself of all His glory, it would mean that He would be at His weakest and He would be vulnerable to his lying campaigns of deceptions, but what Satan did not know and understand is that obedience to God is better than the breaking of God's commandments to satisfy the flesh's passions for the things of earth and the kingdoms of this world. In verse 7 of Matthew chapter 4, Jesus said to Satan,

It is written again, "Thou shalt not tempt the Lord thy God."

Christ stood firm in His obedience to the commandments of God the Father, and as a result, He triumphed over Satan's temptations. Where Adam failed, Christ was victorious, for the Bible says obedience to the commandments of God is better than the sacrifice from a carnal minded nature (1 Samuel 15:22). Some people in the church think they can live a sinful life and then appease God with a sacrifice to prevent the consequences from happening or when the consequence of their sins is operating in their life. God wants our obedience to His Word. That's how you and I will stay out of trouble with sin. The Word of God must be engrained and etched in our heart so that we may not sin against our heavenly Father (Psalm 119.11). Christ gave Satan his lethal blow and "crushed" his dominion and authority over all who will believe in Him. Christ also totally "crushed" Satan's hopes for His demise, both at the cross and in His bodily resurrection from the grave on the third day.

The Bible says in Hebrews 9:11–13,

But Christ being come an high priest of good things to come, by a greater and more perfect tabernacle, not made with hands, that is to say, not of this building; Neither by the blood of goats and calves, but by his own blood he entered in once into the holy place, having obtained eternal redemption for us. For the blood of bulls and of goats, and the ashes of an heifer sprinkling the unclean, sanctifieth to the purifying of the flesh: How much more shall the blood of Christ, who through the eternal Spirit offered himself without spot to God, purge your conscience from dead works to serve the living God?

We also read in Romans 3:25,

Whom God hath set forth to be a propitiation through faith in the blood, to declare his righteousness for the remission of sins that are past, through the forbearance of God.

In 1 John 2:2 we read,

> And he is the propitiation for our sins: and not for ours only, but also for the sins of the whole world.

Christ died for all mankind that whosoever would believe in the name, Jesus, the same shall be saved.

Jesus, the Word Who Spoke in Creation

The Bible states in the book of John 1:1–4,

> In the beginning was the Word, and the Word was with God. The same was in the beginning with God. All things were made by him; and without him was not anything made that was made. In him was life, and the life was the light of men.

Verse 14 of John chapter 1 says,

> And the Word was made flesh and dwelt among us.

Speaking of Christ and His nature, we read in Colossians 2:9,

> For in him dwelleth all the fullness of the Godhead bodily.

All the attributes of God are in Jesus Christ. He is God incarnate, meaning God putting on flesh.

The Word of God is a person (John 1), and He is the voice of God that we read of in Genesis 3:8. It was all three persons of the Godhead who created everything into existence. Christ spoke the things that were in His mind, and whatever He willed it to be, the word became that thing of substance. His Word is the words that changed the life of countless people because He is Almighty God. He is the source of life in all living things, and He is the source of the spiritual rebirth experience of every person that hears His voice. He gives new-life to whoever calls upon the name of the Lord and who believes in his or her heart that He is both Savior and Lord. The Word of God and Jesus Christ are one and the same. He is the Word that was made flesh.

Every human being is born with the knowledge of the basics of good and evil—what's right to do and what's wrong that should not be done.

They know that there is a higher power beyond themselves and He is the unknown God to them, and they know that there is an evil power also. Some of these people, most of which live in remote areas of the world, do not know that that greater power is the God of the Bible who created the universe and all its contents; but when the gospel is preached and the Word of God is planted in the heart of sinners, He reveals Himself as Creator, Redeemer, and Sustainer. Thus, mankind was specially created to be in communion with their Creator, for God created them by forming them, male and female, in His image and in His likeness with His own hands.

The entire Bible is written about Jesus and about the salvation plan that God provided to redeem mankind from the habits and penalty of sin (Hebrews 10:1–19). The Godhead had the plan of redemption in place before the foundations of the world. It must be noted here that according to the Bible, the Holy Spirit is the Spirit of God the Father and the Spirit of God the Son. God is one and He has one Spirit and so it takes faith to believe that the entire Bible is the inerrant Word of God and, therefore, everything that is revealed to us by God must be of faith that comes by hearing the Word of God in our spirit through the power of the Holy Spirit and everything in the Bible that the children of God understands when His Spirit teaches is also by faith. Therefore, faith is the confidence and the assurance that God gives to men and women when they respond to the gospel so that they may understand that He is who He says He is.

We don't understand why God would exist in the form of three persons, from which we get the Godhead description, but we accept it by faith. If the nature of God is to be understood by His creation, then He will cease to be God. There is no genesis with God, for He has no beginning and He has no end. He is infinite in His nature. Nothing God created, neither mankind nor angels, have the mental capacity and ability to understand the infinite nature of God, and so no one can understand God, yet He humbled Himself and became human in the likeness (form and resemblance) of mankind to tabernacle with us. We can know something about His nature to the extent of what the Bible says who He is to us, but we cannot understand the whole nature of God. Without faith, it is impossible to please God, and it takes faith to know Him and to believe that He is God.

In the book of Isaiah 55:8–9, we read,

> For my thoughts are not your thoughts, neither are your ways my ways, saith the Lord. For as the heavens are higher than the earth, so are my ways higher than your ways, and my thoughts than your thoughts.

Has anyone measured the distance between the heavens and the earth? Or is there an instrument that can measure vast distances or the enormous expanse of the universe?

We also read in Job 36:26,

> Behold, God is great, and we know him not, neither can the number of his years be searched out.

And we again read in John 1:18,

> No man hath seen God at any time; the only begotten Son, which is in the bosom of the Father, he hath declared him.

God, in His glorified nature, cannot be seen. As sinful beings, we will be consumed by the brightness of His glory because the presence of God is a consuming fire (Deuteronomy 4:24 and Hebrews 12:29). Christ declared to us who God is. He showed us, by example, how to live a pure and sanctified life before God.

As was stated earlier, the singular God exists in plural form. The plurality of God is the Godhead, which consists of God the Father, God the Son, and the Holy Spirit. All three were equal active persons in creation (Genesis 1), and all three are the same active supernatural persons in the salvation of mankind. God the Father sent God the Son and confirmed Him to be the Father's beloved Son in whom the Father was well pleased. God the Son, who is Jesus Christ, became a man by way of the virgin birth and dwelled on earth with mankind. He lived as the only true example of how mankind ought to live before God. Christ died and shed His blood for the remission of the sins of the whole world so that mankind may have life in Him. He rose on the third day from the dead and is in heaven, seated at the right hand of God the Father. The Holy Spirit, or the Spirit of God, was sent by God the Father in Jesus's name after He returned to heaven to teach and guide the believer to understand what he or she is reading in the Bible. It is the Holy Spirit that Jesus said in John 14 that will also bring to remembrance the things the believer has learned from reading and studying the Word of God.

Let us look at the words only begotten. It is not an accurate translation of the original Greek word monogenes.[10] Only begotten is an English translation of this Greek word monogenes. Monogenes means Jesus Christ is of the same nature, and He has the same attributes of God the Father. Jesus is of the bosom of the Father (John 1:18). So when we use the English translated words only begotten, it gives the interpretation to non-Christians that God procreated Jesus or that God created Jesus as either another God or Godlike being, that is, someone less than God. This would be impossible because God cannot create another God, nor would He create a being having some likeness to Himself, that is, Godlike, but lacking all the attributes the Bible says that are of God. God does not have a wife, and He does not procreate. He only creates.

There is only one God, and besides Him, there is no other (Isaiah 45:5–6). Some non-Christians reading the language of "only begotten Son" bite into Christians, whether of Jewish heritage or are of Gentile background, and try to disannul the credibility of Scripture and invalidate who Jesus is. He is God, and God cannot be invalidated because He is self-existent and self-sustaining, needing nothing and needing no help. Jesus said in John 10:30, "I and my Father are one." In contrast to "in the bosom of the Father," we have the earthly father-and-son relationship, as with Abraham and Isaac (Genesis 18, 20, and 22). In this relationship between Abraham and Isaac, the term "only begotten" is appropriately used in procreation, in which Isaac was of the loins of Abraham. Isaac was the son of promise from God to Abraham and Sarah. This we read in Genesis 17:19 and again in chapter 18 verses 10 and 14.

Because Isaac was the son of promise to Abraham and Sarah, he was typified as the "only begotten son." It meant that Isaac shared the same genes of his parents. Isaac was also the only son, only begotten, of both Abraham and Sarah. Here, monogenes does not apply because Isaac shared the genes of both parents in that he is the offspring of procreation. He is not the same exact image of either parent, and he cannot be the

---

[10]Strong's Greek # 3439, μονογενής (monogenés).

same as his father or his mother. There can be resemblances to a parent but not the same person as either parent.

Jesus is the exact same nature, and He has exactly the same attributes as God the Father and the Holy Spirit. Jesus has no beginning and He has no end because God has no beginning and He has no end. He is eternal.

Jesus Was Not the Result of Procreation

God does not have "a son God," and He does not procreate as was stated before. He made all things by speaking them into existence. God, however, did not just speak mankind into existence. He created them, male and female, by forming them with His hands. God the Father did not procreate Jesus, nor did the Holy Spirit create Jesus. The Bible says in Matthew 1:20 that the conception of Jesus's incarnation into this world, by way of the womb of the virgin Mary, was by the power of the Holy Ghost. Jesus existed in eternity past as God. He wills all things that He creates because all things are always in the mind of God.

What God spoke to create simply became that thing He willed it to become, and in its becoming, the substance of His every Word is good. Christ has no after or second thoughts about anything. His thoughts have no finiteness to them. They are infinite. God's thoughts are beyond the limits of the universe, and so Christ's thoughts never had a beginning, and whatever has no beginning also has no ending to it. God does not "think" before He does what He wants to do, and therefore, Christ, as God, does not do the same. God has no equal to Himself that is outside of Himself. Again, the three-person existence of God is one. Christ has no predecessor, and He has no successor. Isaiah 43:10–11 states,

> That ye may know and believe me, and understand that I am he: before me there was no God formed, neither shall there be after me. I, even I, am the Lord; and beside me there is no savior.

Jesus was not formed nor was He created.

Jesus Typed in Earthly Symbols

In the Old Testament part of the holy Bible, Jesus is typed in many physical symbols. The book of Exodus 25–31 speaks of the tabernacle of God of whom Jesus is the Tabernacle. Every object in the tabernacle painted a perfect picture of Jesus Christ, from the gate to the mercy seat.

Everything (the furnishings) in the tabernacle has meaning as it relates to the atoning work of Christ. There is New Testament fulfillment of the symbolisms of who Jesus is as we read in the four Gospels and in the writings of the apostle Paul. We also read the fulfillment of the symbols in the book of Hebrews chapters 2, 8, and 9.

The Godhead

Jesus said in John 10:30, "I and my Father are one." The one God exists as God the Father, God the Son, and the Holy Spirit. As stated before, this is referred to as the Godhead, and we read this in the books of Acts 17:29, Romans 1:20, and Colossians 2:8–9. God is singular in His nature, but He is plural in His existence, as we see in the name Elohim (Genesis 1:26). Deuteronomy 6:4 says, "Hear, O Israel: The Lord our God is one Lord." Interestingly, the Lord Jesus repeated this Old Testament statement in Mark 12:29, "The first of all the commandments is, Hear, O Israel; The Lord our God is one Lord."

In Genesis 1:26–27, the Word of God says,

> And God said, "Let us make man in our image, after our likeness." So God created man in His own image, in the image of God created He him; male and female created he them.

Here the singular pronoun He is used to refer to the one-person God, but Elohim is also used to denote the three-person existence of one God as we see in the words "let us." He (God) transcends time, space, and matter. Since the expanse of the universe may be impossible to measure to know its exact size and God exists outside its boundaries, then He is immeasurable. He fills every space in the universe and beyond at the same time with His presence. Who God is will be further discussed in chapter 7, "Faith to Believe." Surely God is not asking angels to join Him in creating mankind. Angels are created beings. They have no power to create life. The power to create the universe and everything in it is exclusively God's. Again, the Word of God said in Isaiah 42:8,

> I am the Lord: that is my name: and my glory will I not give to another, neither my praise to graven images.

The glory of God is not only the splendor of God, but the glory of God is also the power of His might and the absolute authority that He has over His entire creation. The glory of God is all of who He is. We saw that earlier when we talked about the attributes of Jesus. God does not share His power, nor does He share any part of His glory with anything He created. All things were created by Him that are in the heavens, on the earth, and under the earth.

I invite you to please read Genesis 18, the encounter of God with Abraham. You will see why some Christians believe it was God who appeared to Abraham in human form at his tent's door in the plains of Mamre. Other Christians believe that the three men were angels. I believe it was the Lord Jesus in His preincarnate form was the one who spoke to Abraham. Please read this chapter with the Spirit of God leading you to the understanding of what's in view. In other words, as with the entire Word of God, prayerfully ask God for His Holy Spirit to give you the understanding of this Scripture. The Hebrew word for Lord, Adonay[11] or Yahweh,[12] is strictly used when it appears in verses 3, 13, 14, 17, 19, 22, 26, 27, 30, 31, 32, and 33 of Genesis 18 instead of the word Adon,[13] meaning "lord" or "sir."

The Bible says in John 1:1–3,

> In the beginning was the word, and the word was with God, and the word was God. All things were made by him; and without him was not anything made that was made.

Jesus is distinct from angels because He is their Creator. In the test of truth, we use multiple witnesses within the Word of God. The Bible defines itself to us through the Holy Spirit, who is the Spirit of God. One such scriptural evidence that shows Christ to be the God of the Bible we read in Hebrews 1:8:

> But unto the Son he said, Thy throne, O God, is forever and ever: a scepter of righteousness is the scepter of thy kingdom.

---

[11]Strong's Hebrew # 136.
[12]Strong's Hebrew # 3068.
[13]Strong's Hebrew # 113.

Another biblical evidence of who Jesus is found in the book of Colossians 1:13–18:

> Who hath delivered us from the power of darkness, and hath translated us into the Kingdom of his dear Son: In whom we have redemption through his blood, even the forgiveness of sins: Who is the image of the invisible God, the firstborn of every creature: For by him were all things created, and that are in heaven, and are in the earth, visible and invisible, whether they be thrones, or dominions, or principalities, or powers: all things were created by him and for him: And he is before all things, and by him all things consist, and he is the head of the body, the church: who is the beginning, the firstborn from the dead; that in all things he might have the preeminence.

We can also look into our lives and into the lives of others and see the miracle of transformation that has taken place and know that there is only one true and living God that transforms men and women from spiritual darkness to having the light of life that is of Jesus Christ. He is the revelation of the invisible God to mankind, and it is He that gives eternal life to whosoever will believe that He is the author of salvation and is the only way to know God. He is Emmanuel, meaning "God with us." No one else can give life but God. For all the changes that have taken place in us, I mean the real substantive changes, from a life of wickedness to one of righteousness, did not happen without God.

Jesus Christ is the changemaker. The word that He speaks to us through the Holy Spirit raises spiritually dead people to spiritual life. Jesus never has to prove His Word. It is the everlasting, unchangeable, the standard bearer of truth, and faith-giving Word. The transformation of the heart is that which God alone does. He takes the stony hearts of men and women that has been made hard by sin and makes them tender enough so that the Word of God may have good ground to root itself. It is the Holy Spirit who waters dried-up and parched lives with the waters of life from the Word of God.

Every new born-again spirit of the people who God has drawn to Himself is not of mankind, nor is it of the forces of the cosmos—it is of God, and thus, every born-again believer has become the evidence of transformation so that people may know that the Bible is true, and it can be trusted for what it says who God is. When we are seeking living examples in whom is the Spirit of righteousness, we are to ask God to show us His true disciples. However, Christ is the redeemed, only true living example of godliness, and the Word of God explains what true godliness looks like, and Christ is it, for there are many false witnesses that are planted by Satan to deceive those whom God is calling out from a life of spiritual darkness and be filled with the light of His presence.

The firstborn of every creature, as stated in Colossians 1:13–18, is referring to Christ's preeminence in all things. The Greek word prototokos,[14] translated firstborn, signify priority or first to experience translation, and since He, meaning Christ, had emptied Himself of all His glory and became human in the very likeness of mankind, He is the first to be changed from corruptible flesh to an incorruptible flesh. This supernatural action was done by the power of God the Father. Christ's transformation in His baptism and translation at His bodily resurrection, in that He was glorified, was also of the power of God the Father. These phases of Jesus's life and His walk with God the Father are examples for us to know and follow and to have that same fellowship with God.

Anyone can have abundant life from God, not by his or her works, but by the grace of God in Jesus. Eternal life is a gift from God. The children of God can avoid the catastrophes and the calamities of sin by doing what God says they must to do in His Word, and if they do sin and then repent because God has troubled them to do so, they are not rejected by Him. His love and mercy still abide over all His children. It is when we refuse to heed God's voice to repent from sin that we are in serious trouble with Him, and thus, it is only when we listen to God that we are reminded that Christ is the only way to a victorious walk with God. He is, by rank, the first born-again example of every redeemed child of God who is transformed from spiritual death to a new spiritually alive person, and so all the redeemed of Christ (they that live the Word of God and have the testimony of Jesus Christ) are awaiting the physical translation to be fully glorified together with Him unto God. Therefore, He, meaning Christ, represents everything that the true children of God would become, such that He is the pattern on earth of what true transformation is to them who are begotten by God the Father.

Now Christ was never spiritually dead because He never sinned. Christ is the first resurrection from the dead for all who die to ungodliness

---

[14]Strong's Greek # 4416.

and are buried with Him in baptism and are resurrected to a new spiritual life in Him. Christ was counted as a sinner because He took upon Himself the sin of sinners. He is the first to receive the inheritance of all heavenly things given to Him by God the Father, and so all those who are begotten of God and are made the righteousness of Christ, through His blood, will receive the same inheritance He received—a right to the tree of life and a crown of righteousness.

All God's children are joint heirs with Christ because of the promise God had made, for if we suffer in this world with Christ, we will also be glorified together with Him (John 8:17). There is only one God, one true Jesus Christ, one truth, one gospel, and one true church. Christ is the head of all the true believers, which He refers to as His sheep (John 10). That true church, I believe, is not a particular denomination, but it's a collection of all the true believers from all denominations who came out and who continue to come out of spiritual Babylon and from under every false teaching and out from every false church and serve the living God in obedience to all His commandments. God knows who these true believers are in all denominations, for there is certainly a mixed multitude in Christendom. Not all who say they are Christians are truly the followers of the Lord Jesus Christ.

Christ, the Son of Man

In Matthew 18:11, Jesus referred to Himself as the "Son of man." There we read,

> For the Son of man is come to save that which was lost.

And in Mark 10:45, Jesus said,

> For the Son of man came not to be ministered unto, but to minister, and to give his life a ransom for many.

This means the Son of Man, Christ, is fully human; yet He is also fully God (John 1:1 and Matthew 1:2). He was human in every sense of what being human is, yet He was sinless (John 1:14).

Jesus is the Son of God, meaning God the Son, the second person of the Godhead, indicating His deity. He is the God of creation, and He is the God of redemption. He is the God of mercy, and He is the God of grace. He is without a genetically related earthly father or a genetically related human mother. He had no bloodline relations with any human being. Christ was not a descendant of any human being, nor was He the product of God the Father and angels. The Bible says in Luke 1:35, that holy thing that was conceived in Mary's womb and He who was born into this world was the action of the power of the Holy Ghost (Holy Spirit). God was 100 percent responsible for the conception and incarnation of Jesus Christ. God Himself came to earth in the person of the Lord Jesus Christ, born into the vessel of weak flesh, and made His abode with a spiritually dead human race, and so Christ, in the power and in the glory of His divine nature, has neither beginning of days nor end of life (John 10:30 and Hebrews 7:3).

Jesus Christ is the Divine One who is the revelation of God to mankind, for the Bible says in John 1:18 that no man has seen God at any time; but Jesus Christ, who is in the bosom of the Father, had declared God to us. The term "Son of man," in addition to describing Jesus's ministering role, also defines His Messianic nature to those whom God had called under the old covenant to be His people. He was the promised spiritual deliverer of the Jewish people, but that is not an automatic conversion. Every sinner must believe and accept Jesus Christ to be their Savior and Lord. Where Adam fell spiritually, Christ resisted Satan and was not overcome by evil. As the perfect Lamb of God, Jesus is the Savior of all who would believe in Him. He is the deliverer of sinners from sin who became God-fearing people, those who God had made righteous through the atonement of Jesus on the cross for the sins of the whole world. They accepted the gift of salvation when their spirit was quickened by God.

Because Christ emptied Himself of all His glory, He had to be given power from God the Father to heal the sick of all manner of diseases. He raised the physically dead, and He gave spiritual life to the spiritually dead. Christ gave sight to the blind, made the deaf to hear, the dumb to speak, He healed the brokenhearted, and He healed all manner of diseases, and the greatest of what Christ did is that He forgave the sins of every sinner seeking salvation from God. These are the people that God the Father draws to Himself through the Holy Spirit. Christ was given a kingdom—not an earthly kingdom but the heavenly kingdom that He had before His incarnation. His kingdom is the kingdom of righteousness, and it is the kingdom of God. He received all these things, not that He did not have the power and the attributes of God before He became the atonement for sin and became mankind's example of what true godly living looks like; He had all the power of being the one true God, but Christ submitted His will to the will of God the Father, and He became the Servant unto God.

Jesus was given the glory and the power of God only because He had emptied Himself of all His glory before He took on the form of a human being (John 17:5). Christ came down to the place of His footstool so that sinners can be transformed from life in sin into life as becoming saints. He will forever be identified in the form and likeness of mankind. He will forever be the God-Man or the Son of Man, as He is referred in John 5:25–27, in Daniel 7:13, and in Revelation 1:13–14. The Bible says in Acts 1:11,

> Ye men of Galilee, why stand ye gazing up into heaven this same Jesus, which is taken up from you into heaven, shall so come in like manner as ye have seen him go into heaven.

In addition to all that the Bible has said about Jesus's return, He will also bear the scars of the nail piercings in His hands and in His feet, and He will have the scar from the piercing of the sword into His side.

As stated earlier in the chapter, there is a mystery of the full nature of God that we will never understand even when all the true believers enter eternity with God. We will be forever learning of the goodness of God for eternity. If it were possible for the redeemed of God to stop learning the wonders of all the things He created and to stop praising and worshiping Him, when we are in eternity with Him, it may mean mischief may not be far from us; for if it were possible, what would a mind and a heart think and do if he or she is no longer praising and worshiping his or her Creator and has nothing else to learn from Him? Those who believe that we will eventually understand God and who teach the same—I believe they are dead wrong, and that may be a dangerous notion to assume that we, the redeemed, will eventually understand our Creator.

Being in the presence of God forever will never get boring. The Word of God says that eyes have not seen nor ears heard nor has it entered the heart of mankind the things that God has in store for them that love Him (1 Corinthians 2:9). If mankind is to ever know and understand God, He will cease to be God. It means that our minds would be the same as His, and therefore, He will cease to be supernatural.

As stated before, in this book, we can know and understand, on a limited level, that aspect of God that has to do with our salvation and who He is—He is the eternal, all-powerful, all-seeing, and omnipresent God. God will always reveal levels of truth in stages as we diligently read and study His Word. When we diligently seek God by faith and search Him out line upon line, scripture by scripture, here a little and there a little, His Spirit will reveal and guide us to truth. The reason Satan tries to discourage people from hearing and reading the Bible and spreads lies about the Word of God is because he knows the power of knowing and receiving information. Mankind's knowledge of right and wrong, good and evil, is because of listening, obeying, and believing the lies of Satan. He knows that the Word of God causes people to be transformed from sinners into saints.

I believe that there is so much information for the redeemed to learn about the immense universe that God did create that it will take time infinitum to know the works of His hands. God is infinite, and His Word is eternal. His kingdom is an everlasting kingdom. God's will that was done on earth is from within Himself, and it is the pattern of that which is in heaven. I also believe that the elect of God will forever be learning about all the wondrous things He has made in this vast universe.

Jesus Christ is the purest among the mighty men of valor and the mightiest among the purest of mortals. He continues to rule and guide the ages with His holy power, and lives are changed and transformed by His gospel. Christ guides men and women with mercy and grace and deposits into their hearts the knowledge of all His goodness. He changes the lives of sinners and purifies the minds of obedient men with His Word. Christ makes men and women find rest, in Him, for their weary feet have trotted, with pain and anguish, the dusty roads of sin.

3

God, the Bible, and You

Because the Bible claims it is the infallible Word of God, then as Christians, we are to believe everything it says about God and about all mankind, for it is the revealed truth of the relationship between God and humanity. God is the bearer of all truth, and this truth is not relative to mankind's interpretation and to his level of intellectualism. One of the attributes of God is truth, for He cannot be anything else but be truthful. Jesus said in the book of John 14:6—to the one who asked him, "How can we know the way?"

> I am the way, the truth, and the life: no man cometh unto the Father, but by me.

As was discussed earlier, every prophecy that is written in the Bible is of no private interpretation, and they were given, in times past, to holy and consecrated men of God. These were men who kept the commandments of God out of obedience even though they were men of like passions and weakness as we are, for they were also redeemed sinners; but they always sought God, who first pursued and chose them to be a peculiar people. There was nothing in the lives of these men that made them special, but rather, they humbled themselves and were obedient to the voice of God as He spoke to them in their hearts. These humble-minded men are they who wrote the Bible as they were inspired by the Holy Spirit of God to write those things God wanted to be written in His book. Please read 2 Peter 1:19–21.

Have you ever asked yourself the question, "Who am I?" "Why am I here?" and "Why was I born?" Well, the answer is in the Word of God, beginning at Genesis and confirmed by God throughout the Bible. The

Bible is all about you and the God who loves you so much that He gave Himself, in the person of the Lord Jesus Christ, to be the payment for your sins and mine so that He may redeem you and I from the hand of Satan, whom you now or once served. You are very important to God, and you are His very best masterpiece.

If I may say so myself, each one of us is the Designer's original. Every person's life is priceless including yours. We are the ones who attach limitations to our lives. We are the ones who put limits on what God can do for us. He wants to fulfill in our lives the true purpose He created us to become. You and I were created to be people of excellence. We must never settle for anything other than always doing our best in every situation.

According to the Bible, God created every human being in His image (Genesis 1:26–27). God created you because He had you in His mind from eternity past. You were never an afterthought in the mind of God. He knows all about you even before you were born. He cares about you specifically, and He wants you to be successful in all things. God wants to be your God and your Lord. He foreknew you and predestined you to be conformed to the image of Jesus Christ. Because God predestined you, He also called you so that He may justify you, for the Bible says whom God justifies, He also glorifies (Romans 8:28–30).

Your beginning and all that you will ever be was always in the incomprehensible mind of God. The holy Scriptures declare the mighty works of God in creation, and they also declare that He sustains all things that He created (Job 38). Surely God did a mighty work in you when He formed you in love. God is the one who sustained you throughout all your circumstances. That's how you made it this far. He protected you from all the attacks of Satan and fought all your battles you could not fight on your own.

When darkness was all around you, Jesus Christ was the one that was the light which made your night become as the day. This great and holy God chose you so that you may become one of His royal, beyond ordinary priesthood saints, and He selected you to be a peculiar person of the Most High God. Your distinctiveness is not in a strange sort of deranged way, but it means that you are specially and specifically different from all others and even different from your old or soon-to-be-old fleshly self. God did choose to create you in His image and in His likeness. He birthed you at the appointed time to be His special vessel that will bear His character upon the earth. That is what God meant when He said in Genesis 1:26, "Let us make man in our image, after our likeness"; and so when we are born again, we do receive the image of God, and His character is formed in us by the renewing of our minds.

The Holy Spirit's presence inside of our being is to help us live godly lives. He expresses the ways of God inside of us. We are to look like God from the inside out. When God was forming you, your name was written in the palm of His hand (Isaiah 49:16). God had chosen you from within Himself from before the foundation of the world (Ephesians 1:4), and so in a very peculiar and remarkable way, you are more than special to God.

God chose that one sperm cell of your father out of an average of two hundred million sperm cells produced and used it to fertilize that one egg from your mother. Any other sperm cell and any other egg fertilized would have been someone else, entirely different from you. The day and the precise hour this fertilization took place were determined and chosen by God. Your father and your mother were both chosen by God to be the vessel that will bear you into this world. Your parents' parents and their parents and their parents, leading all the way back to Adam and his wife, Eve, were chosen and were created by God so He can birth you into this world. If you have children, God has also created them to be His image bearer to the unsaved people of the world.

The year, the month, the day, and the minute, that special time of your birth, were all chosen by Almighty God. Never exaggerate or lie about your age and place of birth because in so doing, you deny God creating you at the appointed time, and you make Him a liar. Making God a liar and denying His power in your life is a serious and a grievous sin to Him. You are not ordinary; you are extraordinary, made and formed in the image of Almighty God. It's not just your spiritual you, but it is every bit of your intricate and very complicated design, which God created, that is a wonder to behold. Every human being is the first wonder of the world because we are fearfully and wonderfully made by God, our Creator.

We read about God's precise timeline of life for the birth of Isaac and the incarnation of Jesus. In Genesis 17:21 and 18:10, God spoke to the time of Isaac's birth. In Galatians 4:4, the Word of God speaks of Jesus's incarnation in the fullness of time.

You may have been the very one that Satan tried to abort from your mother's womb, and maybe he is still attempting to destroy you. The reason you made it this far, in one piece, and that you are alive today is because God kept you safe by protecting you from the deadly arrows of Satan. You did not lose your mind nor your life because God has put a hedge around you with an insurmountable number of heavenly angels. He secured you and saved your life with His presence from all the deadly arrows of the enemy. God saved your life because He had created you for a purpose and with a destiny. There are no useless lives that God has created or will ever create. It is we who have chosen to live lives in rebellion to His commandments. If God is to reveal to us the depth of the constant attacks of the enemy, we may become paralyzed and/or probably die of fear of what could have happened to us. Satan is a cruel and ferocious enemy.

God has equipped each one of us with specific gifts and talents to glorify Him only, and so He has equipped you and me with every good gift that is from above. The gifts and talents that are given to us by God are such that they will bless our lives when used in a God-glorifying way and that they may also be used to be a blessing to others.

The fact is each redeemed child of God reflects the splendor (character) and richness of their Creator in whose image they were created. David, in Psalm 139:14, declares,

> I will praise thee; for I am fearfully and wonderfully made:
> marvelous are thy works; and that my soul knoweth right well.

God has given you His Word that reveals all of who He is to you. You are more than clay or any other earthly matter. You are more than just flesh. You are spirit, and you are life to God. The god of this world, Satan, whom you may now be serving in the flesh, is your enemy, and he has held mankind in chains of rebellion, in bondage to sin. He has yoked all of humanity throughout the ages to do all manner of evil and wicked things. The Bible says,

> But God, who is rich in mercy, for his great love wherewith
> he loved us, even when we were dead in sins, hath quickened us
> together with Christ [by grace are saved]. (Ephesians 2:4–5)

The Bible says that anyone who is living a sinful life is spiritually dead. God will quicken anyone who is spiritually dead to life by His Spirit. The blood of Jesus is powerful enough to thoroughly cleanse all the sins of every repenting sinner. The Word of God is quick and sharper than any two-edged sword. By hearing the Word, you will get faith; and by that same Word, you will be transformed by the renewing of your mind, and after you have been converted to the image of Christ, you will be the fruit-bearing tree of godliness.

The enemy of God knows that his grip on your life will begin to loosen as you begin to hear, meditate, and act on the message of the gospel; and as you believe in your heart that Jesus is your only source of salvation, Satan knows that God will give you a spirit of hatred for sin; and so because the enemy does not want to lose anyone who has been a slave to him, he will fight you with every seed of discouragement, fear, and doubt. Satan will intensify his attacks against you, and he will organize all the forces of darkness to eliminate you; but whatever you do, always trust God, and He will direct your paths so that you may be steadfast in your belief that Christ is your only deliverer from a sinful life.

Satan knows that if God is indeed drawing you to Himself, the likelihood is that you will no longer have the desire to sin. He knows that all those who became the children of God, when Christ became their Savior and Lord, were set free from under his dominion. Satan hates to see anyone in the Word of God because he knows that once we have been enlightened by the holy Scriptures about his lies and about God's truth, his grip on our lives begins to loosen, and so it is crucial for you to intensely seek God in prayer and seek His help to totally transform you if you have been bothered about anything that is wrong in your life. Seek God to give you the strength to withstand all of Satan's attacks, for he knows you will never be the same with Christ Jesus as your Lord and your Savior.

4

GOD'S GRACE

The grace of God is the unmerited favor that is freely given to all who ask God for His forgiveness of all their sins. Grace means that only God can remove all our sins that we have ever committed and totally and unreservedly account them to the Lamb of God, the Lord Jesus Christ. God withholds from us what we truly deserve—that is, to be completely destroyed forever because of our disobedience to His commandments and our rebellion against His holy and righteous ways. The Bible says,

> For by grace are you saved through faith; and that not of yourselves: it is the gift of God: Not of our works that anyone of us should boast. (Ephesians 2:8–9)

Grace is the gift from God to sinful humanity, and that gift is Jesus Christ. He unselfishly gave Himself to be the perfect sacrifice for the sins of all mankind that whosoever believes in Him should not perish but shall have eternal life.

In scripture, the number 5 signifies grace, for it was in Genesis, after the fifth day of creation, that God made man, formed and brought him into existence on the sixth day, into the completed work that He had done. This meant mankind did not have to work for nor did they have to earn what God had freely given them as a possession. In the tabernacle, the ark of the covenant sat in the most holy place. The mercy seat lay on top of the ark that contained the covenant— the bread (the Word of God), the law, and the promised Redeemer of God symbolized by Aaron's rod that budded.

The law of God demanded a blood sacrifice had to be made in order for the sins of mankind to be forgiven, but the mercy of God substituted the blood of the innocent for that of the guilty; and again, mankind is brought into the completed work of atonement that Christ did do on the cross at Calvary. Grace did for humanity what nothing else was able to do for them. It gave mankind the opportunity that whosoever will may experience the immense and perfect love of God and the sweet fellowship of the Holy Spirit.

The blood of the sacrificed animal was sprinkled by the high priest with his own finger in front of and on the mercy seat. It was in the most holy place, or the holy of holies, in the tabernacle that God had made Israel build where the grace of God dwelled. This tabernacle was a pattern of the true tabernacle of heaven of whom Christ is the high priest, ministering in the eternal sanctuary of God (Leviticus 16:14–18 and Hebrews 8:2).

It was Christ who offered Himself as the perfect blood-atoning sacrifice on the seat of mercy so that He is both the ultimate sacrifice and the minister of the reconciliatory gospel of peace. The blood of the healthy animal that was sacrificed was a shadow pointing to what Christ was to be. It was a covenant sign of redemption and forgiveness that God had made with the children of Israel, and since the animal sacrifice was the shadow, it is Christ's blood that is efficacious enough to wash away the sins of every national Israelite and every Gentile who existed outside the camp of Israel under the new covenant. His blood is only effective for cleansing away the sins of the people who are obedient to God to truly confess and repent of all their sins to Him.

Christ was the high priest who shed His own blood as He was wounded on the cross in five places, delivering His own body as the true and only sacrifice that the law of God accepted. Thus, the law of God would no longer overshadow those that Christ Himself would redeem; and as the apostle Paul puts it in Galatians 3:24–26, the law is the schoolmaster that is able to bring every sinner to Jesus Christ that they might be justified by faith in Him.

Christ was pierced in five places on His body, His right and left hand, His right and left foot, and His side, and so it is that grace who showed His mercy into the lives of sinners that believed His gospel and surrendered all of who they are into the care of a loving Savior. Therefore, grace is the unfair exchange of the life of the innocent for that of the guilty. Thus, without the grace of God, no one can be justified and be made righteous through the forgiveness of sins.

Except there be a sacrifice with the shedding of blood, no sin shall be forgiven, and no sinner can be saved. It is because of the grace of God that we have the opportunity to receive His mercy. No one can have the mercy of God without the grace of God, and according to Ephesians 4:11–12, God has equipped the church with five ministerial gifts so that it can be edified by the gospel of Jesus Christ.

God gave some to be apostles and some to be prophets and some to be evangelists, and to some He gave to be pastors and some teachers, for the perfecting of the saints, for the work of the ministry, so that the body of Christ may be edified. God will only give what He has, and so He gives us His grace in exchange for the wages of sin in that we may know Him—that is, search God out in the Scriptures with faith and not search Him out in someone else's private interpretation commentary writings.

Everyone who is in rebellion against God exists in spiritual darkness, and it is only Christ who can totally lead mankind out into His marvelous light for He is the light of a world in total darkness because mankind separated themselves from the presence of their Creator who is the source of light that is the life of a spiritually dead human race.

Jesus Christ reconciled mankind to God by giving His life as the atoning sacrifice to pay the debt of the wages of sin. He settled the account of mankind's rebellion against God. And so every repenting sinner that the Spirit of God quickens, his or her debt was completely paid for because of the love He has for mankind. So Jesus who is the grace of God erased all the debt that those who come to God and are given eternal life are made free from what the law of God demanded from every sinner. The law of God demands that payment for sin be made by a blood sacrifice, and so only the blood of Jesus Christ was sufficient to satisfy the requirements of what the law of God demanded. The law of God demanded a pure and undefiled sacrifice for the payment of every sin every sinner would ever commit. God's nature is absolute holiness, and that's what Jesus Christ is, absolutely holy. His nature has no trace of defilement in it, and so Jesus Christ was the purest and only sufficient sacrifice that existed anywhere in the heavens and in the earth.

This act of God's love, that no one can ever comprehend, is the unselfish gift God gives to all whom He redeems. It's a debt that no one can ever repay. The Word of God says in 1 John 4:19, "We love him, because he first loved us." It is God who shows us His love while we hated Him, and it is He that teaches us to love Him and our fellow man.

With grace, God enters a covenant relationship with the believer, sealed with the blood of Jesus. It was not the blood of animals, nor was it the blood of any man that could or did save those who have gone on before us and that can save you or anyone else from sin. It is only the blood of Jesus that is sufficient to cleanse you and me from all our sins. He was the perfect sinless sacrifice that God the Father did accept.

Without the grace of God, no human being can see the favor of God, and no man can enter His presence. It is because of the grace of God that Christ gave Himself to be sin for us. If it were not for the grace of God, we would not be able to obtain mercy, and we would be unable to have eternal life. There is no salvation without God's grace, and it is because of God's grace that Christ substituted Himself in our place and bore in His body the full wrath of God so that mankind may receive the mercy of God for his sins.

Christ unselfishly gave His life in obedience to God the Father to be the atonement of our sins. We read in Romans 5:1–2,

> Therefore being justified, we have peace with God through our Lord Jesus Christ: By whom also we have access by faith into the grace wherein we stand, and rejoice in hope of the Glory of God.

God's peace with mankind did cost Him something. It cost God the Father to allow His only begotten Son to be nailed to a cross as His only perfect sacrifice, judged for the sins of the whole world. Christ had to die and shed His blood to reconcile mankind to God. However, Christ did not stay dead, for He rose from the grave on the third day and ascended into heaven forty days later. Grace is not free, and it is not fair in that the innocent received the punishment for the sins of the guilty.

How can anyone know the love of God except He gives it to us? How can God give His gift of love, which is Christ, except it is by His grace wherein we receive it? How can anyone receive the gift except it comes by Christ? He is the door by which we enter into the presence of God, for without Christ, we have no access to God the Father, and we cannot see the kingdom of God; and for anyone to see the kingdom of God, he or she must be born again, which is by water and the Spirit (John 3:3, 5–6). The water of the Word of God washes the minds of men and women to clean them from the memory of sin, and the Spirit of God makes alive that which was dead in sin so that the new person who is born of the Spirit is now that new spirit that seeks to serve God.

Type and Shadows of the Work of Christ

It was prohibited by the law of Moses, given in the Old Testament, for any Israelite to touch the dead or to be in the midst of a leper, for such were considered unclean, in which leprosy represented everything sinful, and the dead represented those individuals who were spiritually cut off from God.

Thus, if anyone was ceremonially unclean, that person had to be washed by water outside the camp of Israel for the cleansing of their bodies and was then brought unto the priest, who would examine him to be sure that he was thoroughly cleansed from his leprosy. Read Leviticus 13–14 and Numbers 19:11–14.

The Bible says in Numbers 19:11,

> He that toucheth the dead body of any man shall be unclean seven days.

Spiritually speaking, the dead body represented the sinful state of all mankind. This is so because when Adam sinned, and all mankind sinned because of him, they became separated from the life-giving fellowship they had with God before sin came. Death is the separation of the spirit from the body, and so apart from God, we are spiritually dead because the Spirit of God, which is the presence of God and the source of life, is not in us.

In verse 12 of Numbers chapter 19, the Bible says that he who touches the dead body shall purify himself on the third day; and on the seventh day, he shall be clean. This must be so because by the third day, the decay of the dead body begins. Jesus was raised from the dead on the third day, representing the deliverance before corruption could have occurred. Then on the seventh day, the man who purified himself on the third day by the washing himself was examined by the priest to be sure he was clean. If there is no purification on the inside, then it may be that there was no deliverance from sin.

Christ has to cleanse us from sin with His blood for there to be deliverance. There must be a quickening of our spirit by the Spirit of God for us to be spiritually resurrected to have life in God through Jesus Christ. Thus, the number7, in this case, represented the completed work of deliverance from all uncleanness and sin which Christ did for fallen humanity. This is why we must be born again by the Spirit of God, and the blood of Jesus has to cleanse and purify us from our sin nature for there to be redemption.

Spiritually dead people cannot seek the living God, and holiness cannot behold anything dead in sin except it is for the cause of salvation. As an illustration to show what the state and condition of sin is, as it relates to mankind's pre-fallen nature, which was defiled with the act of sin through disobedience to the commandments of God, a person who touched a corpse and refused to be purified according to the commandment, such that he or she defiled the tabernacle of God, was cut off from Israel. That person no longer was entitled to the benefits of the covenant God made with the nation of Israel. Therefore, as the Bible teaches, the act of sin caused spiritual and physical death to mankind.

Thus, under the new covenant, a person is also cut off from having a life-giving relationship with God because he or she refuses the Spirit of God to lead him or her to Jesus Christ to be cleansed of his or her sins. Such a person has indeed grieved the Holy Spirit from the work that He seeks to do in him or her. Therefore, all things ceremonial in the old covenant were shadows and types pointing to Christ and His work of redemption in the new covenant. It was Christ who took on our leprous nature upon Himself, and He became defiled with the spiritual corpses of sinful mankind so that God did judge Him instead of us. Christ was examined by God the Father and was found to be spotless (clean) when He said,

This is my beloved Son, in whom I am well pleased. (Matthew 3:17)

God's grace to mankind is that all men may indeed live if they would believe that Christ died as the atonement for all their sins. Grace replaced the sentence of total destruction of every repentant sinner with the mercy of God. The redeemed are spared from eternal separation from God.

It is not any of our works that can save us from the wages of sin, but it is the grace of God that saves us from the penalty of disobeying the law of God, for which Christ paid the full cost for our redemption with His own life. We read in Romans 11:6,

And if by grace, then it is no more of works: otherwise grace is no more grace. But if it be of works, then it is no more grace: otherwise work is no more work.

It takes faith to believe that God would be so compassionate, loving, and kind, and that He would totally forgive anyone of all their sins and give them eternal life. Please read John 15.

The whole act of God's goodness and kindness toward a rebellious human race is beyond our understanding. So if you hear the call of God speaking to your heart for you to come out of the shadows of unbelief into the marvelous light of Jesus Christ, you may be one of many He has called to be His chosen son or daughter. No one can choose God, but instead, it is God who chooses us. The Bible says in Romans 3:10–11,

> As it is written, There is none righteous, no not one: There is none that understandeth, there is none that seeketh after God.

The way of life we know and live is not the ways of God, for rebellion is doing the opposite of what God says. Again, the Bible says in Romans 3:12,

> They are all gone out of the way, they are together unprofitable; there is none that doeth good, no, not one.

That, my friend, is the absolute true nature of all mankind. Our right doing is as filthy rags before God (Isaiah 64:6). The Bible also says in John 1:17,

> For the law was given by Moses, but grace and truth came by Jesus Christ.

Christ is the very expression of God the Father, and He is the personification of God's grace and truth.

5

GOD'S MERCY TO YOU

Mercy, like grace, is the very essence of who God is. He is gracious enough to give us His mercy and merciful enough to destroy sin and cover the redeemed with His righteousness. The Word of God says in 2 Chronicles 30:9,

> For if ye turn again unto the Lord, your brethren and your children shall find compassion before them that lead them captive, so that they shall come again into this land: for the Lord your God is gracious and merciful, and will not turn away his face from you, if ye return unto him.

The face of God is His favor. God will, with hands of mercy and with eyes of compassion, render to everyone who hears His voice and harden not their heart against the gift of eternal life through salvation in that no one truly deserves to receive the riches of the mercy of God. He will give you the favor of redemption after He has delivered you totally out of the grave of sin.

The day Adam and Eve sinned; they hid from God. However, God did not leave the man and his wife in the darkness of sin. He sought them out with love and kindness while they were separated from Him by then dark and deadly nature of sin. God did not punish them with His wrath for what they had done wrong. With kindness and compassion, God relieved them of their fear, and He covered their nakedness with His coat of love, for they were naked with sin in the presence of a holy God.

God did remove the judgment that was against both Adam and Eve in which His holy law demanded that the one who transgressed His commandments should die for his and her sins, but the mercy of God, which sat above the law, on the ark of God, in the holy of holies, paid the cost of redemption with His own blood. Christ, who was the voice of God that came in the cool of the day in the garden of Eden, spoke to Adam and his wife about their condition in sin. God saw that mankind had fallen into sin from His presence, for the relationship and fellowship that He had with them was broken by the act of disobedience. He sacrificed an animal as a substitute in their place for their redemption, for they were naked in sin, so that they who believe what God has to offer in exchange for the wages of sin are removed from sin's death row.

Wherefore, the Bible says in John 1:29 that Jesus is the Lamb of God who takes away the sins of the world, and so God showed Adam and Eve, when He made coats of skins and covered them, as is recorded in Genesis 3:21, the type and the shadow of a better sacrifice than that of an innocent animal, which was to come at a set future time under a new and better covenant. Christ is He that was not the shadow but was the object of what the shadow pointed to. He was the perfect and only sacrifice that was sufficient to pay for the sins of the whole world once and for all.

God clothed Adam and his wife, Eve, with coats made from the skins of a sacrificed animal. God covered the man and his wife with His hand of mercy, forgiving them of their sins and the cleansing away of their unrighteousness with His righteousness so that they can be made spiritually alive to God and be made perfect in Him, and so redemption is not free. There was an enormous cost attached to what the law of God required that must be paid to remit mankind's sins, and that is the sacrifice of the innocent dying in place of the guilty. God did redeem Adam and His wife with the love that gives and compassion that He has for all sinners.

God sought Adam out of his hiding place to deliver him and his wife from where they were, spiritually speaking. The Bible says that the man and his wife hid from God among the trees of the garden. Adam was not only hiding behind whatever he thought would make him not be seen by God, but he covered himself with that which makes us still transparent before the all-seeing eye of God, and for sure, no one can hide from His Creator.

The Bible says in Genesis 3 that Adam made aprons of sewed fig leaves to hide both his and his wife's nakedness. This Adam did because their transgression of the Word of God made them shameful before God and vulnerable to every consequence of sin. The spiritual eyes of both Adam and Eve were opened to know and practice evil as a way of life, and as a result of this new reality, immediately they experienced spiritual death. That is because with the ability to do evil and wicked acts, mankind had now disconnected themselves from the spiritual life-sustaining fellowship they had with their Creator. They now knew what good and evil is as the new reality. It is not only that they were now aware of what evil is but that they understood what good was because that was the nature and image they were created with by God.

God is good, and nothing about His nature is evil, and so Adam and Eve became capable of knowing and doing evil; for when they disobeyed God's Word, they were transformed from only knowing to do good to also knowing and doing every wicked and evil act imaginable. Their nature became such that their thoughts were always evil. Since knowing evil is to be capable of doing it, then the evil nature which mankind had become makes him capable of committing the most heinous crimes that are beyond his own imagination. The Bible says in Jeremiah 17:9 that the heart of every human being is deceitful above all things and is desperately wicked; who can understand it? The Bible also says in Romans 3:10–18 that no one seeks to do good but instead does evil. There is none that is righteous, and there is none that search for God on their own.

To sin is a reality and a choice for humanity. A child will learn to lie because it is in his or her nature to do so, but in the light of the law of God, mankind has a choice to sin or not to sin. Evil is the opposite of the nature of what good is. That's why God gave mankind His holy law because it is a frame and a boundary line that is intended to mark everything that is evil and wicked. The law said you have sinned, and there is a consequence to your actions. It also points the sinner to a Savior from whom he or she may receive forgiveness for and redemption from his or her sins.

Adam and Eve lost their innocence to the awareness of what right and wrong are because of their disobedience to the commands of God. They also lost the faith and the trust that they had with their Creator before the act of sin was committed. God became the one that mankind now feared, for one of the consequences that sin produces is the spirit of fear.

Innocence and faith were now replaced with fear and doubt, for what they now saw in themselves made them afraid of what they had now become—sinners, separated by sin from their heavenly Father—and so according to the Bible, in Genesis 3, Adam heard God's voice in the cool of the day; but because he was naked and afraid, fearful and confused, like all of us are when we engage in wrongdoing, he and his wife hid themselves behind the covering of what fear would have us do, and that is to run and hide from God and make excuses for our sinful actions.

The fact is that all unsaved men and women hide behind the fig leaves of excuses that they had sewed together as a covering for their sins. These individuals, some of whom say they are Christians, refuse to commit themselves to do the full counsel of the gospel of Jesus Christ, which is to do all the commandments of God. They forsake the assembly of themselves with believers who do the Word of God as the Bible commands us to do. These dear people make the assertion that churches are just moneymaking machines that suck the possessions out of the pockets of poor people. These people claim that they don't want to fund the preacher's portfolio while they get the curses of poverty. These critics of the church also say that "preachers" are the only ones who become financially rich while poor people receive empty promises in exchange for their meager resources that they possess.

Friends, that might be true about some churches, but we cannot broad-brush all churches to be the same, for it does not take much for Satan to find people in the church who would lend their life to be used as agents of evil to distort the gospel of Jesus Christ. There are, however, a remnant number of true believers who have been faithful in their obedience to the Word of God. The same have been diligent to feed the flock of God and proclaim the good news to the unsaved of the world. There is no excuse that any person can conjure up and use as a reason of not answering the call of God on his or her life. He has made the way to Himself straight and narrow and has done everything necessary for you and me to receive salvation and have eternal life with Him.

When we are born again by God. We are not saved to worship the preacher or the church; we are praising and worshiping our Creator Redeemer. The Word of God is readily available in most places in the world, and if you have one, open it and read its contents and prayerfully allow the Spirit of God to lead and teach you the truth about your spiritual condition.

Some people hide behind the fig leaves of religion. They pretend to be the children of God, but their living—that is, the fruit of their doings—is always inconsistent with what they say they believe. Many people, without truly understanding what they are doing, are robbing themselves from having a productive and life-changing relationship and fellowship with Jesus Christ.

If Satan has got you believing that you can act like and pretend you are a Christian without having a genuine redemptive relationship with God, then it is time for you to come home to Him. Let Him purge and purify you from the toxins of lies that have contaminated your perspective of who God is to you. You cannot pretend to know God. You have to know Him by faith, which is a total surrender of self to Him.

He is your Creator and your Re-Creator. Christ will create a new heart and renew a right spirit within you. Today is the gospel preached in your hearing. Let it sink into your spirit, and let God transform you from pretending to be who you are not into who you were created to be, a child of the Most High God. God is willing to save anyone from the wages of sin if we would come out from behind the veil of our own self-righteousness so that Christ may redeem us and clothe our spiritual nakedness with the robe of His righteousness.

So the question for you to answer is this—will you continue to hide behind the fig leaves of excuses in your rebellion against God? Will you continue to allow Satan to tie you down in chains to sin and allow your iniquity to keep separating you from the forgiving face of God, or are you going to repent right now and turn to Him from all ungodliness and be set free in Jesus? If you are unsaved and you want to live the new life in Christ and be victorious over sin, God will change your life forever in a very profound way, and you will receive the benefits of obedience to the Word of God.

If you are still living a sinful life in the presence of God in that you are hiding an area or areas of sinfulness in your life, He knows all about those hidden areas. Mankind cannot hide anything from God. He sees way beneath the exterior and surface of our lives. When sin is still flourishing in the lives of people who profess to be children of God so that their worship to Him is not as what it should be, God will trouble them in their spirit to confess their sins to Him and turn away from doing evil. We must read the chapters of Revelation 1 and 2 and see what God has to say about all who profess to serve Him.

God is no respecter of persons, but He renders His grace and His mercy to those who humble themselves as He has commanded them to do. The humble are all those who, after they have heard the voice of God in their hearts, see themselves as spiritually helpless sinners in need of the power of God to turn their lives around from one of defeat and unrest to that of victory and is at rest in Jesus Christ. The Bible says in 1 Peter 5:6–7,

> Humble yourselves therefore under the mighty hand of God, that he may exalt you in due time: Casting all of your cares upon him; for he careth for you.

God does not honor, nor does He regard the prayers of those whose words are void of faith.

The Pharisee and the publican spoken of by Christ in Luke 18:9–14 speaks to the phoniness of false prayer and false worship and that of true repentance and true worship, for the Bible says that the sinner who would not look to heaven but smote upon his breast, saying, "God, be merciful to me, a sinner," this man was justified by God for his truthfulness of his spiritual condition, not pretending that he had it all together, comparing himself to other people. He saw himself as spiritually helpless and weak without the transforming power of God in his life.

Some people wear religion when it is convenient for them to do so, and they cloak themselves with religious pretense to cover their sins. Such people bear no fruit of godliness. Their lives are constipated with the toxins of carnality. They live life with no connection to the life-giving and the life-sustaining power of God that makes men and women resist the destructive forces of evil. Exalting oneself is foolishness and it is a sin before Almighty God, and such God rebukes.

None of our good works in life, without God, are good enough for Him to merit us with everlasting life. Every human being's stubborn will must be broken. It is the hardness of mankind's heart that must be tenderized by the love of God so that He can plant in them the life-giving seed that produces the fruit of righteousness. The righteousness of God is available to anyone through the sacrifice of Jesus Christ on the cross at Calvary. It was only for the lost sheep did Jesus Christ die so that the sheep may indeed spiritually live again.

It was God who came down from heaven to earth, the place that is His footstool, to pick up those who are broken and beaten, bruised and battered, those who are wounded by the arrows of sin and are left half dead in the streets of the lost. With love, Christ binds up our wounded lives with the bandages of His love mixed with compassion. He pours into us and anoints us with the oil of His Spirit, and He takes the wine of His blood and pours it on our body, washing us clean from the infection of sin so that we become the sanctuary and the temple of God and the vessel for every good and perfect gift from above.

Jesus Christ is the only One who can remove our sins and mend lives back together again and take His people to the place where He wants them to be nourished—that is, in His temple. It is in the presence of God where His children's mind is fed and is renewed by His Word; their lives are enriched with godly actions, and thus, they become more like Jesus Christ, for it was David who said in Psalm 27:4,

> One thing have I desired of the Lord, that I may seek after; that I may dwell in the house of the Lord all the days of my life, to behold the beauty of the Lord, and to enquire in his temple.

It is in the temple of the Lord that the redeemed of God are to find their daily refreshing word bread from the hand of the caring and compassionate Savior.

Those whom God has given the spirit of reverential fear, to them He has also shown His mercy. You and I deserve nothing but the justice of God, which His law demands for the transgression of His commandments. The punishment of those that remain in rebellion against God is death; it, is the destruction of both body and soul in hell (Matthew 10:28).

We are all guilty of living in rebellion against a holy and just God, but because of His remarkable love for a rebellious and wicked people, God will forgive you of every one of your sins, and He will forget them in the sea of forgetfulness. God's mercy is clearly seen through His compassion for the guilty. God's forbearance and His favor toward you and me are the essence of His long-suffering. God is patient and kind and will wait for you and me to hear His voice speak to us, but His wait will not last forever. The opportunity for salvation is now, today, not tomorrow. No other time is guaranteed to anyone, for no human being knows if he or she will live to see tomorrow.

The fatted calf, which is Christ, was killed for your redemption, and a robe of righteousness was specially made for you by Him. The truth, as it is written, is that God gave His best sacrifice, the Lord Jesus, as an offering for the remission of the sins of the whole world so that everyone who trusts in God shall be forgiven of their sins and have eternal life with Him. The Word of God says in Psalm 85:10–11,

> Mercy and truth are met together; righteousness and peace have kissed each other. Truth shall spring out of the earth; and righteousness shall look down from heaven.

In the Old Testament Word of God, Jesus is pictured as the mercy seat that sat on the ark of the covenant, which bore in it the law of Almighty God (Exodus 25:21–22). Thus, above the law of God is His mercy. Thank God for His mercy, for surely none of us deserves His compassion wrapped in His love.

Every evil and wicked thing that you and I have done, in secret and in the open, God's mercy constrained Him from destroying us. God, in His mercy, is patient to bear with each sinner to hear the gospel of Jesus Christ so that He can separate us from the attachment we have to sin and to the kingdom of Satan. It is Christ who has clothed us when we were naked in unrighteousness, with His covering of mercy, where He forgave us of every evil thing that we have done.

In times past, God looked past when we sinned in ignorance; but now that the knowledge of sin is revealed to us through the law of God, and we also now know what the gift of God is when we hear the gospel of peace preached into our spirit, we have no excuse for remaining in sin. We now know what the Spirit of God has revealed to us that there is the forgiveness of sins and cleansing of all unrighteousness in Jesus Christ.

The Bible says in 1 Corinthians 15:55–57 that the sting of death is sin, and the strength of sin is the law of God. Jesus took the victory out of the hand of the grave, and He took the sting away from the power of death; and if any who are in Christ should die before He returns, they should go to a time of sleep until the bodily resurrection of every elect of God on the last day. The corruptible flesh container will be replaced with the incorruptible flesh.

The grave is just a mark where our corruptible shell container is placed. God has given all those whom Christ has redeemed from the curse of the law the victory of the resurrection over the sting of death and the power of the grave. Mercy demands that we always enter the presence of God with praise and through His gates with thanksgiving in our hearts for all the things He has done for us.

The Bible's record of the relationship between God and mankind is true and trustworthy. Many of us, when we look back into our lives of sin and see where God has brought us from and where He is taking us to, can't help but marvel at the length, breadth, and depth of His love. He is way beyond awesome. God's grace and His mercy were abiding in us while we lived recklessly and we sinned as a way of life in our rebellion against our loving and caring Creator.

Many people have found that the truth the Bible declares about the carnal-minded man cannot be denied. These people have found the Word of God to be consistent and accurate regarding the nature and behaviors of all mankind, whether they lived thousands of years ago or are living today.

The Bible is the only religious book that describes God in the person of Jesus Christ coming into this world that He had created to buy us out from the marketplace of sin and restore us back unto Himself at the cost of His own life. No other religion's writings have documented that their leader died for the sins of mankind, and I have read some of these writings.

There are no specific prophecies in the books of any other religion about a coming Messiah as is predicted in the Bible. There are no references made regarding a Redeemer and a Savior who will save mankind from their sins. These other religions do not regard the Judeo-Christian Bible as their source for truth. What these other religions' books talk about is a do-it-yourself-program recipe for becoming a good person. Thus, what they speak about is that man's good deeds are at the center of their messages. These religious writings make their point, stating that mankind's future depends on how good he can become. Some religions do mention God and that He is all-powerful, but they say nothing about the salvation of mankind from sin.

The Bible is the only book that talks about and describes the plan of salvation, by God, in specific details; that without the shedding of blood, the Bible says there is no remission of sin (Hebrews 9:22), and not only did the Bible describe Jesus Christ's crucifixion on a cross, but it also describes that He rose from the dead on the third day and was seen by many eyewitnesses (1 Corinthians 15:6–7). He ascended back into heaven (Luke 24:36–51).

Many skeptics have questioned, and some have doubted that the resurrection of Jesus Christ as is recorded in the Bible. For the believer, however, the record of the Bible remains the only proof of Jesus's bodily resurrection from the grave, just outside the city of Jerusalem. The Bible's record of Jesus's resurrection is believed by those He has begotten in Himself, through faith, that they did receive from hearing the Word of God.

As Christians, we believe every Word that the Bible says about the nature of mankind—that everyone has sinned and have come short of God's glory—and so we believe the Bible's account of the death, the burial, and the resurrection of Jesus Christ.

Jesus, during His earthly ministry, as is written in many places of the Gospel, spoke of His death, His burial, and His resurrection. One such example is found in John 2:19:

> Jesus answered and said unto them, "Destroy this temple, and in three days I will raise it up."

This He said speaking of the temple of his own body, as is written in verse 21 of the same chapter. In John 10:17–18, Jesus said,

> Therefore doth my Father love me, because I lay down my life, that I might take it again. No man taketh it from me, but I lay it down of myself. I have power to lay it down, and I have power to take it again. This commandment have I received of my Father.

We also read in Luke 9:22,

> The Son of man must suffer many things and be rejected of the elders and the chief priests and scribes and be slain and be raised on the third day.

We have another Scripture reference, as we read in Mark 9:31:

> For he taught his disciples, and said unto them, The Son of man is delivered into the hands of men, and they shall kill him; and after that he is killed, he shall rise the third day.

These are the very words of Christ that He spoke into the ears of many witnesses, which are recorded in the Bible. These prophetic words that were spoken by Jesus Christ, according to the Bible, did come to pass. They are the biblical proofs that the early Christians accepted and believed, and these same Bible proofs are accepted and believed today by God's true children. Their belief in the Bible's record regarding the salvation of mankind and what Jesus did to make it happen is by faith in the truthfulness of the Word of God, given to them by God Himself, through the Holy Spirit.

The fact is mankind is lost forever without a Savior and is hopeless without a Redeemer. No amount of education or the lack thereof, no amount of money or the lack thereof, no amount of prestige or the lack thereof, no amount of influence or the lack thereof, and no amount of power or the lack thereof can save anyone from sin or give them peace with God and receive eternal life from Him. Every human being is lost forever without the blood of Jesus cleansing them from the stain of sin. Unless Jesus is our Savior and Lord, no one can have eternal life from God. His intention and His promise are that no one should remain lost, and no soul should perish. Wherefore, the holy Scriptures declare that the hope of God is that all humanity would come to Him for repentance (2 Peter 3:9).

God does not sit somewhere in the universe and wonder if any one of us will answer the call of the gospel. He knows who will and will not respond to the gospel of Jesus Christ. The fact of the matter is God is relentless with His endless ways to guide us to Himself. That's why the gospel is reaching you at this very moment so that you may not be lost and destroyed forever from the presence of God.

Christ is the only one who can give you true inner peace. It is the kind of peace that puts your heart and mind at ease despite what is going on in your life. With Jesus Christ in your life, you can be at rest in the middle of any storm. The devil's work is to create havoc in the lives of people. He is the source of unrest and torment in the lives of countless numbers of people in our world, but God is bigger than any problem, and He is stronger than all the forces of darkness.

God is the source of all power, and when you have the source of all the power and authority in the entire universe and beyond living on the inside of you, no devil in hell can destroy any of God's true children. Jesus is your hiding place, and He is your shelter in the time of any storm. You may be in the storm, but the storm doesn't have to be in you. There is only one presence that can be in you and me. It is either the presence of God or the presence of Satan; so please, whatever you do, let God be your strength and your peace.

Jesus came so that you and I can know God and have life in Him and have it more abundantly. What does that mean, you may ask? It means that you will have a stress- and worry-free life, even though you will have challenges and the fiery trials of life will come into your life, but none of Satan's powerless weapons of destruction shall be able to do you and me any harm unless you and I allow him the opportunity to do so.

An abundant life in God means that all His children have Him as their true and only source for everything that they would ever need. He is Jehovah Jireh, our Provider. God is He who will meet all His children's needs according to His riches in glory. He owns the universe.

So, friend, why are you consumed with worry about how your needs are going to be met? God is an on-time God, for Jesus said in Mark 11:22 that we are to trust God, and that's for everything and in every situation we're in. Don't you doubt what God alone is able to do; just trust Him. He had already worked it out before creation. He has done it before in your life, and He will do it again. Now stop worrying and leave everything in His hands and go to bed.

God gives to every believer a new perspective on the circumstances of life so that it changes their perception of their situation. God wants us to know that in Him are all the answers to the issues of life, and if we trust and depend on Him only to work things out, we will not have to worry about the things that only God can solve and fix. This new perspective that God gives us comes from the good news that we read in His Word. The Holy Spirit reveals into our spirits who God is to us and all that He is willing to do in our lives. The new perception of who we are, children of the Most High God, helps us to have a new and better outlook regarding our future in Jesus Christ, apart from sin.

The Spirit of God is He who empowers the believer to stand on the promises of the Word of God, by faith, in the day when the acts of sin shall abound, when trouble so intense shall arise in every corner of this planet that will make some wonder if there is a God, where is He, and what is He doing? We will see the lawlessness of unsaved humanity be on the increase in every society; but be not discouraged nor dismayed at what you see happening around you. Just keep your mind stayed on Jesus Christ, and be constant in fervent prayer unto God, never doubting His Word and His presence in your life.

The Word of God encourages the believer to be all that God wants him or her to be so that with the shield of faith, he or she can do all things through Christ who gives them the strength. God is able to carry you through all the fiery trials of life, and He will do so according to His promise to preserve everyone who trusts in Him with all that is within them. The Lord said that He will create the fruit of the lips of them that are redeemed with peace. The Lord will lay the righteous in green pastures and He will plant them by the rivers of still waters and they shall bring forth the fruit of righteousness in its season (Isaiah 57:19 and Psalm 1:3).

The gift of abundant life through Christ means that the sins that we bear and all the burdens that we may be carrying that are wearing us down and wearing us out are all lifted at Calvary. Those things that wear us out are financial problems, sicknesses and diseases, and all the many other problems that distress and cause us to be paralyzed with fear. All these things Christ delivered us from when He said, after He was nailed to the cross, "It is finished." It is with the stripes of God the Father's judgment that Jesus received in His body that the children of God are healed in every area of their lives, and whosoever hears the voice of God speaking to them in their spirit and shall believe in his or her heart and not doubt those things which He has said, the same shall be delivered and be healed from every curse that sin had brought into the world.

Jesus said in Mark 11:22, "Have faith in God"; and again, He said in Mark 9:23, "If thou canst believe, all things are possible to him that believeth." Thus, our faith has to have life (faith that does the Word of God) to be effective in whatever situation we are in. It cannot be fleshly or carnal faith—that is, dead faith.

The Bible also declares in James 5:14 that the prayer of faith shall save the sick, and the Lord shall raise that individual up to a new life in God, and whatever sins that person had committed in his or her life that have confined him or her to strongholds that can only be broken and cast down by the authority of Jesus Christ, they shall be forgiven him or her. For when sin appeared because of mankind's disobedience, its consequences, which is the curse, also appeared with it. Every truly born-again believer, according to the Bible, is spiritually revived again by the life-giving power of God through the Jesus Christ, and the same are called to live a life of holiness unto Him, and so every born-again child of God is delivered to Him from Satan, the power of darkness who is the prince of unrighteousness.

The Word of God must be the only guide for every Christian to follow that they may live holy lives unto God, and they must allow Him, through His Spirit, to teach them how to manage who and what they listen to; for the voice we pay attention to, the same we will believe. We must also allow God, through His Word, to teach us how to manage our finances and to be the good stewards over everything He has put into our care, and that includes our family. We must trust God to be Lord over every area of and everything in our lives. We must not leave anything out of His control. He is His children's Provider and Sustainer.

In this life, we do not have to bear what God has taken away. Trials will come, but they would not have any power over any of God's people whose trust is in Him. Our problems may not simply go away, but if you and I truly believe God to do all that is in His Word, He will give us the victory over every one of them.

More abundant life also means that God, if we will allow Him to, will mend our broken marriages. God will give us the wisdom and patience to work with a difficult child. He will be our help in all the challenging and difficult situations that are robbing us of the rich experiences of true and lasting peace with Him.

The Bible declares that Christ will break the chains of sin and its curses if we would cast our burdens and the cares of life over to Him, and in a miraculous way, God will set you and me free from everything that has oppressed, suppressed, and depressed us in this life until now. God is mightier than any power from hell, and He is stronger than the prince of darkness. His love is stronger, wider, deeper, and kinder than the power of hate that Satan and wicked men may be using to destroy you. You have not known true love nor ever experienced it until you meet Jesus, the God of the Bible.

The Bible says in Isaiah 61:1–3 and in Luke 4:18, speaking about Jesus and His Ministry, that the Spirit of God was upon Him, for He had anointed Him to preach the good news unto the hopeless, that He will mend the brokenhearted, proclaim liberty to them that are held captive by the circumstances of life and by Satan, and release us all from the prison of sin.

Christ came to comfort all that mourn. His promise is that He will give anyone beauty for ashes, putting peace in their hearts and a smile on their faces. He will give to everyone whom He has called to Himself the oil of His joy for mourning, for the joy of the Lord is the strength of the children of God. The Lord will replace the sorrow of those who have not known peace in this world with the blessed assurance that when we give everything over to Him, all things are possible, including eternal life. He has given to all whom He calls the desire to seek to know who He is by searching the Scriptures, and God will also give to them that diligently search Him out in the Scriptures the desire to truly serve Him and their fellow man. God will give any repentant sinner seeking His help the garment of praise for the spirit of heaviness. Thus, the darkness of sin that covers every human being is consumed in the presence of God by the light of the Lord Jesus when a sinner's spiritual ears are opened and he or she responds to the voice of God.

Allowing the Lord Jesus to wash your sins away and to cleanse you from every sin must begin with you confessing all your sins—not some but all sins that God has troubled you in your spirit to confess and repent. Jesus says in John 12:46–47,

> I am come as a light into the world, that whosoever believeth on me should not abide in darkness, and if any man hears my words, and believe not, I judge him not: for I came not to judge the world, but save the world.

If anyone rejects Jesus to be their Savior and Lord and refuses to receive His Word as the words of life that can raise them from spiritual death to spiritual life, then he or she has denied themselves salvation from God. For salvation is not in any other, nor is there a redeemer besides Christ by which sinful mankind can be saved and according to the Bible, the same eternal, unchangeable Word of God shall judge everyone that rejects salvation from Jesus Christ as the only way to have eternal life.

God always keeps His promises. He will never let anyone down, never! God has never gone back on His Word. He is a covenant-keeping God. God is not slack concerning His promise as men count slackness (2 Peter 3:9). God says what He means and means what He says. If God is going to save anyone, He will (that is, His will be done) use the problems that are in his or her life to trouble him or her in his or her spirit regarding his or her sinful ways.

If your spirit bothers you about any wrong behavior, it may be a sign that God, through His Holy Spirit, is speaking to you. He may trouble you about a wrong way of living or the worship of some other god, or He may bother you about an inappropriate or an unhealthy relationship that you are in. Whatever it is that you are bothered about, by God, allow Him to create a new heart in you and renew that right spirit within you. Do not ignore God, and do not shut Him out of your mind.

There is a lie Satan has sewed into minds of some people that they can just believe that there is no God and so all they have to do is to believe in the forces of energy that are in the environment, and they will protect them. What a lie. What Satan is doing is persuading those individuals to think and believe that they can live life recklessly and be uncaring of their spiritual condition so that he can get the opportunity to destroy their lives. Such individuals neglect to use common sense to evaluate danger, thinking that "the forces" would protect them.

Whatever forces they are talking about is of the demonic world, and when danger is averted and calamity does not touch them, it is not the forces that protected them. Don't be fooled; it is God who protects us even when we are not mindful of Him. It is God who surrounds us from all harm Satan will use destroy your life but God fights him off from getting to us. You may not know it was God protecting you, or if you are aware that it is Him operating in your life even though you are resisting the God that loves you so much that He will not give up on redeeming you from the power of darkness unto Himself. I am sure it breaks the heart of God to see so many of people self-destruct in sin. The very forces of darkness God is protecting some people from the forces of darkness they want to behold. Why would anyone choose to believe the lie of the devil and be tormented and even be destroyed? I ask you to listen and hear the Holy Spirit of God speak to you and be transformed by God from a life of rebellion to one of obedience and live soberly, righteously, and godly in this present world.

As stated before, a person who refuses to heed the voice of the Spirit of God pleading with him or her to turn away from sin and lead him or her to the knowledge of Jesus Christ so that he or she may have eternal life, that person has indeed rejected God (John 12:48). If anyone denies Christ and His message of salvation, it may well be that Satan has overcome that person with his lies about the only way the Bible speaks about knowing who God is and what He has to offer. Whatever lying words he has used to have anyone fooled such that he or she may not understand that their way of living life apart from God is based on lies the enemy has told them of who God is and who He is not. The Bible has unmasked this impostor for who he really is—a liar.

So many of people have believed the cliché "If it feels good, then do it." The deceiver has deceived so many people to believe they can trust their feelings; after all that is how you were made—to rely on your senses. It is the same lies he told Adam and Eve in the garden of Eden about God's commandments, and they were deceived (Genesis 2), for nothing has changed in his program of lies.

However, the time has come for God to open your spiritual ears to hear the melodies of the gospel of peace and rest which is of Jesus Christ alone. He has quickened your spirit to hear and know the way, the truth, and the life (Jesus Christ). I sincerely hope and pray that you do not reject the gift of God but instead accept salvation as the only true gift from Him that would change your life forever. I also pray that you would continue to seek after God in His Word as He draws you to Himself. You may have tried everything in this world to satisfy the thirst that you have on the inside, but for any human being who has tried everything in his or her own power outside of Christ to find lasting peace and the joy of living, they have discovered that they were still empty while drinking the polluted waters of this world.

Without the presence of God in our lives, we will remain empty and void of what really matters: to have peace with God and with our fellow mankind, wherefore we are at rest in Jesus Christ; and after all, isn't that what we are looking for as we live in this world—to have the unshakeable peace of God? Friend, make the best decision of your life. Choose God today, for He is the only source of true peace, and in Him only is rest found for weary souls (Matthew 11:28–30). The fact is many people are still dry on the inside because they may have drunk from the cisterns of vain philosophies. The pleasures of this world and any other way to find God will not give anyone the peace that only Jesus Christ gives.

Don't be fooled by the devil's tricks and his lies. He is a cunning deceiver. He will outfox you when you do spiritual combat with him without the full armor of God. Nothing about Satan's tricks and lying ways has changed since the garden of Eden. He takes advantage of our weaknesses, and he capitalizes on our vulnerabilities and innocence to the ways of this world. Not one iota of your life should be left unguarded without the whole armor of God. If you want to have a deeper relationship with God, ask Christ in earnest prayer, and seek Him diligently and daily in His Word. It is only from Jesus Christ that anyone can receive rest for their souls and the peace of God that surpasses anything that they can find on this earth.

If you (the reader) are unsaved, whereby you have not committed your life to Jesus Christ, please do so today. Please do not reject so great a salvation, for if you do, the Bible calls your decision "quenching the Spirit," which is recorded in 1 Thessalonians 5:19; and when anyone quenches the Spirit of God, they have indeed rejected the Holy Spirit, and there remain no more opportunities for them to receive salvation. Do not allow the enemy to steal, kill, and destroy the opportunities God may be giving you to have every one of your sins forgiven. The Bible says in 2 Peter 3:9,

> The Lord is not slack concerning his promise as some men count slackness; but is longsuffering to us-ward, not willing that any should perish, but that all should come to repentance.

It is God who has said in His Word that it is our iniquities——the iniquities of mankind without exception that have separated them from Him, and it's our sins that have hidden His face from us in that He would not hear our cry (Isaiah 59:2); but God has made a promise to them that turn from evil in that the Redeemer shall come to Zion to deliver them, and the Lord has made a covenant with the redeemed, for He has caused His Spirit to come upon them that seek Him. His Words that He has put in their mouth shall not depart from them, nor shall it depart out of the mouth of their children nor out of the mouth of their children's children from this time forth and forever (Isaiah 59:20–21).

God has not left us, but instead, all humanity has left Him for our own self-destructive ways. All of us, like sheep, have gone astray and have done foolishly. We all have turned everyone to his own way away from God to serve the father of disobedience and rebellion———Satan (Isaiah 53). We all have chosen the way that leads to death. Jeremiah 17:9 says,

> The heart is deceitful above all things, and desperately wicked: who can know it?

> The Bible also says that there is a way that seemeth right unto a man, but the ends thereof are the ways of death. (Proverbs 14:12)

Friend, God is willing to give His mercy to you and to your neighbor and to the stranger that comes across your path. Allow Him to do His work in your life. If you are being convicted by God in your heart, please, wherever you are, ask Him with everything that is within you for His mercy so that He may give you His grace that takes away the consequences of a sinful life. You may not have another opportunity like this moment, so please hearken unto the voice of God today, and make the decision to follow Him every day for the rest of your life. The pleasures of living a sinful life will only last for a season, but then there is the judgment of God who will judge every unsaved person who is naked in unrighteousness. On the other hand, the gift of God, which is eternal life, is His to give to whosoever will hear Him and believe His gospel of peace.

Satan's desire is for people to reject the convictions of God that He may have placed in their hearts for them to turn away from sin. The chief devil and his cohorts want to kill any opportunity you may have to receive peace with God. Satan desires to steal any potential you may have for having the joy of knowing Jesus, and he wants to destroy any hope you may have in Christ for all the promises that the Bible says God will bring to pass in your life. This chief devil wants to also destroy your hope in Christ's soon return for the people whom He did redeem from sin.

Call upon God, and let Him keep your mind stayed on Him so that you do not become discouraged from becoming His true child. God has opened the door of opportunity for you to know Him as your Savior and as your God. Do not postpone the opportunities God is giving you today to surrender your life to Him. Say yes to God now and have the blessed assurance that you are Jesus's and Jesus is your's from this very moment onwards to live with Him in eternity. The Bible says in Isaiah 55:6–7,

> Let the wicked forsake his way, and the unrighteous man his thoughts: and let him return unto the Lord, and he will have mercy upon him; and to our God, for he will abundantly pardon.

Now is the guaranteed time given to everyone to accept the grace and mercy of Almighty God. Today is the day of salvation (2 Corinthians 2:6). My friend, come now boldly to the throne of grace that you may obtain mercy from the One who is merciful and is full of compassion. In Christ, you can find grace to help you in the time of your need (Hebrews 4:16).

The Bible has in it the record that God, made in the likeness of men, born of a woman, as noted before, lived and demonstrated an exemplary sinless life. Jesus Christ did not escape the temptations of Satan, for it is Satan's desire to dethrone God. However, Jesus was triumphant over every temptation of the devil in that He destroyed his dominion that he had over those who were once living in sin. Satan is made powerless against every one of God's true children, and so you too, my friend, can be born again.

In His ministry, Jesus preached the salvation message of redemption so that people everywhere may have eternal life in Him. Jesus is the only way to everlasting life with God. Read Romans 5 and Hebrews 10. The absolutely just and eternal God taking on the form of a man, in the person of the Lord Jesus, to be the sacrifice for unjust mankind does not make sense at all to any of us who believe the Word of God; but it is by faith alone that we, the true Christians, believe all that the Bible says about Jesus Christ, who is the image of the invisible God and in whom also is the fullness of the nature of God (Colossians 1).

Because the nature of mankind became sinful, when they disobeyed God back in the garden of Eden, it was the shedding of the blood of Jesus that was God's full remedy for the sin problem, and thus, through the atoning sacrifice of Jesus Christ, God activated the only solution (salvation by grace) He had so that mankind may once again have fellowship with their Creator, for Jesus alone is the way to know God. Jesus stated these powerful words in John 15:13–14:

> Greater love hath no man than this that a man lay down his life for his friends. Ye are my friends, if ye do whatsoever I command you.

The fact is that God's agape love is so unselfishly pure that when it is given to anyone, they are totally transformed by it.

Every human being, regardless of our background, needs to know that it is God's desire to save us all from the wrath which He said will come upon the children of disobedience. The Bible also says that hell was created for the devil and his angels (Matthew 25:41), but because we all did disobey God's commandments, wherefore we all have sinned against Him, then it is only the redeeming power of God, through Jesus Christ, that could restore any human being to a place in his or her heavenly Father's kingdom; and if we refuse to believe that Jesus is the only atonement for sin, then the soul that rejects the gift of God and continue in sin—it shall die (Ezekiel 18:4).

Who We Are to God

The Bible says that mankind was created in the image of God. We were all created to serve God and to serve Him only and not anything or anyone else. Every human being was created with his and her very own gifts, talents, and identity of who they are in the eyes of Almighty God. Everyone is made to reflect God's image in them. Each of our lives is to be lived in such a way that glorifies God. There is nothing wrong in boasting in the Lord about the things that He has done in and for us, but when we forget God and when we allow pride and arrogance to overtake us because we've lost our minds and believe that we are totally in charge of our lives and the Lord Jesus has nothing to do with what you and I have, we have sinned against the One who alone has been our help in ages past and who alone is our hope for years to come. When we glorify God in all things and we humble ourselves under the mighty hand of God, He will exalt us in due time.

It is a fact that God made us all different, and none of us is a carbon copy of any other person. We were created by God to fulfill the unique purposes He has designed us to become. He has put in us all the possibilities for good successes to be fulfilled in our lives here on earth, but it is God who gets the credit, and it is He who gets the glory when we become what He created us to be.

Some of us try to be other people, or we attempt to improve on the externals, thinking that makes us acceptable to those who say we should be different. The question is—different from what? And what is to be changed? We are not answerable to anyone but God. The only change that we are to have is the one that God does perfectly. He gives His redeemed a new spirit nature so that they may live a life of right doing because he or she is covered by the righteousness of Christ, and so by living godly before the Lord, the righteous is able to bear the fruit of the Spirit (Galatians 5:22–24).

Since we are all created in God's image—that is, we have God consciousness—and you and I are created in His likeness, we are to let God alone change us from the inside out because it is before Him that we all have fallen short of who He had made us to become, and so we are to let Him make us that new creature in Christ Jesus. We are to make Jesus Christ our object lesson starting today. Every believer in Jesus need to learn who we are in Him from the Word of God, and we are to get the right perspective of who we are from the teachings of the Holy Spirit. He alone knows everything about each of us, for it is in God we live and move and have our being; and since we were created by God, we owe Him and no one else the life that we have. Our lives should be lived in a way that glorifies Him and not us.

The Bible says in Romans 12:1–2,

> I beseech you therefore brethren, by the mercies of God, that ye present your bodies a living sacrifice, holy, acceptable unto God, which is your reasonable service, and be not conformed to this world: but be ye transformed by the renewing of your mind, that ye may prove what is that good, and acceptable, and perfect will of God.

God wants His children to be transformed by the renewing of their minds so that when the mind is renewed, the man is changed. God commands us to bring everything to the altar of sacrifice because we are to be His temple that He dwells in.

There is a battle in the spirit realm for your mind. Satan wants you to be fixated on the pleasures of sin. He does not want you to be productive with your life. Satan does not want your works to be that of godliness so that all your doings do follow after your faith and trust in Jesus.

He wants you to waste every day and every minute of your life being unproductive. He wants you to spend the time, the talents and gifts that God has given you doing foolishness. Satan wants to persuade you to believe that God is unfair and controlling. He wants you to believe that the Christian life is dull and boring. The devil wants you to think and believe that there is no joy in living a godly life—but he is a liar—and the fact of the matter is it is far better for our flesh to be afflicted by the Word of God, bringing it under the subjection and under the authority of Christ, than to enjoy the pleasures of sin that Satan has to offer.

Romans 8:10, 13–14 says,

> And if Christ be in you, the body is dead to sin; but the Spirit is life because of righteousness. For if ye live after the flesh, ye shall die: but if ye through the Spirit do mortify the deeds of the body, ye shall live. For as many as are led by the Spirit of God, they are the sons of God.

I encourage you to always pray, read, and study the Word of God diligently and never let it depart out of your mouth, for out of our mouth are spoken that which will surely come to pass. That which we profess, that is what we will eventually become. That which we think on says a lot about who we are, and if our minds stay on Christ, we will not willfully sin against God; and if we do sin, not presumptuously, we have Christ as our advocate before God the Father, representing our case when Satan brings railing accusations against us to God.

God wants us to repent of every sin He has troubled us to confess and repent, and so every human being that hears the Word of God must do what He says because the consequence of disobedience of the commandments of God is very severe and deadly. So when we obey God's Word to turn away from the practice of and indulgence in sin as a way of life, His mercy is powerful enough to forgive us of every sin that is in our lives, and His blood is powerful and sufficient to wash away the stains of sin.

Our flesh must yield to the control of the spirit that God has birthed in us, and it is to be managed by us living the Word of God, for our bodies are to be the house and temple of the living God. Your body and mine must be made holy and acceptable unto God. No evil thought and no act of sin should we behold. Unless our mind is transformed by God's Word, we remain unchanged in our living, and the memory of sin is still present in us. God has given us in His Word the blueprint for victorious living, and He has given us His Holy Spirit so that He may teach, instruct, lead, and guide us into all truth of the Bible.

God feeds us His Word in stages. He takes His sons and His daughters from the milk of His Word to the meat of His Word until they become perfectly established in the ways of Jesus Christ. If every Christian would continually grow into what the Word of God says they ought to become, holy and faithful saints, then as a person thinks in his or her heart, that's what he or she will become. Every seed would only produce fruit after its kind. What's in our hearts will bear out in our lives who we really are. God renews our minds, and He transforms our lives by revealing into our minds measures of His truths. If anyone needs wisdom and understanding, God gives it to us when we ask Him.

God is the only architect that rebuilds every life into the image of Himself. It is He that designs our future to be filled with victories, and yes, you can have victory even if you are in the worst of circumstances. It is in war that we fight our way to victory that Christ had already won on the cross at Calvary. It is in tribulations where our faith is tested and strengthened by adversity. It is the place where we are preserved by God.

Don't allow Satan to wear you down and wear you out with negative thoughts. If you used to be a worry worm, Satan knows it because he keeps a record of all that we do. We must tell ourselves, "That is not who I am. I am a new creation in Christ, and I have the mind of Christ in me. I will continually set my mind on things above"; and then we must always tell ourselves and believe in our heart, "I am better than my circumstances because I have the Holy Spirit living inside of me. I am who God says I am. Ye though I walk through the valley of the shadow of death, I will not fear Satan or any evil that he may put in my way."

Friend, we are not our own; we are the Lord's. Brothers and Sisters, please read Psalm 97. It tells us what our enemies are up against and our chief enemy is Satan and it tells us how great and mighty our God is.

Everyone who is born of the Spirit of God has received the righteousness of God through Christ Jesus, and so we are never to rejoice over the tribulations of others for we all have sinned, the Bible declares, and we all have come short of God's glory. Just remember that it is by the sheer mercy, and goodness of God that He has not put our sin out there except that we have done so by our own behavior; but if we should continue in sin in spite of the pleadings the Holy Spirit is doing to influence our decision to turn away from doing evil, it will only be a matter of time before we are put to an open shame.

CALLED TO BE CHOSEN

First Corinthians 15:10 says,

> But by the grace of God I am what I am: and his grace which
> was bestowed upon me was not in vain.

Each one of us needs to cry out to God in faith-filled prayers for Him to release the power of His Spirit to help us resist the temptations of Satan. We must allow God to give us a hatred for sin so that we can be set free from its power. If you are being afflicted in any or in all areas of your life because of sin, ask God for His help, and He will deliver you and cleanse you from all unrighteousness. We have to always talk with God. If we are not talking with God, who are we talking to? I encourage myself, and I will encourage you as well, to stay in the Word of God no matter what season you and I are in; for when we remain in God's Word and we meditate on it always, it becomes that treasure and that jewel that is hidden in our hearts.

Seasons are times of change, so when we lose some things in life, it's because God is about to replace those things with something much better. Hiding God's Word in our hearts must be every child of God's act of stewardship so that we may not deliberately sin against Him. We all must do what pleases our heavenly Father, for the Word of God is that which is able to replace fear and doubt with faith. God will use His Word to transform you by the renewing of your mind. God has obligated Himself to care for His sheep, and if we would do all that He has commanded us to do, with His strength and with the power of the Holy Spirit in us, we shall overcome every crisis that we face.

It is not we, by ourselves, who are able to do the commandments of God, but it is Christ in us that we are able to keep ourselves from sin. We will go through some storms, but the storms will not go through us. We will be in troubled waters, but the troubled waters would not be in us, and we will see some dark days, but the light of God shall consume the darkness, and at the end of our fiery trials, we will come out stronger and better than when we went in. We are made stronger in adversity with Christ's blood covering us and with the Spirit of God on the inside of us.

God's blessings are in His mercies, for we read in Lamentations 3:22–23,

> It is of the LORD's mercies that we are not consumed, because
> his compassion fail not. They are new every morning: great is thy
> faithfulness.

We may not be always faithful to keep the commandments of God, but He is always faithful in His promises to do for us when we cannot do for ourselves. He will help us in the areas of our lives that we need help in because He knows that the spirit is indeed willing, but our flesh is weak.

It is God's will and my prayer that all of us thank Him more for what we do have for He is all we really need and thank Him for what He has given us for He has given us eternal life. A heart that is thankful for the mercies of God is a heart that is content with what he or she has received from Him, for the things that did remain from the storms that were sent to shake off the dead things that were killing us were of God's doing.

Some Christians constantly complain and whine about the trouble that come into their lives rather than ask God for the faith and confidence to know that He is in every situation with them. Please read Isaiah 43:1–3 to see and meditate on the sure promises of God, and know this—as the children of our heavenly Father, we will in this life go through some trials, but they are only allowed into our lives to strengthen our faith in the One who created and then saved us from the wages of sin, by the act of His own will, unto Himself.

The Bible says in Psalm 34:19,

> Many are the afflictions of the righteous, but the Lord delivers
> His people out of them all.

In some cases, God is subtracting things from our lives that we thought we could not do without; and at times, God has to teach us to be content with what we have rather than complain about the things that have been taken away, for those things usually interfere with our relationship and fellowship with Him. Let us be grateful and thank God for what we do have. We are alive because of the mercies of God, which are renewed every day, and we do have a measure of health.

There are people all over this world who did not make it alive through to the end of yesterday, and some went to bed and never woke up. Who knows how they would be judged in the resurrection and where they will spend eternity? Only God knows. Many people who may have had the greatest potential to do great things in their lifetime are buried somewhere on this earth, for many of them may have died before they did accomplish the great things God had created them to do, so you and I need to be thankful to God that we did not die with an unfinished assignment. If we are employed, let us be thankful and not take things for granted. God protects and watches over us and our family. If we lose anything in this life, then let's thank Him anyway. If it were not for the goodness and the mercy of God, where would we be?

We may not fully understand why we go through tribulations, but that's okay. We can still give God thanks for His protection and His provision that He has given us during these temporary challenges. If we had no tests, how would we know what victory is?

The Bible says in Philippians 4:11–13,

> Not that I speak in respect of want: for I have learned, in whatsoever state I am, therewith to be content. I know both how to be abased, and I know how to abound: every where and in all things I am instructed both to be full and to be hungry, both to abound and to suffer need. I can do all things through Christ who strengtheneth me.

Friend, why worry and be stressed out about the things God has under His control. He is not trying to ruin our lives. He is preparing us for better things. What we, as Bible-believing Christians, need to do is to thank God for making us into different people from who we once were. We asked Him to change us, and did we think that the process would be smooth and easy? No, change is never easy and comfortable, but it is the vehicle and the course that God uses to take us to the next level in our walk with Him.

Some of us want to get to the top of life, but we don't want to use the steps and directions that God uses to get His willing and obedient children there, and so God has to train us in the way we should go using tests and trials. Thus, when tribulations and fiery trials come into our lives—and they will come—we will be prepared with the strength of Christ to withstand those things and not depart from the faith we have in God.

Some people have had more trouble—I mean serious trouble—than we can ever imagine or live through, yet they persevered and overcame every adversity with the help of God because they trusted in Jesus.

In my life, I had tasted some severe trouble at a time when I did not know Jesus Christ as Savior and Lord. It was trouble in my finances because of unemployment, which affected my self-worth. The enemy had tormented me to the point I did not want to live. I grew up believing I was never good enough to become somebody productive, but God saved me from myself. I began to spend time with God by searching the Scriptures and in prayer. What He did was take away the appetite I had for sin and gave me a hunger and a thirst for righteousness.

I have also seen more trouble after I became born again. I had allowed the spirits of discouragement and doubt to overrun me. I wondered why all hell was breaking loose in my life if I was saved by God. Then I remembered John 16:33. I have also seen the goodness of God operate in my life, and every time I thought that I would not make it through, God made a way and delivered me through the storm because His presence was with me all the way. God has told us in His Word to count it all joy when we are in trouble because greater is He that is in us than Satan, who is in the world. Satan and his imps get nervous when they see God's people glorifying Him (praise and worship) in tribulation.

God is our portion, our refuge, and our strength, a timely help in the time of trouble. Therefore, let all God's people hope in the Lord, for He will bring all His promises to pass in our lives. Christ has promised that He would never leave nor forsake any of His redeemed people even in the time of trouble. The Bible says that the joy of the Lord is our strength. Joy cannot flourish where there is no hope, for hopelessness leads to despair.

Often what we do not have is more of a blessing. What God is doing when He withholds some things from us is shielding us from the calamities and troubles that we are unable to see because we cannot perceive the troubling end of those things which are beyond our understanding. God is not trying to keep good things from us—He desires to give us His goods—but He is careful not to give us the things that we may not be prepared to handle at that moment in our lives.

God would not allow anything or anyone to lead us away from Him and destroy us unless we insist on being stubborn and rebellious and get those things by ungodly means. God wants to prepare His people to be good stewards of the gifts He has for them. Trust God: He has your best interest in His mind. Please know that God has better things for us that are of eternal value. Some of us dwell on the troubled waters around us such that we do not see Jesus in the ship with us. When we are drowning in trouble because of fear, God has an outstretched hand for us to hold on to. Many of God's people are so focused on the trouble that they do not see the provisions that He made specifically for them in their situation. Christ wants all His people to keep their eyes on Him, for when we keep our minds stayed on Him, we would be more thankful for the great things He has done and is still doing in and for us each and every day.

Once God has decreed a thing to happen and once He has prophesied His will and His purpose for our lives, there is no person, no power, and no principality that can stop them from coming to pass—except it is of our own doing. Great is the faithfulness and the mercies of God toward His children who deserve none of His generous benefits. In our troubles, Christ delivers us out of them all. God calms the rough waters in our lives. He brings light where there is darkness, and He brings the rain where there is drought. God gathers His children together as a hen gathers her chicks so that they are not scattered, divided, and destroyed by fear.

Christ covers His people with His love when they are hated and despised by sinful people. It does not matter what others say of us when the Lord is by our side. He is our shelter in all the storms of life. God cuts off our enemies in their pursuits so that you and I are not destroyed. God is a fire that goes before Him and burns up His enemies round about (Psalm 97:3). He opens and divides the sea of impossibilities and will make for you and for me—if we doubt not—a clear, dry way for us to get to the other side from the pursuits of the enemy.

It is God who prepares for us a table with every good thing that is from within Himself in the presence of our enemies. He anoints our head with the oil of His Spirit, and our cup of all His blessings overflows from our life into the lives of others. O that we would praise the Lord and magnify His name, unafraid of what people may say for all God's goodness He puts in our life and for the mercies that He gives to the children of men each and every day; and it was God who remembered us in our low estate, when we had none of this world's goods and when we were not regarded by the rich and the powerful because we were not as influential as they are.

God has given His people an overflowing measure of His heavenly blessings, and He has given every sinner space to repent, for the Lord is long-suffering. He is patient, and He is kind. The Lord's name is excellent in all the earth. The Creator of all things who is sovereign over the universe and beyond has made Himself to tabernacle with men, and He sups with them to show them the way to have peace with God, for He is the way, the truth, and the life. He has promised if anyone would call upon Him, He will come and abode in and sup together with him or her.

God made His habitat with corrupt humanity who is infected with sin, and He became a servant of God in the person of the Lord Jesus Christ unto mankind as the example of righteousness and as the perfect atonement for the sins of the whole world. Christ wrote the check for the payment of sin with the ink of His own blood to execute His will so that every person who repents of his or her sins and receives forgiveness from God may inherit eternal life. The cross was His table to write on, and His tongue was His pen to write with.

The Word of God stands forever. If I am unable to convince you in words the power of the Word of God that causes people to come to Christ and be changed forever, the Spirit of God is the only one who can do what I or any other person is unable to do—to open your ears to hear and your eyes to see the wonders of His will for your life in His Word, and so you have a choice to make: either you accept God's invitation to renounce sin and follow Him all the way, or you reject Him and continue in total rebellion. Light will shine in darkness, but not for long, for God will eventually withdraw Himself from pursuing anyone who insist on being stubborn to the gospel of peace.

Nothing but the blood of Jesus can wash away your sins and mine and is able to cleanse us from all unrighteousness. Jesus Christ is God's light given to a dark world which hates the light because the spirit of the wicked one is in it. No one can see their way out of darkness except the light that came into the world removes the darkness from their heart. Jesus does not save anyone in darkness. He only saves men and women out of darkness to freedom in God; wherefore, they are at peace with Him and with their fellow man. Thus, they have found true rest for their souls, and so the Word of God says in Revelation 12:11 that the saints, whom Christ have redeemed, overcame Satan by the blood of the Lamb and the word of their testimony and love not their lives unto death. The blood of Jesus and the power it has to completely erase the sinful past of anyone is beyond mankind's comprehension.

No being in this universe and beyond can alter God or His Word. No power or authority on earth can change the sacred Word of God, and in their attempt to do so, God's fierce wrath will abide upon them. God's promises for our lives are in His Word, and yes, the mercies of God are much better than anything this earth can give. Praise the Lord for His wonderful works to the children of men, for Christ still forgives iniquities, and He is still saving men and women out of a life of sin.

6

GOD'S FORGIVENESS

Forgiving someone is one of the hardest things for any of us to do. It is not something that is natural to us, for we would rather be right when in many instances we are indeed wrong. Saying the words "I completely forgive you for the wrong you have done to me" is not natural for any of us to say and really mean it if those words are to be uttered. The spirit of forgiveness is a gift from God, and until we receive it, many of us live lives with a spirit of unforgiveness and with bitterness and resentment in our hearts toward the wrongdoer.

All the wrong that you and I have done—that is, the sins that we have committed throughout our lifetime—can and are forgiven by God, but God wants us to forgive one another in the same manner He forgives us. We all, at some point in our lives, may have been hurt by someone; and in some way, we sought their apology with little or no success. Nevertheless, God forgives sins. Ask Him, and He will forgive you. Being bitter and resentful leaves us angry, and unless we forgive, we will never be free in our own minds, and it may be impossible for us to live the blessed life, one of joy and peace.

Bitterness and anger rob us of the freedom to form meaningful relationships with others because of what was done to us in the past, and because we are afraid of being hurt again, we isolate ourselves from other people; and as a result of our isolation, we become imprisoned by an unforgiving spirit.

Some of us who have been wounded by the fiery darts of others develop an antidote of poison that is deadlier than the wounds we may have received from the wrong that was done to us. We attack the innocent and the guilty alike, and sometimes we find pleasure in doing so.

Some people are guilty of finding pleasure in being miserable, and they want the entire atmosphere around them to be an area of misery. How sad it is that some of us will allow that spirit from Satan to control and, ultimately, destroy us if we are living this way.

Many of us who live in bitterness because of unforgiveness don't recognize genuine friendships others may try to forge with us, and we can't appreciate the love and kindness that they show toward us. Our negative disposition is usually because we have become so infected with the cancer of bitterness that we self-destruct, and it's only the healing hand of God that can make us whole again. We should not be blaming others for our condition, but instead, we should seek God in His Word and be in constant prayer with Him so that we can be made new in Christ.

God will always help us recover from our falls in life and restore us to the place of true peace with Him, so when we are challenged to confront our sins, we are to allow God to take us through the difficulties of life with Him to redeem us from the state of unhappiness and from the destructive nature of unforgiveness.

Studies have shown that bitterness and anger, because of unforgiveness, can make us sick and delay our healing from illnesses.[15] We are very much susceptible to physical sicknesses resulting from a weakened immune system.

> When harbored for a long time, bitterness may forecast patterns of biological dysregulation (a physiological impairment that can affect metabolism, immune response or organ function) and physical disease.[16]

Healing and recovering from illnesses are very difficult when we are not at rest, and we age much faster because we are at disease (dis-ease)

Some of us separate ourselves from others who love us. We do this because we are angry. We may even become verbally abusive to other people that we are close to, and sometimes they, in turn, develop a negative attitude toward us, and eventually there is a vicious cycle of bitterness and

---

[15]K. A. Lawler-Row, J. C. Karremans, C. Scott, et. al. "Forgiveness, Physiological Reactivity and Health: The Role of Anger." Department of Psychology, East Carolina University, Greenville, NC, International Journal of Psychophysiology: Official Journal of the International Organization of Psychophysiology, 2008 Apr;68(1):51–8. Epub 2008 Jan 17.

[16]Carsten Wrosch, a professor in Montreal's Concordia University Department of Psychology and a member of the Centre for Research in Human Development.

resentment. Yes, we may not realize it, but unresolved bitterness from an unforgiving spirit can develop into hate. I know it is a strong word to use, but because we have encapsulated ourselves with the spirit of unforgiveness for so long, we move farther and farther away from being able to sense and see where unresolved unforgiveness can lead.

This is why God wants to give us His peace so that it may be that we can find rest for our souls. The Bible says in Ephesians 4:26–27, 31–32,

> Be ye angry, and sin not: let not the sun go down upon your wrath: Neither give place to the devil. Let all bitterness, and wrath, and anger, and clamor, and evil speaking, be put away from you, with all malice: And be ye kind one to another, tenderhearted, forgiving one another, even as God for Christ's sake hath forgiven you.

A Vessel of God's Love and Peace, Not a Vessel Bitterness and Unrest

Maybe God is calling you to be His chosen vessel, whereby He wants to show you what true love looks like, and He wants to give you His peace that only He can give. God will give you, if you diligently seek Him, the spirit of peace with the fullness of joy—not as the world gives but as God alone is able to abundantly give to anyone that seeks Him out and ask Him for the spirit of forgiveness. If you are seeking God, it is because He is drawing you to Himself. Matthew 11:28 says,

> Come unto me, all ye that labor and are heavy laden, and I will give you rest.

God is the only source from whom we may receive true rest. It is rest in the midst of all the chaos, confusion, and the turbulences of life.

It is spiritual rest that puts our minds at ease and that keeps us from worrying about the things that God has under His control and is more than able to take care and richly supply our needs, and if we seek genuine and unselfish love from any human being, we will not find it.

Many times, we unrealistically expect from one another that which only God can give. However, God expects us to truly forgive one another, and that's our responsibility. Using sex as a form of manipulation does not define what true love is, and nothing but God-led forgiveness, that which is pure, godly, and undefiled, should be the practice of the true child of God.

Let's be clear—sex outside of marriage is defined by the Bible as fornication. Secondly, no one should make it difficult or hard to forgive the people who have wronged them, and we who have been wronged should readily accept their forgiveness. Our attitude of doing the commandment of God to forgive should be out of a pure and sincere heart. God knows the intents of our actions, and therefore, He knows our heart. Nothing is hidden from God's sight. Everything in the universe and beyond is naked and exposed before the eyes of Him to whom every unrepentant sinner must give an account for living sinful lives, (Hebrews 4:13).

When we sin against God and we confess and repent to Him the sin(s) we have committed, we would like to know that He has accepted our sincere sorrow for sinning against Him and that He has forgiven us. There are some people in the church of God who have been hurt by others but refuse to forgive the wrongdoer and accept their forgiveness. These people refuse to accept forgiveness from the people who hurt them because they want those individuals to be unhappy and miserable just as they are. These individuals who refuse to accept forgiveness from the wrongdoer want that person to live in an atmosphere of misery with the constant reminder of the unpleasant memory of their sinful past, and it almost seems like such individuals prefer to allow Satan to control their thoughts and behavior rather than do the things that God will be pleased with.

When we have an unforgiving spirit, God will not forgive us of our sins against Him, and He will deal with us in a manner that brings us to our senses. When we engage in such behaviors, we have created another layer of sin into our lives, and we have involved others as accomplices to our foolishness.

We need to get to God fast, without delay, and let Him help us turn from our sinful lives and let Him destroy that attitude of unforgiveness that was contrived by a conniving demonic spirit that has bound some in the church under its control. The Bible's definition of true love is that it is pure, kind, and does not manipulate anyone. True and honest forgiveness cleans the human heart from the toxins of bitterness and anger. Our forgiving one another allows God to hear our prayers and forgive us of our sins. He forgives our wrongdoings on the condition that we forgive others of their wrongdoings toward us.

Unforgiveness will kill any relationship, and it can make us rotten on the inside. Sex is just a part of the communion between the husband and his wife that makes them one with each other. God created sex to be a part of the wholeness in marriage between a husband and his wife. Sex is not the answer to unforgiveness within the marriage relationship. It may be one of the places where we go after we have truly dealt with that which did set both partners apart and have soured the husband-wife relationship. Sex is the vehicle for procreation within husband-wife relationship.

Sex has been merchandised as a commodity for just about anything and has been wrongly defined as a condition and as a test of the love a man may have for a woman and vice versa. We are to seek God in earnest for His forgiveness if indeed any of us, like so many others have done in the past, have acted in ways that dishonored God and has poisoned us on the inside.

So, men and women, please do not abuse each other in the flesh to fix that which only God can fix. Our actions may bring us temporary pleasures, but they will cause more pain than we care to have; and for sure, sex is not the definition of love, and it cannot be used in the place of truly forgiving one another; for when sex is misused to connive others and selfishly get what we want, it leaves deep scars from the wounds we receive when we mismanage our bodies and misuse what God has made sacred to be used exclusively in marriage. The greatest benefit of marriage is sharing ourselves unselfishly with the spouse God has given us. We should always be ready to forgive one another, for none of us are perfect, and that is the truth.

No Forgiveness, No Rest

We cannot find rest in God if we have not forgiven others as Christ has commanded us to do, and we cannot have peace if we are bitter on the inside; and if we think that just having enough stuff would take care of all our problems, we are sadly mistaken. Having notoriety and fame in and of themselves would not give anyone rest, wherewith we are at peace with all men and with ourselves, but what we may get instead is more trouble.

Having power and authority alone, in and of themselves, would not give anyone rest. As a matter of fact, these may bring more problems than we may care to have. God is the only real place where we may find rest, for when we have God, we have everything. Nothing can take the place of our unrest—only God can be that place of rest, wherein we have forgiven those who have trespassed against us, and God has forgiven us of our sins against Him.

In the Bible, God commands all of us to forgive others for the wrong they may have done to us so that we may receive the forgiveness of our sins from Him. How do we know that we have done something wrong? Well, according to the Bible, God reveals to every person that which is wrong and that which is sin. He does this in a loving way through the Holy Spirit (John 14). The Bible says in Colossians 3:13–15,

> Forbearing one another, and forgiving one another, if any man has a quarrel against any: even as Christ forgave you, so also do ye, and above all these things put on charity which is the bond of perfectness, and let the peace of God rule in your heart, to the which also ye are called in one body; and be ye thankful.

The spirit of forgiveness is of faith, given by God to everyone that believe and obey His Word to do whatever He says for us to do. As Jesus was being crucified on the cross at Calvary, He said as He hung his head, "Father, forgive them; for they know not what they do" (Luke 23:34).

God forgave us when we were the ones that offended Him and did all manner of evil against His Christ, who came to save all mankind from the wages of sin. Jesus demonstrated the ultimate act of forgiveness. He highlighted the lack of understanding of those that committed the act of crucifying Him, which really is all of us.

Is it possible that sometimes those who may have offended us really and truly did not understand what they did was wrong? We sometimes feel that way—that what we were accused of doing was not intended to harm anyone and that we really did not know that what we did was offensive to the other person—but all mankind is guilty of hating God and His commandments. That is what the Bible declares of every human being.

Forgiveness through Repentance

If we would confess all our sins to God, for He will reveal them to us, He will totally forgive us of every sin! It does not matter to God the wrong things we have done, for He desires that every living person turn to Him and repent of his or her sins; and according to the Bible, God has promised that He will forgive any person of all his or her transgressions if he or she believes in his or her heart that Jesus Christ is his or her true and only deliverer. The Bible says in 1 John 1:9,

> If we confess our sins, he is faithful and just to forgive us our sins, and to cleanse us from all unrighteousness.

But if we refuse to heed the Spirit of God calling us to repentance, then we remain unforgiven of our sins, for the Word of God says in Proverbs 28:13,

> He that covereth his sins shall not prosper: but whoso confesseth and forsaketh them shall have mercy.

God will not forgive any sin we refuse to acknowledge and confess to Him even though He knows every sin that we have ever committed. It does not matter to God the magnitude of our sin or sins, for God can totally forgive us of all sins. No one is beyond God's forgiveness. In the book of Titus 2:14, the Word of God says

> Who gave himself for us, that he might redeem us from all iniquity, and purify unto himself a peculiar people, zealous of good works.

As we cry out to God in faith to repent of our sins, God will attend to the voice of our supplications. If God did not forgive sins, then where would we be?

> If thou, Lord, shouldest mark iniquities, O Lord, who shall stand? But there is forgiveness with thee, that thou mayest be feared. (Psalm 130:3–4)

God invites us to reason with Him about our condition in sin, for God can totally forgive us of all sins.

No one is beyond God's forgiveness. He wants us to know that there is forgiveness for all our sins from Him, but this does not mean that we go and sin presumptuously and then seek God for His forgiveness after He has forgiven us. If we continue to premeditatedly sin, the possibility is that we can die in the act of committing willful sins. God is not to be fooled with. He is reasonable, and He is fair-minded, but He is not a fool, nor is He senile.

How can God, who is absolutely holy and just in all His ways, forgive sin when the penalty for breaking His law is death? How could God be so interested in any of us when by nature we are not interested in Him? It is all because of His mercy. God has been so merciful to so many of us who are the recipients of His unspeakable and immeasurable love. It would be next to impossible for the true children of God not to testify that if it were not for the forgiving nature and mercy of God, through the sacrifice and shed blood of Jesus, to forgive them of every wicked and evil thing they have done; they all would still be bound for destruction in the lake of fire. It is amazing to me that God would forgive any of us of our multitude of sins and charge them all to the name that is given above every name, the unblemished lamb of God, the Lord Jesus Christ.

It was Jesus Christ, the perfect and sinless sacrifice, who was covered with the sins of the whole world, who stood before the judgment of God the Father. He was judged as though He was the sinner. He was found guilty before God with the guilt of our sins and received the punishment for our iniquities in His body. Jesus was the innocent dying for the guilty. Yes, friend, Jesus Christ is the only one that can and will forgive you completely if you would believe and go to Him, just the way you are. Jesus said in Mark 2:10,

> But that ye may know that the Son of man hath power on earth to forgive sins, [he said to the sick of the palsy].

Every human being is indeed sick of the palsy of which sin is.

Jesus, through His love for us, took our place on death row, as it were, for He was made sin for us. It is God, through Christ, who pursues sinful mankind and meets them in the desolate places and in the wilderness of life and forgives all who confess their sins to Him and cleanses them from all unrighteousness.

In the holy Scriptures and by the testimony of many recipients of the goodness of God, we see the grandness of God's forgiveness for all manner of sins. He forgave the nation of Israel of their multitude of sins, for He saw their affliction and delivered them out of their suffering. God's people in the Old Testament have on many occasions stubbornly disobeyed His commandments. God, in His mercy, forgave them every time they backslid into practicing sin, and so as it was with the nation of Israel, so it is with mankind today, that He forgives those He calls and leads by His Spirit to acknowledge they have sinned and that they need to repent.

The Bible says that

> The Lord God, is merciful and gracious, longsuffering, and abundant in goodness and truth, Keeping mercy for thousands forgiving iniquity and transgression and sin that will by no means clear the guilty. (Exodus 34:6–7)

Another example of God's goodness and grace toward sinners is the forgiveness of the woman in John 8:1–11, who was caught in adultery by the religious church folks, who themselves may have committed similar sins; but because we usually are troubled by the guilt of our conscience by the memory of the same unrepented sins we have committed that we see others do, we want to hang them so we may quiet our own storms.

These men did not seek to forgive this woman, for she is a true picture of every sinner, but they, instead, sought to have her killed by stoning her. She was to be stoned by men whose hearts were heart of stone.

But Christ did not condemn her, He forgave her, though the law of God demanded that anyone who was guilty of the sin of adultery should be stoned. Jesus said in Mark 2:10,

> But that ye may know that the Son of man hath power on earth to forgive sins. [He said to the sick of the palsy]

Every human being is indeed sick of the palsy of which sin is.

God also forgave Rahab of her sin of harlotry (Joshua 2), and He forgave King David of his sin with Bathsheba (2 Samuel 11:13). God forgave Saul of Tarsus of his sins that included the consent to have many of God's people killed just because Christ was their Savior and their Lord, and at his conversion, he became Paul, the preacher, the one who bore the stripes of suffering for the cause of Christ. He preached the gospel of Jesus Christ with boldness (Acts 9).

God also forgave the woman at the well (John 4:5–29), for she thought rest from unrest could be found by pleasing our carnal nature, the physical and the fleshly part of who we are as sinful human beings. The men that this daughter of God had in her life were not the source of living water, for they, most likely, had their own issues. They probably were thirsty, and they may have been restless, seeking rest in parched and dried-up places.

I don't mean to cast stones at anyone or to be judgmental, but how many of us are living this way today? God is not pleased when we put ourselves in vulnerable positions to be bruised and scarred with the injuries of short-lived pleasures. God can and will forgive any person if he or she is willing to come to Him and confess their sins and receive His forgiveness. God is not out to rob us of peace and happiness. He gives them to us, unreserved.

Christ is the God of peace, and He has the keys to true happiness. The blessings of God that He has for His people are so much better than we could have ever imagined or could ever find in earthly things. God has also forgiven a countless number of people, some whose testimony we may never hear in this life until we all meet God together in heaven. To all who God had made to overcome all manner of adversities, because they were born again, He has also given them the right to eat of the tree of life, and so you too, my friend, can receive the forgiveness of your sins today from a caring and loving God and be a partaker of His heavenly gift——eternal life. No one is beyond God's forgiveness, and everyone can forgive his and her brother and sister if they make God be their help.

It's the goodness of God that draws us all to Christ, and it is He through the leading of the Holy Spirit who leads us to repentance; for unless we repent of our sins, no person is able to see the forgiveness of God.

Romans 2:4 says,

> Not knowing that the goodness of God leadeth thee to repentance?

We also read in Jeremiah 31:3,

> The Lord hath appeared of old unto me saying, Yea, I have loved thee with an everlasting love: therefore, with lovingkindness have I drawn thee.

Every unsaved person is spiritually dead, and his or her dry bones lay in the grave of sin of the spiritually dead. Mankind is spiritually dead because they have transgressed the commandments of God, for the Bible says in John 8:34, "Whosoever committeth sin is the servant of sin." Only God can speak the words of life to spiritually dead people such that they that are made spiritually alive by God now live because God raised them up from the grave of sin and from the valley of dry bones. He gives to the spiritually resurrected His life-bearing seed so that seeing they see and hearing, they hear the words of life from God, the life-giver.

God breathes into every spiritually dead person's life the breath of the new life. He puts together our disconnected, scattered, and discombobulated parts so that you and I may be able to stand and live again, for God is He who is our redeemer, protector, provider, and sustainer. The Lord is our bone connector. He forgives sin, and He gives life to all who are spiritually dead; and after God has raised us up again and has given us the new life, He makes us one in Him so that in Christ we live.

> Whosoever is born of God doth not commit sin; for the seed of God remaineth in him: and he cannot sin, because he is born of God. (1 John 3:9)

The seed of God is His Word, the Bible.

The Love of God Forgives

Romans 5:8, says,

> But God commendeth his love toward us, in that, while we were yet sinners, Christ died for us.

The death of Christ on the cross was the act of the great love God has for mankind. God has made the opportunity for salvation possible, and He made it simple in Christ so that no person may have an excuse for not knowing the gift of God. We deny the gift of God when we deny Christ by refusing to believe His Word and accept the goodness of God. There is no greater love than that what God did for sinners on the cross at Calvary.

It is impossible for anyone to live a godly life apart from God except it is God who gives him or her life, for the Word of God says in 1 John 4:9,

> In this was manifested the love of God toward us, because that God sent his only begotten Son into the world, that we might live through him.

Our finite minds cannot fathom the magnitude and the depth of the love that God has for us. It is past our understanding to comprehend the love that God has toward sinners and that He would save sinners like you and me.

The riches of the blessings of God are made available to His children through Christ Jesus. This we read in Ephesians 1:7,

> In whom we have redemption through his blood, the forgiveness of sins, according to the riches of his grace.

God made all whom He has redeemed alive together with Christ, through the richness of His mercy and the greatness of His love, wherewith He indeed first loved us, raised us up, and made us sit together in heavenly places with Christ Jesus (Ephesians 2:4–6). Despite the love that God has shown to every person, many still despise Him and refuse to receive His gift of love.

God Shows Us How to Forgive

God, our Heavenly Father, not only loves all of us, but He wants to forgive everyone who would hear the voice of His Spirit speak to their heart. In Luke 15:11-32, the parable of the Prodigal Son, Jesus shows us the love God has for mankind. He shows us how the love of God forgives.

And the Bible says that after many days and after living his life foolishly, away from the presence of his father, this young man found himself empty of all the possessions he received from his father, and this impatient younger son spent everything he had: his time, his money, and his energy.

What he spent is what many would pay for short-lived pleasures in exchange for a life with God, for this younger son had everything in the house of his father, and the greatest of what the father gave his sons was his love, but the pleasures of this world would only last for a short time; and when the season of pleasure is over, we are all left empty, for what we have that are of this world are just shallow dreams with empty promises and temporary happiness.

The emptiness that we experience is the feelings of hopelessness and despair, a broken heart and anguish. The fame that we may have in this world, where there are many vipers and parasites, is only because of our possessions and its worth to those who only care about the things we have; and we thought they were our friends, but they all vanished quickly when what we had evaporated.

Everyone, the invited and the uninvited, became our circle of friends when we are rich with the stuff that many people are envious of, and with greed in their heart, they covet our earthly possessions. We are the life of the party when our pockets are full, but when the fun is over and all is spent and we are left with nothing to share, there is no one to be found to help us clean up our messed-up lives.

But God is just a prayer away. One word for help from our lips is enough to have the Almighty and all His holy angels assemble right to the place where we are and fight against Satan and his imps. Yes, God is more than able to set you and I free from the bondage to sin and bring us back home to Himself; and so God wants His children to always seek Him in His Word, through His Spirit, and in much prayer to Him. So many Christians are being attacked relentlessly by Satan and his demons because they have not allowed God to be in full control of every area of their lives, and some have wandered away from the presence of God, from under His protection, and attached themselves to vain philosophies.

You may have wondered why wrong behaviors and attitudes in your life are compulsive. It's because they are demonic strongholds with deep roots, going back several generations. Some of these behaviors and attitudes are depression, suicidal thoughts, anger, pornography, sexual perversion, adultery, fornication, homosexuality, drug and alcohol use, bitterness, low self-esteem, worry, fear, doubt and unbelief, double-mindedness, discouragement, gossip, pride, dealing with any part of the occult, strife, disobedience, slumber or laziness, stealing, lying, etc. If any of these things is in our lives, they must be seriously dealt with as stated in the Bible (2 Corinthians 10:3–6, Mark 11:22–26, Matthew 11:28–30, and throughout the rest of the Scriptures).

The way back home is now long and lonely, and no one can be found who is able to give you rest, for they did not tell you that they had their own issues; but God, who is very rich in mercy, wherewith He first loved us with an everlasting love such that He will spend the only thing of value, that is worth more than anything that He has, to find us and to bring us home to Himself.

The Bible says in Matthew 13:45–46,

> Again, the kingdom of heaven is like unto a merchant man, seeking goodly pearls: Who when he had found one pearl of great price, went and sold all that he had, and bought it.

God spent His most valuable possession, Himself, to purchase mankind's freedom with His own life from the dominion of Satan. He called us pearls of great value. Pearls are found in oysters, which are scavenger sea creatures that are unclean. We are the treasure hidden inside the shell of sin, for in sin we are unclean, but God sees beyond our sin and calls us what He will make us become.

It was God that asked the question in heaven, "Who can go for us to deliver my people out of the hand of sin? But He did not get an answer, for no other created being could answer Him. No one could understand what was at stake. None of the angels in heaven could relate to mankind's plight because they had no connection to us. There was absolute silence in heaven. No one could speak except God the Son. It was He that spoke in the beginning at Creation and the Godhead created and formed man in the image of God, and so when God (Father, Son, Holy Spirit) saw that mankind was wounded and he was brutally and viciously attacked in the street of evildoers and that he was being persecuted and mistreated, beaten and then killed by Satan in this dark world, it broke His heart; for God saw Himself in mankind, whom He had created in His image and formed in His likeness.

And so God was determined to redeem mankind at the cost of His own life in the person of the Lord Jesus Christ, and thus, according to the Bible, God prepared Himself a body, wrapped Himself in human flesh, and came to Jericho from Jerusalem as the Good Samaritan, the Son of Man, and the Son of God wrapped in one body to redeem His wounded and lost sheep.

God has prepared a house with many mansions for His redeemed sons and daughters. A house with many mansions we cannot comprehend, but nevertheless, God does not withhold His best from His lost people. It is with love and mercy that He avails His best for His lost sons and daughters. God is not worried about where we are, for He knows where all His lost sheep are hiding. He is concerned about our lost condition, and He is concerned about our nakedness in an unforgiving world ruled by Satan.

It saddens God to see our lives desolate and barren, dry and thirsty on the inside of who we are, and when we have become so hungry for the Bread of Heaven, for we have nothing left to eat after you and I have spent all that we had. God offered Himself as the Bread of Life, for the only thing that we will eat when we are apart from God, in sin, is swine's food. Swine's food is filth. That's what swine eats.

We eat spiritual swine's food when we sin against God and partake of the leavened bread of sinful men. We become so desperate for meat when the famines of life have come into our lives such that we have nothing to eat, we will compromise who we are, sons and daughters of the Most High God, and join ourselves to corrupt men who do not know our heavenly Father.

We eat the culinary dainties of those whose hands are covered with the blood of the innocent. We are the people who have lost our way back to God because we became drunk with the wine of foolishness, and we defile ourselves with the taste for the leeks and onions because the spirit of bondage is in us, and we lust for old wine, the wine of sorrows and regrets, whose effects, in many instances, leaves us with lasting scars, and somehow wrong became right, and evil men became our masters, for whoever we join ourselves to, we become one with them.

We thought life would have turned out different, even though we were warned by the foreknowing and foreseeing One who knows infinitely more than we do, but we just had to find out for ourselves what was so different from what we had in our heavenly Father's house; and in spite of all the mess we have made, God still loves us so much that He is willing to bring us home to Himself—at the cost of His best gift, Himself.

God does all that is in His power to show us the way back to His home by using the signposts of the gospel, and as He leads us along the straight and narrow way back to Himself, He does not wait until we reach all the way home. He instead meets us along the way with the sparkle of compassion in His eyes and with glee on His face. God embraces His redeemed sons and daughters with loving-kindness only a true father can give.

With the best robe that God has, Christ covers our nakedness with His love to hide our shame. It was God who shut the doors of vain opportunities along the dusty roads of sin, for God knows quite well that the lost is a vulnerable prey to a ferocious and relentless enemy, and that's why the only door of opportunity that was open was the door of God's love and forgiveness, His compassion, and His peace.

The lost and confused search for love and belongingness in all the wrong places where the predator and devourer of our peace seek to devour his prey, but God fights him off when we are too weak to know who is behind us, at our heels. Those who are lost and weary look for peace and meaning to life in dark and lonely places, thinking they might find God in many false religions with New Age thinking and vain philosophies, using self-willed efforts, but God cannot be found in any of those places. He is not the one lost, for God is an overflowing presence who is everywhere at the same time, and certainly, He is not a god made by human hands, where he is placed in a corner until needed, as if he is a convenience god. God is not a concept and a figment of someone's imagination. He cannot be accessed by having positive energy flow through your life. He is not a force, and He is not energy; but God is He who created you and me in the beginning, and He desperately wants to recreate us into His image, making us vessels of pure gold unto Himself. Thus, we become the temple of the Holy Spirit, a sanctuary holy onto God.

In jubilant celebration, God throws a party that beats all parties for His returning children. He kills His best fatted calf so that there is always meat in His house for those that are hungry for peace and rest in God, and they that eat of the sacrifice of God are transformed from the state of sin and are given eternal life from His own hands (John 6:53–58).

God's wine presses are filled with the best wine, and they that drink it directly from its Maker's veins are cleansed by its power. Every sinner who drinks of the new wine are never intoxicated, for it is only the blood of Christ which can wash and scrub away every sin out of the lives of those who believe Jesus Christ is the only source of eternal life so that the inner man, of who you once were, is made new again by the blood of the Lamb, for they that are begotten of God are given eternal life from Him (John 6:54).

God invites all His holy angels of heaven as witnesses to the celebration of every sinner's redemption. All the host of heaven takes notice. The sun shines its brightest. The stars twinkle with glee, and every created thing take note of the joy that is in the house of God. Now, no one can deny the great love your heavenly Father has for you.

There is no power in the heavens that is created by God, neither is there any in the earth or under the earth, nor is there any principality or any devil in hell that can separate any of God's children from the love of their heavenly Father, for God's love is stronger than any hate. It is stronger than any envy, and it is mightier than any plot from the pit of hell. To every redeemed of God, your haters would have to admit that it is beyond them to understand such indescribable display of agape love that

CALLED TO BE CHOSEN

our Father, who is in heaven, would have for His "once lost in a life of sin but now found" children.

Lost sons and daughters of God, come home to Him now, for no one has your back but Him. When the fun is over, which of your so-called friends are going to have your back without a knife in their hands? Who will help you clean up the messes of your life, and which of them would take away the pain and the sorrows that are in your life? Who is going to fill you with happiness and joy for the emptiness you have inside?

You feel used, for many came into your life and just took what they wanted while others stole from you whatever was left. The predators took advantage of your innocence, and they violated your unspoiled beauty to the harsh realities of life just because you were unwise to the ways of this world; and after a few moments of pleasure that appealed only to the senses, you feel dirty and shameful, used and abused. Everyone stripped you naked of all that you had and left you with nothing.

But God is calling you back home to His house not to violate you but to bind up your wounds you endured from a cruel and a hateful world. He is determined to take care and rebrand you as a new creation in Christ Jesus. God has prepared the water of compassion and hyssop to purge you of all uncleanness and to wash clean not just your feet but all of you in baptism, cleansing you from the stains of iniquity that covers you.

It is by God and His Word that your mind is made new. He has the best clothes made especially for you as He hides you in Himself. It is the robe of righteousness that God puts on you to redress you into what you have now become—a child of the King of kings—so that you are grafted into the vine of Christ. He will change everything about you from the inside out and dress you with ornaments of godliness. It is the blood of Christ that gets the stains of sin out, deep from within the very core of your being, and makes you clean from within. It is His blood that makes your robe whiter than anything anyone has ever seen.

Your past life is cast away by God to as far as the east is from the west and God has made you a new person and He has sanctified you unto Himself. God has promised to protect you at all cost from the roaming predator and from his cunning devices. If this is you, and if this is the picture God has given you to see what He will do in your life, please turn to Him today, for He will deliver you from sin's grip, and He will put you in the house that praises His name, that gives Him honor, and glory. God is ready to have a coming-home celebration for His sons' and daughters' return. Our heavenly Father, the Creator of all things, has killed the unspotted calf, who was never touched by sin, for He was His only and best sacrifice, in celebration of the reunion between Father and child, shepherd and sheep.

The Bible said that the lost son arose and came to his father, but when he was yet a great way off, his father saw him and had compassion and ran and fell on his neck and kissed him (Luke 15:20). The kisses of God are His mercies and His grace wrapped in His forgiveness and in His indescribable love for us. This is a demonstration of how God, our heavenly Father, sees us and treats those whose hearts have heard His Word. God does not hold us to our sin and to our past as He receives us, but He welcomes each sinner home with forgiveness and with love. God justifies every sinner whom He has called, with the blood of Jesus. Romans 3:24 says,

> Being justified freely by his grace through the redemption that is in Christ Jesus.

In Luke 7:47, we see another example of the rich compassion of God toward the humble, where we read what Jesus said:

> Wherefore I say unto thee, Her sins, which are many, are forgiven; for she loved much: but to whom little is forgiven, the same loveth little.

Jesus had compassion on this sinner, which is an example for us to follow regarding how we treat our fellow brothers and sisters. Friends, we must remember that in the same manner that Christ forgave this woman, with bowels of mercy, we are to forgive those who may have wronged us. She had a grateful attitude with a spirit of thankfulness to God.

God forgave this woman of all her sins, for indeed she is a picture of all humanity. The Scriptures did not say God examined her life to see if she was worthy of His forgiveness. He knew who she was, and He embraced her into His loving care. Christ bound up and nourished her wounded soul. This woman was recreated into the image of her loving Creator and Savior. Her response to what God had done in her life was to worship Him with the most precious thing she had. God gave His best to redeem every sinner from the wages of sin, and so the redeemed of God gives to Him his or her life on the altar of real sacrifice.

Some of the religious people who were present were angry about what had happened and what Christ had done for this woman. They were hateful toward those who were not like them, just like some do today in some churches. These people resented this woman's act of praise and worship, in her thankfulness to God, just like some today also do in some churches. We must not allow the critics who critique our manner of praise and worship to our Redeemer to affect our relationship and fellowship with Him. We are not answerable to those who have religion but no relationship with their Creator. If they only knew what things God had delivered us from and if they would see what a magnificent change He had begotten in us, they would have no other choice but to believe that God can do the same for them.

The Bible says that this daughter of God broke the alabaster box and poured out the very precious spikenard ointment and anointed the feet of Jesus with her hair. This redeemed child of God was still slanderously referred to in the religious community as the harlot, the sinner woman, even after she was forgiven of her sins by God, but she knew who she was—a child of the King of kings. Her hair was the representation of her glory.

So when God is glorified in the life of the redeemed, he or she glorifies Him with everything they have been given by their heavenly Father. The children of God must never withhold their best from God. After all, He did not withhold His best gift, Himself, in the person of the Lord Jesus Christ, and so the ointment that was poured on the feet of her Savior, in thanksgiving to Him, was the perfume of genuine praise and the fragrance of true worship.

Some of us are so stingy with that which belongs to God that we steal from ourselves, and we suffocate and stifle our own blessings from flowing into our lives. This woman is an accurate picture of all who are redeemed by Christ. O, the joy of knowing God, my friend, is better than all this world has to offer. He is a kind and compassionate friend. God hears the voice of the true worshiper. He attends to the heart whose lips give Him praise, and He blesses the soul whose mind stays on Him. God will save anyone from the wages of sin by remaking the vessel of flesh that was broken when it fell into sin. He looks into the mirror of His redeemed children's lives and sees Himself in them and says to Himself, "Very good." What God sees when He looks into the heart of every born-again person is His children wrapped in the righteousness of Jesus Christ.

The sinner who was nailed to a cross next to Jesus repented of all his sins, seeing that he had justly received his due reward for his deeds, and so Jesus forgave him also of his sins.

Every human being justly deserves the wrath of God as the penalty for breaking His law. The penalty for remaining in rebellion and in sin in the presence of God is the destruction of both soul and body in hell (Matthew 10:28), and we not only disobeyed the commandments of a loving, caring, gracious, and merciful God, but we also disregarded His presence and authority in the affairs of our lives and His guidance in showing us how to live in this world. We have not considered His ways into our lives, and we have not respected the life that He created; but God, in Christ, through His love for all of us, can forgive anyone of all their sins if they would hear the Word of God as the message of the good news. It is God's great desire to have all mankind turn to Him from sin, confess, and repent of their sins and receive from Him true forgiveness.

My friend, I encourage you to receive God's peace, the Lord Jesus, into your life. We read in Isaiah 30:18,

> And therefore will the LORD wait, that He may be gracious unto you, and therefore will be exalted, that he may have mercy on you: for the Lord is a God of judgment: and blessed are all they that wait on him.

In God, there is endless mercy available to anyone who seek to know Christ as He calls them to Himself. God will always answer us when we knock on the door of His mercy, and He will pour out His endless measures of favor, by His grace, into our lives. My friend, why waste the rest of your life searching for opportunities that will vaporize in the land of illusions? Call on God today in prayer, and see if He would not answer you with the answers that will change your life forever.

According to the Bible and according to the testimony of a multitude of witnesses who are the recipients of the goodness of God, they have all been transformed by what He had spoken into their hearts. God's prayer line is always open to all sinners seeking rest from the vain pursuits of life. You may be desperate for help, and you may feel as if you are running out of time, but God is just a prayer away from the answer to a profound change in your life. That answer is Jesus Christ. He will turn any impossible situation around if you and I give everything over to Him.

Don't waste another minute trying to find answers in places where there are only questions. Only Christ can help troubled and desperate sinners.

The Word of God says in Luke 15:10,

> Likewise, I say unto you, there is joy in the presence of the angels of God over one sinner that repenteth.

There is absolute joy in heaven when any sinner confesses and repents of his or her sins and lives the life that Christ gives. The hurt line to God is never busy. He does not need call waiting, nor does He need call forwarding. There are no drop calls, and there are no static interferences. No one can tap into God's prayer line; neither can anyone, including the devil, eavesdrop our conversations with God. Trust what the Bible says about God, for He is the most dependable and trustworthy friend you can ever have.

All Is Forgotten

As the redeemed of God, we are all made the new creation in Christ Jesus. When God forgives you and me of all the sins that we did commit, He completely forgets them. It is not that God cannot remember what things we did, but our forgiven sins are no longer attached to our new nature in Christ, of who we have become. They are buried with the old nature of who we once were.

God has committed Himself not to remember the sins He has forgiven us of. God has given all who He has redeemed, through Christ, a fresh new start, and that new beginning does not contain anything from our past. The vessel of clay that was marred in the hand of the Potter, He made it again, another vessel, as it seemed good to Him to make it (Jeremiah 18:4). In 2 Corinthians 5:17, we read,

> Therefore if any man be in Christ, he is a new creature: old things are passed away; behold all things are become new.

New things are new. They don't contain any old parts, nor do they have any imperfections in them; and so God says old things are passed away, and we have to believe the Word of God and not allow our minds to wander into the graveyard of our past, where the memories of our old nature are buried. We are to behold that which God has made new and stay in His Word and live that new life that He made for you and me to live in.

There is no condemnation nor is there retribution from Satan that can undo what God has done in the life of each believer, for the old things are passed away, and behold, all things are made new in Christ. If Satan has troubled you about your forgiven sins, and you are one of the true believers that God has begotten to Himself, submit yourself unto the counsel of God, resist the devil by obeying the Word of God as it is written, and he will flee from you.

How do we submit to God? We must stay in His Word and do all that it says and trust Him completely to deliver us from the hour of temptation. Christ is your way of escape. The Bible says we who are in Christ are to abstain from all appearance of evil (1 Thessalonians 5:22). As the redeemed of God, we must not give any opportunity to the devil to operate his works of deception into our lives. Satan cannot condemn you when you are in Christ even though he may try. Romans 8:1 says,

> There is therefore now no condemnation to them which are in Christ Jesus who walk not after the flesh, but after the spirit.

Jesus said that He came not to condemn anyone but that He may save them from their sins (John 3:17). So who can lay a charge against you, for if Christ be for you and He is Almighty God, who can be against you? In Isaiah 43:25, God says,

> I, even I, am he that blotteth out thy transgressions for mine own sake, and will not remember thy sins.

Also, we read in Hebrews 10:16–17,

> This is the covenant that I will make with them after those days, saith the Lord, I will put my laws into their hearts and in their minds will write them, and their sins and iniquities will I remember no more.

In Psalm 103:12, the Word of God says,

> As far as the east is from the west, so far hath he removed our transgressions from us.

And again, we read in Micah 7:19,

> He will turn again, he will have compassion upon us; he will
> subdue our iniquities; and thou wilt cast all their sins into the depths
> of the sea.

The redeemed of God must not allow the things that have happened to them in the past—those things that were meant for their destruction—to suffocate and strangulate their bright future that they have with their heavenly Father, but they must live life in the promises of God and in the hope of Christ's second advent. When we stay in the Word of God and we heed His commandments, we instead suffocate the old and sinful habits away from our lives.

As the people of God, you and I cannot have a bright future by looking backward. We cannot plow the new ground going in the direction we came from, and so we must be onward Christian soldiers marching forward into the promises of God. Thus, it is that the memories of our old nature that God had taken away when we received grace and mercy from Him are destroyed. They are buried in the grave of the perished and the forgotten, and such must stay buried in that place.

None of God's people should continue living with the decomposed past of who they were. That which is sown in corruption, it is raised up in incorruption. Whatever is sown in dishonor is raised up in glory, and that which is sown in weakness is also raised up in power, for unto God are the redeemed made in the likeness of Him who has drawn them out of darkness into His marvelous light; wherewith, they who are in Christ do live unto Him with a spiritual body. Those who are born from above do live in the spirit that they did receive from God, and so we should not return to the cemetery of the forgotten and postmortem the buried past of our carnal nature. All things are new in Christ, for the redeemed of the Lord have all received the victory over sin and Satan through their Redeemer.

We are at a fresh new start in life in that God has given us the opportunity to walk with Him in the spirit. We read in Philippians 3:13,

> Brethren, I count not myself to have apprehended: but this one
> thing I do, forgetting those things which are behind, and reaching
> forth unto those things which are before.

Those things that are before us are the promises that God had made concerning our future in and with Him. Since God does not remember our sins, once we are forgiven by Him, we shouldn't either. We must always be in communion with our heavenly Father through prayer and studying His Word. Our sinful past must be erased by the renewing of our mind with the Word of God, and the sinful images of our past life, when you and I were in bondage to sin and Satan, are erased from our mind with God's Word. It is sharper than any two-edged sword (Hebrews 4:12).

We cannot be the transformed people of God living a lie in sin. Changed people live consistent lives with the Word of God they believe in. God's Word must be studied and meditated upon at every opportunity we get (night and day). Do not allow your mind to go into idle mode because Satan, without warning, will overwhelm you with strong temptations; and before you know it, you are in a headlock in sin—the one(s) that so easily besets us—in other words, the strongholds of sin.

Friend, put on the whole armor of God that you may be able to withstand the schemes the serpent (Satan) uses to lure and destroy anyone in the evil day who profess to be a child of God (Ephesians 6). Satan uses tricks, tactics, schemes, and deceptions to trap and destroy his prey.

We cannot allow ourselves to be in situations that will allow Satan to get an advantage over us. We are not to allow him the opportunity to choke the Word of God out of our hearts with the cares of this world. When we submit ourselves to the will of God by setting our minds on Jesus Christ and we do those things that He has asked us to do, we are able to resist Satan and the urges we get in our flesh to sin. Submitting our wills to the will of God is not an oppressive relationship that suffocates us from growing and reaching new heights on the ladder of good success, but submitting our wills to that of God's is to allow Him to lead us in how we are to live in this world.

God wants Hid children to always commune with Him in prayer and to abode in His Word so that the memories of who we were in sin are replaced by the mind of Christ in us. The Bible says that we are buried in baptism with Christ and resurrected with Him unto a new life, so we are to live only in the resurrected life, forgetting everything that is behind us. Let us reach for those things that God has prepared for us to live in.

The past is the past, and what's buried, let it stay buried, and it is our responsibility to forget it. God has done His part by blotting out our sinful past. God has forgiven us, and so must we. Let's stop allowing the enemy from having us look backward into the dark past. God is light, and in Him there is no darkness at all; and since the redeemed dwell in Christ and He in us, let's live as children of the light. We waste precious time not trusting God, who has promised to take His faithful children to higher heights in this life. We must find encouragement in the Word of God to help us become more like our heavenly Father. We must remember that it is the blood of Christ that purges us from all our sins. What Christ has done for us, no man nor the devil and his ministers can undo from the hands of God. Hebrews 9:14 says,

> How much more shall the blood of Christ, who through the eternal Spirit offered himself without spot to God, purge your conscience from dead works to serve the living God?

All to Jesus we surrender, all to Him we must freely give, reserving nothing from Christ for comfort's sake. There is nothing comforting about our past life. Holding on to any part of our past is letting go of the hand of God. We cannot serve the pleasures of sin and the memories of yesteryear and serve God at the same time. Don't allow the devil to tempt and to trick you into preserving any part of your past for just in case your relationship with God does not work out. The devil is a liar. God is very clear about past unhealthy relationships and habits; they must be completely severed from our lives. God's Word and His Spirit, when He convicts us, is able to show every true believer what unhealthy relationships and habits are.

One of the biggest areas of trouble for men and women who say they believe the Word of God is to keep themselves from sex before marriage. Sex is a celebratory benefit for legally married men and women in the eyes of God. If we believe the Word of God, it follows that we are to be obedient to everything He says we are to do and not do. The Bible says in 1 Corinthians 8:18 that we are to flee fornication. That's a clear commandment from God, and yet people who purposefully, by habit, violate God's law seems unmindful to the consequence of continuing to live in disobedience.

So many people make promises to themselves to make the present and the future better to live in than how they have lived life in the past, but can we really live life differently without God changing us from the inside out? God will not put new wine into old wineskins. He will not give any of us His blessings unless we allow Him to first change us into vessels made to handle the blessings which He has for us.

We read in Romans 12:2, "But, be ye transformed by the renewing of your mind." Transformation is, at best, difficult, but it is always possible if God is leading the way in our lives. It begins with letting go the hand of sin we have been holding on to and allow God to remake and rebrand us into His image. Please, let us give every fragment of "self" and the memory of our past to God, for the Lord Jesus is our only hope for total restoration. The only true rest that you and I will ever find in this world is in Jesus Christ.

7

FAITH TO BELIEVE

What is faith, you may ask? We will define faith from the Word of God, the Bible. The Bible says in Romans 10:17, "So then faith cometh by hearing, and hearing by the Word of God." That verse means that the only source anyone can receive faith to know God is from God Himself. It is received by consistently hearing the words that are spoken in the pages of the Bible, but what we read, we must understand; and so the Holy Spirit must be the One who speaks to our spirit, helping us understand that which is written. Faith, in general, is a complete confidence in God to bring to pass all the things He has put in our heart to ask Him for, no matter how impossible they may seem in the natural.

All the understanding that God wants us to receive about who He is and how He wants us to live comes from the teaching that the Holy Spirit gives as we read the Bible, and so whenever we are troubled in our spirit by the Spirit of God about what He may be saying to us, we must listen to His voice. God may trouble us in our conscience repeatedly about a particular issue until we either acknowledge His presence speaking to us or we reject Him out of our conscience; but they that hear the still small voice of God speak to them, a voice who confirms and is consistent with the words of the Bible as they read and study it, will always be guided by Him to do all things through Christ who strengthens the children of God.

There will be peculiar convictions from God, way down on the inside, as He speaks to us. It's a consistent and persistent voice that we hear deep within the center of who we are, that born-again spirit nature we received from God. These convictions are also always consistent with what we read in the Word of God, so that which we hear in our spirit is really the voice of God speaking to us. What we are convicted of in our spirit, that inner voice, is always in connection with what we read in or hear that which is preached from the Word of God.

The convictions of God that we may experience are not produced in our senses—that is, our feelings and sensations that cause us to react in a euphoric manner without our thoughts bothering us. The convictions of God are not mind tricks that cause us to go into a religious trance. They are the inner core revelations of God that trouble us in our spirit and causes us to think and to pay attention to what was said by Him. What God will say to us is always the truth about who we are and the right and wrong things we have done or are doing. He will speak to us about the things that we are doing that are displeasing to Him and are destroying our lives. The convictions of God are supernatural, and they are indeed the voice of God talking to us.

The Bible says the believer is to try the spirits to see whether they are of God—therefore the Spirit that speaks to us and is consistent with that which is written in the Bible is of God. Hebrews 11:1 says,

> Now faith is the substance of things hoped for, the evidence of things not seen.

The substance of the things that we hope for has not yet materialized; it has not yet come into existence in the natural, but they are in the spiritual realm, and because we can trust God and His Word, what He promises will always come to pass.

God is just, and He is faithful to bring everything to pass that is of His will—those things which He has promised that He will do for those who put their trust in Him. He is not like mankind in that we cannot always trust ourselves with the promises we make to each other regarding our commitment to do what we say we will do, and the reason we cannot trust ourselves is because so often, what we promise to do for someone else is usually motivated by how we feel at that moment. We do not evaluate whether we are able and capable of doing what we say we will do, and when we cannot, or we are unable to make good on what we promised to do for the individual, you and I make excuses for why we cannot do what we say we will do for that person. One day we feel one way, and the next day we feel different about others and their situations; and surely God is not like us, and we ought to praise Him for who He is. His ways are not our ways, for they are far above anything we can ever imagine and measure.

The Bible says in James 1:17,

> With whom there is no variableness, neither shadow of turning.

So when the promises of God that He has promised to give to whoever will believe His Word are not manifested in their lives, it is because they have doubted His Word. He did not change His mind about doing what He said He would do for us, and when we are not in agreement with what God's Word says for us to do, the troubles that are in our lives will continue to exist. There are so many of us Christians who, for whatever reason, find it difficult to truly trust God to do what He alone is able to do for us far beyond what we are able to do for ourselves, and so we will always be oppressed by and distressed about the troubles that are on every side of our lives.

God is the only one who is able and is more than capable of helping us from drowning in troubled waters, and so we must have an unwavering trust in God for all that we ask of Him. He will give us the answer when the need is legitimate, and it is not born out of greed. We may not always get what we wanted—only because God always sees our situation differently from our perspective—and besides, He has much better things for us, and that is why it is most important for us to let His will be done regarding what we are seeking Him for; but regardless of how bad our situation might be, God will give us the answer to our prayers, which we make to Him in faith, and that will best address our needs in our current situation. God does not want us to be afraid of Him, but He wants us to be bold and respectful when we need to talk one on one with Him.

The Word of God says in Acts 16:30–31 when the jailer asked Paul and Silas, "Sirs, what must I do to be saved," and they replied to the jailer by saying, "Believe on the Lord Jesus Christ, and thou shalt be saved, and thy house." First of all, God designed the experiences that Paul and Silas went through to demonstrate to us that trusting Him is an exercise of faith, and when we begin to trust God out of the experiences we have had with Him that He uses to reveal who He is to us, you and I will begin to understand that we can trust Him in all things in any given situation.

One experience with God is credit for all future experiences we will have with Him. Paul and Silas trusted God, doubting not His Word but, rather, believing that He is faithful to do what He said He will do for them and not only just do it but do His best—not that He can do any less. So when these men of God prayed, it was a prayer of faith which was produced by the power of God in them to believe that He will answer and deliver them out of their present circumstance.

There is another fascinating objective that God was accomplishing through Paul and Silas's faith and obedience to His Word—if only we all would allow God to use us in similar ways—and that is to use their supernatural deliverance as miraculous proofs and as a witness of what God can do for others when He uses us as His examples for His glory. It is always—permit me to use the phrase—a win-win experience we will always have with God in that all who God intended to be the recipients of His blessings, their lives are changed, and ours are richly blessed.

What God did for Paul and Silas physically was the evidence for the jailer to see and believe the wonderful workings of God to set free all those who were spiritually imprisoned in sin. This jailer was convicted in his spirit by God to seek salvation from Him because of the miracles he had witnessed in Paul's and Silas's experience with the Lord. He saw what God did for Paul and Silas, and he was troubled in his heart by the things he both saw and heard. He received salvation, through faith, by believing the things that were done by God in the lives of these two men of God. So we see the Word of God can be heard by the things He does and shows us in the lives of others.

The Bible says faith comes to us by the hearing of the Word of God. When we believe and trust God with everything that is within us, He gives us a stress-free life, and so we know that God can make the impossible possible and the hard things of life simple. He is the only source of our faith, and we are to use it to trust Him in all things. Thank the Lord that He is ever so merciful, so loving, and is so kind to forgive us of our sins and to show us His workings through tangible evidence.

The Lord Jesus has repeatedly forgiven the transgressions of a great number of saints who have asked Him, in prayer, for the forgiveness of their sins. He has forgiven the sins that so easily beset many, and as we read the Word of God, we see so many examples of those who were healed from all manner of demonic possessions just because they trusted in the power and the authority of God.

Because of the faith the believers in the Bible had exercised to always trust God, others saw them as examples of what God can do in their lives, and so they too were delivered from all manner of sins and from demonic possessions. If we truly trust God, by faith, and allow Him to be the God of every area of our lives, He will deliver us from all our sins and make a clear way for us out of our troubles. As we look at the hall of faith in Hebrews 11, we see a parade of ordinary people who overcame many different types of adversities. These people came through the trials and tests in complete victory because they trusted God to be their strength and provider. He was their help in overcoming every obstacle they had encountered, and because of their victories, we too can be encouraged to trust God with all that is within us so that He can guide us through the paths of life.

We are to celebrate what God has done and is still doing in our lives each and every day. We are to be thankful for the deposits of courage and faith that God has put into our lives so that we have the ingredients to be the successful people of God. We are not just God's witness agents, but we are God's special people with whom He dwells. The God of the universe literally lives on the inside of His faithful children. We have all the power of heaven dwelling on the inside of us so that we can do all things through Christ who strengthens us. Christ is always with us in every good thing that we do and in every obstacle we face in this life, in the good times and in the tough times, so it grieves God when we sin in our thoughts and in our bodies. Abide in Christ by abiding in His Word, and allow His Spirit, who lives on the inside of our lives, to lead and teach us the ways of God so that we would do His works and please our heavenly Father.

We must never forget our roots, of where God started us from, and we are to never despise those small beginnings, for God is He who will see us through from the beginning to the end of our journey in this life. As it was in David's life, God uses lessons in the classroom of life those situations that He allows into our lives so that we may learn how to fight the good fight of faith and subdue those giants that seek to destroy our joy, peace, and faith in Jesus Christ—giants like doubt and discouragement, fear, and confusion, worry and anxiety.

The experiences of our past with God are His training exercises that He gives us to strengthen our faith in Him, so the tribulations that you are going through right now that are not of your own doing are meant to prepare you for better things from God; but remember, the resistance from the enemy does not get any easier; they become stronger and quicker, like the birth pains of a pregnant mother as she nears the delivery of her child. What a friend we have in Jesus; all our cares and sorrows He bears.

In Isaiah 41:10, we read,

> Fear thou not; for I am with thee: be not dismayed; for I am thy God: I will strengthen thee; yea, I will help thee; yea I will uphold thee with the right hand of my righteousness.

Trusting God with every area of our lives is letting go of our control and letting God direct us in the paths He wants us to walk in. Through faith, we are more than conquerors in Christ, for we were created and made to win every time, at every trial. As believers in Jesus Christ, we do have the best defense attorney in the entire universe. It does not matter how bad our case is, how messed up your life and mine have been. It could be the worst of crimes that we may have committed, but the fact of the matter is that our defense attorney, the Lord Jesus, did win every case on our behalf, on the cross at Calvary.

You see, when we find ourselves in the struggles of this life, and if we truly trust God and we are faithfully obeying His commandments through Christ, we are the declared winners in every battle against the enemy just because Christ, our advocate, has already won the battles of life on the cross. God does not hear any appeals from Satan to retry our case although he does his best to bring false evidence to accuse the redeemed of forgiven sins. He is an enemy that does not forget the past. He replays repeatedly in temptations, the sins, and bad habits of our past; but because we have a born-again spirit from God, we no longer live in the flesh, but we live in the righteousness of Christ because of the power of the Spirit of God living on the inside of our lives. If we did not have challenges in this life, how would we know how good God is? And how would our faith be strengthened without any opposition from the enemy? And how would we be able to trust God if there were no resistances pushing against us?

We must understand that strength and endurance, patience and hope are made in adversity. God can and will fight all our battles if our minds are fixed on Him and we unreservedly trust Him with everything that is within us. We must purpose in our hearts to believe all that God says He will do for us. My friend, let us believe that God is able to make us more than conquerors through Jesus Christ.

God did not make us to have struggles in our lives. Nevertheless, He allows the trials to refine everything about us to become as pure gold. If we can withstand the temperature of the refining process because of Christ's presence with us in the furnace of affliction, then we can withstand any attack of the devil because He is also there with us in every situation. God created all His children to win—and win we must, for the prize is too great and the cost of losing in the fight against all unrighteousness is too expensive. We may not swiftly cross the finish line as number one, but it is more important that we continue even if we fall along the way. We may have been wounded in many of life's battles and injured by some of life's struggles, but we cannot give up because we stumbled and fell along the way in the journey of doing everything God's way. We must get back up, with the helping hand of God, and stay on course and stay in the race, for there is a crown of life that is laid up for you and for me if we do endure to the finish when Christ returns. Never give up on what God has for you. Never give up on the process in the metamorphosis of your life.

Do not allow Satan to steal your joy, do not permit him to steal your peace, and never allow him to take your focus from always looking unto Christ. He is very "good" at putting distractions in our way when we are doing the Word of God. You can do all things through Christ who strengthens you. God will always encourage and strengthen us to finish the race no matter what obstacles come into our way. God will always help each one of us along life's journey. The way of God is straight but bumpy. It may even be a winding path, but it is still the only way to God. Do not allow yourself to be sidetracked by the distractions and the discouragements that the enemy sends to cause God's people to doubt what He said He will do for them. Always wait on God no matter what.

With God, it's everything of who we are, or it's nothing at all. We cannot submit parts of our lives to Christ and then expect Him to take full control of everything especially when we are in trouble. Friend, it doesn't work that way with God. There can only be one master who is on the throne and who is in control of our lives. When we are at rest in Him, He is at work for us, doing what we cannot do for ourselves. The Bible says in 1 Peter 5:7,

> Casting all your care upon him; for he careth for you.

And so one of the two masters has to go, and that master is Satan. God is to be His children's only master, so let go and let God be all that He wants to be in your life. God is complete in every measure of His existence, and so the people of God are made totally and completely new in Christ Jesus; and with His Spirit in us, we have the power of Almighty God to help us finish the course we are given to complete in this life. Because God was faithful to us in all that He did to redeem us from the curse of the law, He expects us to be faithful in our worship to Him, and thus, as the true people of God, we will bless the Lord at all times for His endless benefits, for His goodness, and for His wonderful works that He has done in our lives. His praise shall continually be in our mouth. Every moment of our lives, we should reflect on the goodness of God toward us even when we are not good to Him and our behavior toward our brothers and sisters has, at times, been less than godly.

We must not treat our brothers and our sisters, whom God has also created and recreated in His image, with ugly behaviors and then expect God to bless us. We are surely deceiving ourselves if we are behaving that way. If anyone thinks that he or she can get away with that which displeases God, he or she is sadly mistaken; and as always, God can and will forgive every sin He troubles us to confess and repent.

It does not matter what others may say of us, for we have been set apart from the standard operating procedures and systems of this world— not that we are made any better than others, but the fact of the matter is that we are made the beneficiaries of heavenly things that God has for those who trust only in Him. It is only by the grace and mercy of God alone that we receive His favor into our lives. There is nothing about us that makes us deserve the blessings that are deposited into our lives by God. Obedience to the Word of God and faith in Jesus Christ are the keys that will allow the true children of God to be used as examples to others and be the beneficiaries of His goodness, and so nothing but our faithful obedience to the Word of God moves Him into action to help us in the time of our need. We are upheld by the right hand of God when we trust Him—completely—with every bit of our lives. There is nothing and there is no one that can come between the Lord and us, for greater is He that is in us than he that is in the world.

Friend, never give up in your fight to win in the struggles of life. Never give in to adversities, and never surrender to tribulations, for the battles that are in this life, Christ has won them all, and the victory over life's challenges is ours to receive by faith. Let the shield of faith that God has given you and I not only protect us, but let it be the power of God that helps all of us move those mountains of trouble out of our lives, and let it help us to believe that God will open new doors of opportunities for your family and mine. These are the opportunities that seem impossible in the natural for us to have. Never stand still or retreat in the face of challenges when it is our duty to push forward in the pursuit of the victory.

The living hope that God has given us to trust Him is that which gives us our strength. It is faith for today and the hope for tomorrow that will make us to never grow weary in doing the will of our heavenly Father. The Bible says that we must carry our cross. This we must do to crucify and put to death our carnal nature, thus destroying its power over our lives; and as such, we are able to truly follow Jesus wherever He takes us, for when we follow Christ, we are able to walk on what other people sink and perish in, but our eyes must stay focused on Him.

If you are out of the way with God, He will turn your messes into a message of victory. We are to be honest to God about everything that troubles us, confessing all our sins to Him so that we can be made whole from our brokenness. Let the words that come out of our lips be "Teach me thy ways, O God, and show me thy path to the victory of obedience to your Word."

God is a covenant-keeping God. He has never broken a promise, nor will He ever break any of His promises to anyone, specifically to them that believe that Jesus Christ is their Lord and their Redeemer, for He has promised His people that He will never leave nor forsake them no matter what trouble they fall into. The Bible says that God is faithful. He is faithful to do all He has said He will do for His people, for we read in Deuteronomy 7:9,

> Know therefore that the Lord thy God, he is God, the faithful
> God, which keepeth covenant and mercy with them that love him
> and keep his commandments to a thousand generations.

God has given His children the tenacity to be resilient in courage, fortified with hope, and waxed strong with the strength of Christ, conquering today and marching forward to tomorrow. Onward, Christian soldiers, marching as to war with the blood of Jesus covering us. We will never fail, for even if we fall while we are in the race, God is able to pick us up and lead us to victory.

When other people cast stones with their lips at who you are just because you are a different you, not who you used to be, but a blood-bought, blood-covered, cleaned-up you, just remember that God has forgiven you, and there is no agent from hell that can undo what God has done in your life.

As the children of God, each one of us must have the absolute confidence that He will fulfill all His promises in our lives even when things seem absolutely impossible for them to happen. God does not operate under the natural laws that control this world. All God's workings are supernatural, and so His doings are outside of time, and they are outside the realm of our understanding, but God will deliver each one of us victoriously through every circumstance that is meant to stifle our spiritual growth and development and prevent us from reaching our destiny of where God had destined us to be.

No human being can understand the nonexistence of time, but God exists and operates outside of time. Such existence is exclusive to God alone, and that makes Him absolute and infinite. He is always in the now. There is no past, present, and future with God's existence. Time and change are inseparable. Change is the result of the passage of time, and the Bible says that there is no variableness nor shadow of turning with God. He changes not.

God never asks anyone to trust Him for things He is unable to fulfill for He can fulfill all things that are good and that are of His will for our lives. God will not fulfill our sinful desires, for nothing about Him and in Him is evil, and there reside in Him no wickedness, and so anyone who is being drawn to God by His Spirit must believe that He is and that He rewards all those who diligently seek Him in His Word (Hebrews 11:6).

The good news of the Bible is the gospel of Jesus Christ, and it is God's declaration of His love for a spiritually fallen and sinful human race. The gospel is a clear message of God's love and hope, grace and mercy, peace and rest to all those that God the Father leads to Christ. The good news is not only about the deliverance of the lives of others, but the good news of the gospel also shines the light of Christ into every dark and secret place in our lives that are the closets of our dysfunctionalities. They are the repressed and unresolved issues that produce fear, discouragement, doubt, worry, and low self-esteem. These are the things that weaken our faith to completely trust the Lord to deliver us from the torment and the pain that those issues are causing us.

God can destroy every stronghold that has held us in bondage to living in sin. With the weapons of true godliness, which is the full armor of God (Ephesians 6), the strength of Jesus Christ, and the power of the

Holy Spirit, every child of God is well equipped and is commanded in the Scriptures, by Him, to live a holy life evidenced by good works. The children of God are to live holy and consecrated lives which alone can pull down and destroy evil imaginations, suffocate every wicked thought, and destroy every high thing that exalts, magnifies, and boasts itself against the knowledge of God. The power of God in the life of every true Christian is able to bring into captivity, every thought to the obedience of Christ (2 Corinthians 10:4–5).

The entire Bible is a faith book. Finite minds cannot comprehend an infinite God who created both the visible and the invisible things of the universe. Jesus Christ not only created all things, but He has absolute control over everything. Even hell and all the forces of darkness are under His control. Satan and his imps must have permission from God before they can wage their attacks on His redeemed children. Our God is big, infinitely big. No space in the universe can contain Him. God does not expect us to understand Him, but He expects us to know Him for who He is to us through the study of His Word.

The Word of God is understood through the teaching of the Holy Spirit, and so everything we know and understand about God, as to who He is to us, we receive them by faith through the teaching of the Holy Spirit. Whatsoever we do in obedience to His commandments, which is the Word of God, must also be done through faith, for the Bible says that it is impossible to please God without faith (Hebrews 11:6). Faith to know and believe that there is a God who is holy and is all powerful yet merciful and gracious is not supposed to make any sense to us. It takes faith to believe that God is He who is the only true and wise God, that every soul that He has birthed into this world has to give an account to Christ of the life that he or she has lived.

If faith that is of God was the product of mankind's reason, then God would be the product of their reason and the product of their invention. Whatever is not of faith from God is of human reasoning and logic. Real faith—that is, faith that comes from the hearing of the Word of God—is not the product of probability and chance. True faith is total reliability on the trustworthiness in the Word of God. It cannot be proven with physical facts and tangible evidence, but faith is the undeniable convictions and the assured promises that God gives to the one He will save (because He foreknew his or her response to the gospel) and to those who are His Word-believing children.

There aren't that many things that can be explained in the classroom of science, but whatever is explained in science, God has allowed such revelation to occur to point us to His existence as Creator and Sustainer. All that mankind may reason about how the universe came into existence but cannot find the answers to the unexplained—and that's everything—takes faith to believe.

Some secular-minded scholars and intellectuals in many of our institutions of learning claim that the contents of the Bible are unacceptable because it requires faith to believe there is a God they cannot see even though the science of evolution takes an extreme measure of faith to believe its theories. They claim that biblical faith is not logical, and it cannot be accepted in the classroom of physical observation and provable science. They claim it cannot be tested, and it is not measurable, like matter and substance can be measured. They are right. Faith cannot be tested in a laboratory like matter is tested in the laboratory by the rules of science. It is not measurable like matter and substance. These individuals want the evidence of the existence of God to be revealed by scientific testing. We can only study and test matter and substance using finite and the limited rules of science. We cannot know an infinite God by validating His existence using scientific data collection. What are they hoping to find? God is immeasurable. We cannot estimate God's location. He is a Spirit and He fills the universe and beyond with His presence. His mysterious nature is beyond finding out.

Matter exists in three forms—solid, liquid, and gas—and God is none of these. It is God who created matter, and He is not defined like matter and substance are defined, and so we cannot believe that there is an infinite God without accepting the claims of the Bible regarding His existence. It is by faith we believe what the Bible says of God, who He is, and His authority over the vast expanse of the universe. Regardless of the skeptics' view of what they think and believe the Bible is and is not, it remains the only true source of absolute truth —of who God is and the revelation of an omniscient, all-knowing, omnipotent, all-ruling, and omnipresent God everywhere at the same time. It is God who created matter, space, and time, and they were created simultaneously to coexist. There is no one who can show how time came into existence outside the all-intelligent God of the Bible, and if it was always in existence, can anyone prove it without producing a dead-end answer which does not explain anything?

The simple truth is that time is the creation of an all-intelligent Designer Creator who created it, as well as matter and space in the beginning, as is recorded in Genesis 1. The Word of God says in the beginning God created the heavens and the earth. Here we see "in the beginning (time), the heavens (space), and the earth (matter) were created simultaneously by God. If time did not exist, but there was matter, when would it have been made? Time is required for something to come into existence based on the theory of evolution, but God exists outside of time, and He is self-existent. He has life within Himself. He always is. God does not have a beginning nor does Have an end.

Who knows or can understand the incomprehensible infinite mind of God? The fact is that there is no one. No created being anywhere in the universe and beyond has the mental capacity to understand the nature of God. He is a Spirit. He is a mysterious being, and His full nature of who He is infinitely beyond mankind's understanding, but He is accessible to anyone who diligently seeks Him out in His Word, the Bible, and seek Him out in faith-filled prayers. God (Father, Son, Holy Spirit) is One God, and beside Him is no other God.

Outside of God, time cannot exist. He had to create it into existence, and He did so at creation. If there was matter but no space, where would one put it? The past, the present, and the future are intrinsic of time. Space has length, breath, and depth; and matter exists as solid, liquid, and gas; and all these entities are finite. God is infinite. He is not made up with finite substance. Everything that exist God spoke into existence in the creation of the universe and beyond. The substance of everything God that appear when God spoke them into existence was in the mind of God.

The history of how the universe came into existence and when God created the heavens and the earth is explained in terms of time. Time tells us about the sequence in which the things appear (came into existence) when the all-powerful Creator God made them by Himself with the words of His all-wise and all-powerful mind. God exists outside His creation. He is not limited or confined by His creation. He is outside and exists infinitely beyond the universe, yet He controls everything He created. He is intimately involved in the operation of everything in the universe and beyond. Everything that God created are under His control. He controls and sustains the universe with His own power.

There is a mystery about the nature of God and how He works. He is absolutely holy. The Bible says in Isaiah 40:22 that God sits upon the circle of the earth. Heaven is the throne, and earth is the footstool of God (Father, Son, and Holy Spirit).

God reveals Himself to mankind regarding His existence through the convictions they receive from His Spirit in their hearts when they hear the Word of God speak to them as they read the Bible. There are scientific principles that describe the states of matter, but these principles cannot describe God, for He is an extremely complicated and mysterious Supernatural Being who is separate and way beyond His creation.

I would say this—that faith as a substantive reality has no measurable predictableness. Faith is not guesswork. There is no article of speculation or presumption in what faith is. It is not defined as the probability of what may occur. We Bible-believing Christians don't hang our hopes on what may happen in the future, for faith is the assurance that what God has said will happen shall come to pass. He foreknows, and He foresees everything that will happen in the future because He is the future, and He controls all things in it.

All things in the present and in the future are under the control of and are in God, and so our faith in God takes us beyond our limited thinking to where He is, for us to see and receive those things that had already come to pass when He decreed it in eternity past. Faith that is of God opens our spiritual eyes to see all that He had already determined for us and has set in place those things that are of His will that we may believe His Word and receive them with thanksgiving.

God cannot be located in any defined area like matter can be located. He does not exist in our finite three-dimensional world, nor does He exist in the fourth or fifth or sixth dimension and so on. Quantum mechanics and fine particle physics are limited to what they can do. All physical and chemical laws are under the control of and are contained in God.

Gravity was created by God to be on planet earth to support the livability of life. He calculated its dimensions and coordinated its position to be exactly where He wanted biological life to exist, and so everything God made came out from Him when He spoke them into existence, for He is before all things and in Him all things consist (Colossians 1:17). God did not have to make modifications to His creation because of flaws in any of the visible and invisible substance He spoke into existence. Everything God made was created with remarkable precision. The level of specificity and complexity of everything in the universe points to an all-intelligent Creator Designer. He is the only Architect, Creator, and

Sustainer of the entire universe and beyond. The human body is the most amazing lifeform anywhere in the universe. Mankind was created in the image of his Creator and formed in His likeness.

The level of complexity of the human body, especially the brain, is simply remarkable. I believe even though mankind use a small percentage of their brain's operational capacity, it functions way above and beyond anything in the universe outside of God for David said, "I am fearfully and wonderfully made." He was referring to the Creator God who made him and the entire human race. Nothing was left up to chance by God to become whatever. Every living and nonliving thing in the universe was made with a purpose. Everything God made has purpose for God made them to perform specific functions in their specific locations. God has fine-tuned His creation to such a degree when He spoke it into existence that it would take time infinitum for mankind to unravel the simplest yet complex thing in the universe and beyond. Everything operates with remarkable precision within extremely narrow limits. That is the handy work of an intelligent creator. The universe did not come into existence the theories of evolution nor chance. For it is impossible for the kind of universe that exist to come into existence without someone guiding and orchestrating its formation and guiding it into its position and location in the universe.

God knows about the visible and invisible things in the universe and beyond simply because He made them all, and He made them fit perfectly into the environment He created for them to be in, and so true and objective investigative science will always show that God created the laws of physics and chemistry, which makes everything work the way they do in the universe. God is outside of and is beyond what He creates. He is the all-powerful and invisible God that operates this universe. Mankind has not begun to scratch the surface of the operation of this vast and very complex creation of God.

No one can locate God anywhere within the universe to prove His existence. He is bigger than the universe He created. His nature is outside the laws of physics and chemistry. God is not a mathematical or chemical formula. All scientific research and testing take time to measure that which it is trying to find out, and God exists outside of time even though He can transform Himself into time while at the same exist outside of it simply because He made it. The earth was precisely created by God to support life. Before sin came by Adam and Eve disobedience to their

Creator, the earth and life on the planet existed in perfect harmony with God and mankind. The universe and mankind were created good by God because He said so in Genesis 1. And so disharmony between mankind and his environment came immediately after Adam and Eve sinned and everything was now affected by the curse that sin wrought. So what we see in the earth now is the aftermath of the occurrence and effects of mankind's sin. Nothing was created by God to die——everything was created to exist forever. Death and decay are the result of sin entering into existence the moment mankind transgressed the law of God—— it affected the universe for disobedience to the Word of God has far reaching consequences.

The Bible bears the record that God transformed Himself into several forms of known substances so that He is known and is described by what those things represent. He was the "Shekinah glory," an extrabiblical word coined by Jewish scholars, meaning "He caused to dwell." He was a pillar of fire by night and a pillar of cloud by day as the Israelites journeyed from Egypt to the Red Sea on their way to the Promised Land. The examples we see in Scripture of who and what God is described as are seen in many places in the book of Exodus, starting at chapter 13 and in Numbers chapters 9 and 10.

God appeared to Moses as a flame of fire in a burning bush (Exodus 3:2). He was a wrestling angel with Jacob (Genesis 32). He appeared in limited brightness of His glory veiled in a cloud in a vision that Ezekiel saw in Ezekiel chapter 1. The glory of God was in the midst of the wheels and in the midst of the four living creatures with the cloud and the fire enfolding upon itself. There was a noise that was like the voice of the Almighty that Ezekiel heard, proceeding out of this indescribable and very complicated image, and God became a man, incarnated to be the atonement for sin and the example of godliness for mankind to follow. This was prophesied about in the Old and fulfilled in the New Testament books of the Bible.

For our limited understanding, the simplest reference that we can use to describe where God is that He is in the infinite past and He is in the infinite future at the same time, as in the now. Now what instrument of science is there that can figure out such existence? We can't even comprehend that God has no beginning. He always is. We will literally get a headache just trying to go there. The fact of the matter is it is God who said it takes faith to believe that He exists, and it takes faith to know

Him. Let us stop trying to rationalize the things we don't and cannot understand and instead accept who the Bible says God is and praise and worship Him for who He is—Creator, Sustainer, Redeemer, Healer, and Provider. What the Holy Spirit has revealed to us in His Word and in true and honest science and what we see in nature is enough for us to believe that God exists. We must always be careful about coming to our own conclusions of what the Bible is saying as well as what it is not saying, for we can be tricked by our senses about the thing we may be trying to find answers to.

Not every answer we receive nor every conclusion we come to about the hidden things of God and of the universe is from God. We must include earnest prayer to God for the teaching of the Holy Spirit to instruct us in the things we must know that pertains to our salvation and what God expects of us as we are led to truth.

The Bible says in Proverbs 25:2,

> It is the glory of God to conceal a thing: but the honor of kings is to search out a matter.

In other words, what God is saying is that revelation and understanding of the Scriptures are hidden from mankind by God until they use the desire given to them by Him to search the Scriptures daily for truth and find it with the help of His Spirit. Please also read what Jesus said in John 5:39.

Satan knows quite well how to trick mankind with his counterfeits. Faith is not of the senses. Faith is not seeing what God has for us. It is not a feeling that we get what we cannot see, nor is it a smell we get for what God is about to do for His people; but we know that according to His perfect will, He will meet our needs perfectly, and He will meet the need right on time.

Faith is trusting God when we cannot trace Him. It is holding on to Him when we cannot feel His presence, and faith believes that God is working our situation out for our good when we cannot understand what He is doing. It does not make sense that God would give Himself in the person of Jesus Christ to pay the cost of our sins and bear them on Himself on the cross, but the Bible says that He did, and it is by faith that we believe that Christ paid it all (the full cost of the wages of sin) on the cross at Calvary, and so it is by faith that we know that there is a God, and it is by faith that we can receive anything from Him, even eternal life.

God speaks to us in the still voice of the Holy Spirit during our turmoil and chaos. God will always tell us to be still and know that He is God in the midst of what may seem to be the impossible. The things we cannot control are under the control of God. The human mind is incapable of reasoning out and unraveling the mysterious workings of God, which are infinitely beyond our understanding; and when we get in the way of what God is doing for us, we mess things up worse than they already are.

When it is impossible for anything to come to pass or to happen, it is God who will do it; for whatever is impossible with mankind, it is possible with God. God has given us the skills and abilities to perform what we are to do, and when we have diligently done all that is possible for us to do, it is by faith we are to trust Him to do for us what we are unable do for ourselves.

No problem is too hard for God to solve, and there is no difficulty that He cannot bring us through. When we are fearful of doing the things that are unfamiliar to us and when we are uncertain about what the future holds, it is in God's Word where we find encouragement. He gives us directions on how to do those things that seem impossible for us to do. Christ is He who gives us our strength to bear and to do all things. God the Father gives us the confidence to move boldly forward in life, and His Spirit is the source of power that we need when we are empty of strength. When we need examples of how to have good success, then Christ is our perfect object lesson. We also have a cloud of witnesses who accomplished great things because God was their only source of help. None of us is any less or any better than our fellow man. We were all created to be sparkling jewels in God's crown. So when you feel discouraged and disappointed about how your life has turned out, look up to your heavenly Father, for He can help you turn things around. Give all of who you are to Him, and He will make successes out of your mess. It is never too late to start over and redeem the time you've lost. Just trust God completely, and He will take you places you have never been before. If you are in the valley of the shadow of death, He will set your feet on higher ground. Have faith in God.

I encourage you to read the account and summary of the hall of faith of the men and women in Hebrews chapter 11 of the Bible. The topic of faith has been written about by so many, yet its depth no one can exhaust, for all areas and character of faith is inexhaustible. Faith is from God, and He is faithful in His promise to do what He said He would do.

As stated earlier in several places in this book, faith comes to us by hearing, and it is hearing the Word of God (Romans 10:17). If we say we believe the Word of God, then our faith must and will be tested. Faith is the vehicle that drives us into the presence of God, and in His presence, there are never any dark days, nor are there any disappointments; and so the object and source of our faith is of God in Christ Jesus.

The recipients of faith are those who are called by God and are chosen to be His children. The substance of faith is hope and complete confidence that God will always work things out in miraculous ways. Where there is faith, there is no doubt, worry, and there is no fear, for faith assures us that God will do whatever His perfect will is for us. The proof of our faith is what God had provided for us when we did not know how He was going to fulfill His promise He made to us. The fruit of faith is obedience to the Word of God. The reward of our faith is eternal life in Christ Jesus through salvation.

The Bible says in Ephesians 2:8,

> For by grace ye are saved through faith; and that not of yourselves: it is the gift the gift of God.

Here we see that grace and faith are both gifts from God, for it is not we who have found God, but it is God who finds us. God isn't the one who is lost. It is mankind who is lost because of their sins. He gives us the faith to respond and believe He is eternal God, and He rewards those who diligently seek Him.

Our faith will stand trial. This is what the Word of God says as we read in 1 Peter 1:7,

> That the trial of your faith, being much more precious than of gold that perisheth, though it be tried with fire, might be found unto praise and honour and glory at the appearing of Jesus Christ.

The Bible declares that for sure our faith will come under constant attack from Satan. His objective is to raise doubt in our minds about the truthfulness of the Word of God and to also raise doubt about the faithfulness and the promises of God to all who believe. We read in

Daniel 3:16–18 that the faith of the three Hebrew young men was tested because of what and who they professed to believe in. They believed in the only true and living God, that He was their only hope and their only savior from destruction.

These men of God knew and believed that He was their deliverer, and they believed that God would indeed deliver them out from the fiery furnace of affliction; and in a further measure of how strong their faith was, they made it known to the king that if God did not deliver them out from the flames of the furnace, they would not surrender their trust in God to Satan; but the Bible says that one like unto the Son of God was with them in the furnace throughout their ordeal, so if God chooses to do or not do for us, we must still believe that He is our God and our Lord.

The exercise of faith in God does not have conditions or restrictions of what you and I want Him to do for us, but rather, the exercise of faith in God is whatever His will is for us in any situation that would bless our lives and that would bring Him glory in the face of the enemy. Just remember, the taller any structure, the deeper its foundation, and so is our faith when it is exercised in the gymnasium of life. Trusting God, in obedience to always do His will, will guarantee the true people of God victory over the enemy.

The deeper you go into the Word of God and the more challenges God allows into your life, the stronger your faith will become. Every trial in your life is meant to increase and strengthen your faith in God. If you don't have enough faith or you are weak in faith, ask God, and He will give it to you. He will let situations or events that is humanly impossible for you to find the answers to come into your life and test your trust in Him.

Tithing is an area of test for many Christians where God will test us for us to see if we really trust God by the exercise of our faith in Him. The tests and trials that God allows us to go through are lessons to help us understand that no matter what, if anything is important, nothing is ever more important than the God we say we love and trust. God must be first in everything, for He selflessly gave Himself, in the person of the Lord Jesus Christ, as the only perfect sacrifice in that He was made the complete atonement for all sins. As the redeemed of God, we must praise and glorify Him always for all that He has done and is doing for them.

If you do not have any faith, then faith will come by hearing and hearing the Word of God. Every trial in the life of the true child of God is meant to prepare him or her for the battle between good and evil. Be not deceived, my friend, Satan will attack you relentlessly, and so God is dressing you with His armor, including the shield of faith.

> And we know that all things work together for good to them that love God, to them who are the called according to his promise. (Romans 8:28)

Just remember that who the Lord loves, He also chastens.

The Palm Tree Christian

In Psalm 92:12–15, God talks about the righteous man flourishing like the palm tree and how he shall grow like the cedar in Lebanon. The palm tree is a unique tree with unique characteristics. Most palm trees grow straight up and are unbranched. Their leaves grow directly from the tree trunk on thin stems. The child of God is directly connected to Jesus Christ, the true Vine (John 15). God has not given His children any human mediators to go before Him on behalf of the children of God to know what He is saying to them. God has said in the Scriptures to come to Him directly, in Jesus's name, beyond where the veil was which prevented His Old Testament people from going directly to Him——that Christ did remove so that anyone can go directly to God and make their petitions known unto God.

Always looking up toward heaven, the palm tree grows to great heights. Sometimes its height is as tall as 110 feet. We will look at the unique characteristics of this tree so that we can glean life lessons that are Bible-based in that we may be nurtured to produce godly fruits in our living for others to see and go to God to receive forgiveness of their sins and receive eternal life by salvation through Jesus Christ. The true children of God will always, in their hearts and minds, look heavenward to God as their only dependable source for direction to know how they must walk spiritually in this world. It is by faith, with the help of God, that the children of God obey His commandments; and if anyone falls short, Christ the righteous is their strength to get back up and carry onward in the ways of God.

The palm tree grows and flourishes in either dry or wet ground. It can be found in desert or swamp places. Wherever it is planted, it thrives well. Its roots grow deep into the ground to find all the nutrients it needs to develop and flourish. These deep roots also make the tree stand stronger and more resistant to any tempest that may come its way. The life of the children of God must grow in a way that is consistent with whatever God says in His Word they must do and not do.

Every true Christian who knows the voice of their Shepherd can do all things through Christ, who is the source of their strength. The Word of God is the good seed, and when it is planted into the heart of good ground, it grows to great heights and produces the fruit of the Spirit, and the fruitful life of such a person is profitable unto God and his fellow man. As the children of God, we must grow deeper each day by carefully and diligently studying the inexhaustible Word of God. Constant growth means that we constantly seek the light of the fruit-producing Word of God that the Holy Spirit shines into our heart. Without sunlight, the palm tree dies, and so the person who remains in spiritual darkness is spiritually dead without the presence of the Spirit of God. The light of the Word of God is necessary for all to see their way in this world. Without God guiding us as our Shepherd, we would be lost in the darkness of this world.

The life of the children of God must grow in a way that is consistent with whatever God says they are to do and not do. Every true Christian who knows the voice of their Shepherd can do all things through Christ, who is the source of their strength. The Word of God is the good seed, and when it is planted into the heart of good ground, it grows to great heights and produces the fruit of the Spirit, and the fruitful life of such a person is profitable unto God and his fellow man. As the children of God, we must grow deeper each day by carefully and diligently studying the inexhaustible Word of God.

Constant growth means that we constantly seek the light of the fruit-producing Word of God that the Holy Spirit shines into our heart. Without sunlight, the palm tree dies, and so the person who remains in spiritual darkness is dead without God. The light of the Word of God is necessary for all to see their way in this world. Without God guiding us as our Shepherd, we would be lost in the darkness of this world.

The palm tree is known for its many uses. Every part of the tree is useful. It provides shade for the younger and the tenderer and immature plants. It also provides shelter for the passing traveler. As the children of God, we are entrusted to be His ambassadors of the gospel to others who may not know Him as their Savior and Lord.

The palm tree has many other uses which include oils, sugars, syrups, and medicinal therapy. In fact, the palm tree was also used in building constructions and was used in making writing materials. In the same manner of the palm tree's usefulness, all of us who are in Christ are useful to God to be His servant disciples to all those who He will lead into our lives. You may not be the oil, but you may be the sugar that God can use for His glory to be a blessing in someone else's life. While the oil softens and moisturizes, the sugar sweetens. Your genuine smile can be a testimony of the peace of God that is within you so that you become a true witness of God's mercy to a searching sinner seeking rest. Faithfully ask God what He would have you do for His kingdom. It will amaze you what the Lord Jesus can and will do through His willing children disciples in the lives of the unsaved.

The life of the apostle Paul can be used as one of our examples. God transformed him from a persecutor of the Christian church to one who was persecuted for the faith, defending the cause of Christ. God used him in a remarkable and extraordinary way to write two thirds of the New Testament portion of the Bible. As a palm tree Christian, what would you have God do through you? Are we asking Him to show us His ways and the plans that He has for us so that we may know what things we can do for the kingdom? Are we asking God to give us the spirit of humility to serve Him by serving others, whoever they may be? As Christians growing in Christ, we are expected to live Christlike lives so that we are the examples for others to see and follow as Christ has commanded the church to be.

The child of God is to be a faithful witness of His love, with Christlike actions, to his or her brothers and sisters so that all people may know that we are the disciples of Christ, and we know that love shows itself in acts of righteousness, mercy, and compassion to others. John 13:34–35 say,

> A new commandment I give unto you, That ye love one another; as I have loved you, that ye also love one another. By this shall all men know that ye are my disciples, if ye have love one to another.

We also read in 1 Corinthians 10:33,

> Even as I please all men in all things, not seeking my own profit, but the profit of many, that they may be saved.

Seeking the same for others, as Christ has done for us, must be of a selfless spirit, for God selflessly transformed us from what we once were into the image of Himself. We are all saved to be of service to whomever God would have us disciple the gospel of peace. The good news is not for us to keep, but it is for us to share selflessly with all people, irrespective of their position or their station in this life.

Because the palm tree is well rooted in the ground, it can withstand any adverse weather condition. The winds may beat on it violently, but with motions of an unconcerned attitude, it moves in the face of the wind ever so graceful as if it is dancing during the storm. As the children of God, we must be rooted in His Word. Our foundation is God, and our maker is Christ the King of Glory, who had begotten His children in Himself. It is He who preserves His people in the fiery furnaces of afflictions so that there is not even the smell of smoke on them. Though we are troubled on every side in this life, we are not distressed. We are not distressed about life's perplexities because Christ has assured us in His Word that He will never leave nor forsake us, and we are not destroyed even though we are sometimes cast down by fear.

The Bible says we have this treasure in this, our earthen vessels, that the excellency of the power may be of God and not of us (2 Corinthians 4:7–9). Though the just man may fall several times, he rises again because the Lord God picks him up with His right hand. Even though the storms of life may cause God's children to bend in the face of the adversity, they are not broken and destroyed; and when the storms are over, the redeemed of God stand upright for it is they that live upright in all their ways before God survive the adversities of life; and because of the purging process, the upright in spirit are more refined and polished in their character than before the storms came. This is because the true believers in Christ are anchored, steadfast, and unshakeable in Jesus. It is the faithful who shall endure until the end.

The Bible says that we are more than conquerors through Christ Jesus who first loved us (Romans 8:37), and so you and I are more than conquerors as the children of God. Conquerors do not accept defeat, neither do they hesitate regarding the promises of God that He has made concerning who they are, children of the Most High God. They do not waver in the midst of the distresses of life even when things don't look good from the outside. The child of God must stand firm, anchored on the promises of Christ their Savior. No matter what, every child of God must keep on fighting the good fight of faith until the battle is won.

Like David, as a boy and as king of Israel, the child of God needs to know that the Lord is his or her Shepherd and is his or her strength in every battle. The Lord Jesus goes before us in every crisis and quenches the fiery darts of Satan, no matter how relentless the attacks are, for He is our shield and our buckler. God will always work your situation out perfectly no matter how difficult it may be. Don't worry and be not dismayed at the storm that is around you. Only trust God who is in you. He knows what you are going through, and He will bring you through your personal storm. Even though we sometimes are in the shadow of death, God wants us not to fear any evil or fear any fiery dart from the enemy.

David knew that the Lord of hosts was always with him when he faced every enemy that rose up against him because he was always in communion with God through prayer and in the reading of His Word. This attitude of holiness in fellowship with the Lord should be in the children of God. Only trust God who is in you. He knows what you are going through, and He will bring you through your personal storms. Even though we sometimes are in the shadow of death to the point we are despaired of life itself, God wants us not to fear any evil or fear any arrow from the enemy.

Though we may have battle scars, the fight is not over until the battle against any adversity is won, for then we can surely say like David in Psalm 124:2–3,

> If it had not been the Lord who was on our side, when men rose up against us: Then they had swallowed us quick.

If it had not been for the Lord fighting our battles, where would we be? God is a present help in the time of our need—whatever that need may be. Nothing shall be able to separate any of God's children from His love and from His care. Not even the perils of this world and the tribulations of life are able to break emotionally and spiritually the true children of God when Christ is the captain of their ship in life's rough seas. They may bend but not break. Christ will always steer His faithful believers into the port of victory. Only trust Him completely in everything.

The palm tree is always green, regardless of the season. Because it is planted deep in the ground, where food and water are in the soil, its leaves never withers. As the children of God, He wants us to meditate on His Word day and night so that we may grow deeper into the richness and knowledge of who He is and how we are to live according to Word. Thus, by living the Word, we will know the voice of God, our Shepherd, and to a stranger we would not answer.

God's people are the trees that are planted by the life-sustaining streams of His gospel so that they may never wither and die. If we are not watering our spirit with the Word of God like we should, then it would not be long before we dry up and wither away. Being planted in the Word of God does not prevent the storms of life from coming against us, but because we are planted in His Word, God is only able to take us through the storms because of our faith in Him. The true children of God are, thus, referred to as palm tree Christians because of the characteristics of the palm tree.

The true child of God, as he or she matures from a baby Christian to a constant doer of the Word of God, do so in adversity. God grows our faith by allowing situations and circumstances to stretch us according to His Word we say we believe. Because the child of God is anchored in Christ and is fully armored with the armor of God, he or she knows that they are able to withstand and resist the constant bombardment of tricks and acts of deceptions from Satan.

No weapon formed against any of God's children shall be able to prosper, and no tongue shall rise up and have anything against any of the true people of God. Whatever people may say about them that is not truthful does not define who they are as followers of Christ, so please do not pay any attention to what others may say about you. It is a distraction tactic of Satan to get you out of focus from what God said who you are. You are Christ's, a child of the Most High God.

Because the life of every child of God is covered with the blood of Jesus, no devil in hell can destroy him or her unless he or she gives Satan that opportunity to do so. God's children are covered by the impenetrable presence of Jesus Christ Christ, and so the fiery darts of Satan will not prevail against them. The children of God are sealed from within with the grace of God, and they are sealed on the outside with the mercy of God.

As you go through tribulations, just know that God is establishing you. He is making you over into His image. God is making you be a person of faith by allowing situations that are meant to make your faith stronger. Trust in the Lord with all might, your mind soul, and lean not unto your own understanding; but in all your ways acknowledge God—that is, trust Him, and He will direct the paths you are to walk in. God is taking us higher in righteousness and deeper in faith when we trust Him so that our trust in Him is firm and steadfast.

The cedar tree is an impenetrable wood tree. It resists extreme heat. It is also resistant to many botanical diseases, and so Satan's hope is to raise doubt in the heart of God's people. He wants the people of God to believe that God manipulates His faithful followers with enticements to buy their obedience to Him; but despite Satan's attacks, Job trusted in God while he was in the crucible of affliction, and he trusted Him even when those of his household doubted the God of his salvation and they perished. Job's friends wrongly accused him, stating that his sudden condition was the result of some sin, which they assumed he had done. They also falsely advocated God's position on Job's situation.

However, despite how wrong Job was judged by the church in his day, he continually and steadfastly trusted God, knowing that He was his deliverer from the troubles that were in his life. Isn't it funny how some people can come to the wrong conclusion about your life because of what they see on the outside? Some people in the church today behave no different from those back then. They have read what God has said in His Word about the judgment of others, and some of us have been the victims of being falsely judged and falsely accused by other people within and without the church. I thought that the Word of God says that the things written in times past were written for our learning so that we may know the things we are not to do and those things we are to do (Romans 15:4). They are our Bible examples of the lives of others as they were tempted and tried by the circumstances of life

Because of the perils that Job faced, his wife bowed her knees in surrender to Satan, and she perished because she lacked the faith to trust God; and assumedly, she may have blamed God for the loss of Job's earthly possessions. Mrs. Job may have also doubted the fact that God was in control of Job's life during his tests and trials. The same kinds that everyone goes through.

Like Lot's wife, who looked back in greed at the perishing things of this earth, many Christians are themselves looking back into their past and are lusting for the perishables and the dainties of this world that inevitably will be destroyed, according to the Bible, and for sure every unrepentant sinner will also be destroyed by God. No Christian can serve God and serve the material things of this world at the same time. We have to choose one or the other. God wants us to have things, but He does not want the things to have us. Oh, how it would be so much better in our lives if we will just let God do for us those things we cannot do for ourselves. If we would say to God, as the psalmist did in Psalm 86:11, "Teach me thy way, O Lord; I will walk in thy truth."

There are many other accounts of faith in action that are in the Bible that are powerful and compelling examples written by God to encourage us all to depend on Him for our victories in this life, and if we shall overcome in this life, if we endure to the end of the war between good and evil, when Christ will conclude this present world, we shall receive the crown of life for the crosses that we carried, all because of what God did in and for us, when Christ bore our sins on the cross.

Faith, being by itself—that is, without the actions of trusting God—is meaningless. The Bible says in James 2:17, "Even so faith, if it hath not works, is dead being alone." Our faith, my friend, must be with patience for God's answers to our prayers. We must never waver at His promises no matter how the situation is that we are in or how dire the circumstances we are facing are, for if we do, it means that we are operating in the spirits of fear and doubt.

Each one of us is to trust God for His provision of what we do need no matter what that trust out of obedience to the Word of God may cost us. The cost of obedience to God is nothing compared to the cost of sin's wages. Nothing is costlier than not waiting on God in every situation. Anything done in haste, without careful and strategic planning, will lead to disaster.

If you have asked God for His help in an area or assistance in all areas of your life, don't give Him time restraints, for He will not grant the answer if you do not truly trust Him. God looks at the heart of mankind, for with the mouth we make lofty promises to Him, but with the heart, we may believe differently from the things we say. For surely whatever a person thinks, that is what they will eventually live out in practice.

Our faith is made evident by the actions that follow what we say we believe, and our actions will testify how strong or weak our faith is. Faith is a verb, and it acts. If we believe that there is one God, we do well; but also know that devils also believe, and they tremble (James 2:19). Only those who are well rooted in the ways of God can withstand any storm that will try their faith.

Fear is the contrast of faith. Faith lets you rest and trust God in all things, in every situation, knowing that He will take care of you while the perils of life are raging around you. Fear, on the other hand, keeps us up in worry for we trouble ourselves with the things only God can fix, and so worry flourishes where there is doubt. Faith pushes us to release all our troubles from our hands onto the shoulders of God.

Fear paralyzes us from trusting God with the problems of life, and fear paralyzes us from relying on Him with our lives for the answers we are seeking Him for. It is when we exercise our faith to believe God can work out the impossible solutions to our problems that we understand how much we need Him and how good He is to us. The things He has done for us in the past are reminders that He can do it again in every situation. God is the sinner's only hope for true deliverance from sin. Fear drives us away from God into the pit of despair and distress. Worrying about tomorrow does not make the day, which has not yet come, any easier. It just makes today that much harder to live in.

Satan's job is to persecute and torment God's people with fear. His intention is to make us believe that there is no help for our troubles and that our sin is too great for God to forgive and cleanse away; but the Bible says that the Lord will not forsake the redeemed, and He will hear the cry of any of His lost sheep seeking to repent and is seeking the Shepherd's forgiveness for his or her sins. Faith shields us from the fiery darts of the enemy. Fear takes our armor off and makes us vulnerable, wherein we are naked to Satan's lethal blows. Satan is a defeated foe, and every child of God should live life through faith in their Savior's care and not live life in fear of a defeated enemy.

Satan cannot make anyone sin; only we can consent to his temptations and sin. Therefore, let the people of God exercise faith in Him, for it is He who created every human being to be born into this world, and it is He who recreates sinners to be His true and faithful children who are born from above by way of the new spirit man in them. Therefore, what you could not do before in the spirit because you were spiritually dead in sin and separated from God, you could now do by the power of the Holy Spirit, which quickened you to God and by the strength of Christ which He gives to every born-again believer. Have faith in God, and He will take you places and into some daunting situations you have never been before.

8

GOD'S GIFT OF SALVATION

Salvation is God's gift to all who hears and responds to the gospel message of peace, to the deliverance of their souls from being destroyed in the lake of fire by God in the day of judgment. God expressed His indescribable love that while we were yet sinners, Christ died for us (Romans 5:8). The Bible says in Titus 2:11,

> For the grace of God that bringeth salvation hath appeared to all men.

Mankind's deliverance from sin is through Jesus Christ and Jesus Christ alone. There is no salvation in any other source, for there is no other name under heaven, given among men, whereby we are saved (Acts 4:12). There is one God and one mediator between God and mankind—that is, the man Christ Jesus (1 Timothy 2:5). He gave Himself as a ransom for all who will obey the Master's voice calling them out of darkness into His marvelous light. No human being took Jesus's life, but instead, He laid it down by Himself, and He picked it up with the power that God the Father had given Him.

No human being can contribute anything to or do any work that would make him or her a worthy candidate to receive salvation from God, but rather, it is God who seeks out lost sinners so that it is by His grace alone that people are saved, and it is not by any work that they have done. It is a gift from God to everyone that answers the voice of His Spirit speaking to them in their heart.

The apostle Paul states in Philippians 2:12,

> Wherefore, my beloved, as ye have always obeyed, not as in my presence only, but much more in my absence, work out your own salvation with fear and trembling.

Here the apostle Paul is admonishing and teaching the redeemed of God to always be in the study and in meditation with the Word of God. We can only live out that which we have learned from God's Word. The apostle Paul is also saying that our deliverance is done once and that every child of God must continue to study the holy Scriptures to know the truth and to grow into the image and character of Jesus Christ. In other words, we are to become more like the Lord Jesus whom we follow. By beholding, we do become changed into that which we imitate, so we must imitate all the actions and habits of Jesus Christ. The Bible says that the follower of Jesus Christ must let His thinking habits be our thinking habits in every situation, and so this way we become more like Jesus Christ who is the sinner's perfect example of perfect obedience to God and as we, the children of our heavenly Father, become more like Jesus whom God the Father was very pleased with our will that gets things done our way will fade away and God's will which is far mor powerful that all the forces in the universe and beyond will be the only operating power in the lives of His true children. The Bible also says, in 2 Corinthians 3:17–18, as it speaks about the transformation and freedom from the stronghold of Satan that takes place in the lives of all those who behold the Word of God daily,

> Now the Lord is that Spirit: and where the Spirit of the Lord is, there is Liberty. But we all, with open face beholding as in a glass the glory of the Lord, are changed into the same image from glory to glory, even as by the Spirit of the Lord.

Those who refuse to look daily into the Word of God and allow Him to transform them into the image of Jesus Christ are at serious risk of backsliding into sin, for the veil of unbelief may not have been totally removed from their heart and their mind. Just as we eat to nourish our bodies to stay in good physical health, the same is true about our spirit man. We must feast upon the Word of God daily to nourish our minds with the things of God so that we are always in good spiritual health to endure the temptations of Satan and fight the good fight of faith.

The life that is sick because of inadequate nourishment will eventually die from that which is preventable, and that is because we refuse to give our bodies the nutrition it really needs. Jesus said, in Luke 22:31–32 that Satan had desired Simon Peter to sift him like wheat in that Peter may be destroyed by the spirits of deception and unbelief, but Jesus said,

> I have prayed for thee, that thy faith fail not: and that when thou art converted, strengthen the brethren.

So as it was with Peter, Satan is desirous of everyone who has received the gift of God to also sift them as wheat; but God will protect His true children from the enemy. Of course, we must trust Him all the way even when things look bad, and so, friend, whatever you and I do, we are to put on the whole armor of God and stand in faith in the Word of God so that our commitment to do all that God says keeps us standing against the relentless attacks of Satan. We cannot throw in the towel or surrender in the fight against this defeated foe. No believer should ever let his or her guard down in the war against this chief demon. Christ, our advocate, encourages us daily to press toward the mark for the prize of the high calling of God in Christ Jesus (Philippians 3:14).

No one should ever take the faithfulness of God for granted. He demands reverence—that is, fear Him with respect to the obedience of His every Word. No one can obey the commandments of God by themselves; they need His help. There are some who are about the letter of the law and not the spirit of the law. They make the law of God to be heavy burdens on many of the flock of God, teaching rather the doctrines of men and not the life-giving and fruit-bearing Word of God.

Keeping the commandments of God can only be done with the help of the Holy Spirit, who dwells inside of every true believer in Jesus Christ. Whatever God says to do, that we do—nothing more and nothing less. Whatever He says not to do, we ought to immediately confess and repent of the sin(s) that we are committing and behold the commandments of God. Christ will help you keep your eyes on Him so that you will not willfully sin. He is our strength in a weak flesh vessel, and the Holy Spirit is our helper to become who God wants us to be.

Repentance is the sincere sorrow for sin, and it must be followed by the turning away from living a sinful life and to obey the commandments of God. Thus, all who receive the gift of salvation are delivered from sin by accepting Jesus Christ as the only Savior there is. The Bible says that mankind should not live by bread alone but that they should live by every Word out of the mouth of God (Luke 4:4).

Salvation from God will cost you nothing. Eternal life from God is a gift made available to every living person, and it is impossible for any of us to repay the debt that Christ paid with His own life. It cost God the shedding of the blood of Jesus Christ, and as stated before, God's law demands that blood must be shed for the remission of the sins of all mankind, for the Bible says in Hebrews 9:22,

> And almost all things are by the law purged with blood; and without the shedding of blood there is no remission.

The salvation of mankind required a perfect sacrifice be made, and that sacrifice was the Lord Jesus Christ. The blood of Jesus is the covenant sign of the New Testament that God Himself has given to us so that all whom He has brought to Himself are passed from death unto life in Christ. The Bible says in John 3:36,

> He that believeth on the Son hath everlasting life: and he that believeth not on the Son shall not see life; but the wrath of God abideth on him.

The Bible also states in John 8:24 that if anyone does not believe that Jesus is God with us——-Emmanuel, who is the living bread from heaven and that without Him as their only hope for a life with God, they shall die in their sins. The "I Am" we find in verse 24 is the Greek words that have the same meaning in the Hebrew words "I Am" found in Exodus 3:14 as God was speaking to Moses. Again, we find the same meaning of the Hebrew and Greek statements made by Jesus in verse 58 of John chapter 8. It is by Jesus alone that salvation is given. It is not found in the wisest of men. Salvation is not found in the goodness of any man. There is no earthly spiritual leader outside of Christ, nor is there written in any of the writings of any other religion the offer of eternal life through Christ.

The Bible is the only book that describes mankind to be sinners and that they indeed need a Savior to save them from the penalty of remaining in disobedience to the entire counsel of God's Word. It is God who will judge all those who refuse salvation from Him. Everything that remain affected and blemished with sin, including Satan and his followers, will be destroyed.

Many of the writings of the other religions' spiritual leaders are messages that do not offer the seeker of rest any promise of true and lasting peace with God. It is God who showed me the way to true peace in Jesus Christ and that He was the only atonement for my sins. I could not find what my soul was searching for in any of the other religions that I tried. Searching for the meaning of life in another source apart from God is fruitless, and according to the Bible, there is no other savior besides Christ that can save any human being from his or her sins.

Salvation is personal, and it is a personal gift from Almighty God to anyone who hears and believes His gospel. Jesus said in John 14:6,

> I am the way, the truth, and the life: and no man cometh unto the Father, but by me.

Jesus is also teaching in verses 6 and 7 of the same chapter that if anyone says they believe in God, then they must also believe that Jesus and God the Father are one and that He, Jesus, is the eternal God of creation and salvation.

Jesus is the light of the world (John 6:35), and the world is in darkness because of its sin. First John 5:11–12 says,

> And this is the record, that God hath given us eternal life, and eternal life is in his Son. He that hath the Son hath life; and he that hath not the Son of God hath not life.

The Bible consistently reveals in the pages of the New Testament that Jesus Christ is God who manifested Himself in the flesh (in the form of a man) through the virgin birth, and it is only He who can give any person eternal life and rest from a restless life. It is only from Him that any sinner can receive the gift of repentance. Jesus, being in the form of God, thought it not robbery to be equal with God (Philippians 2:6); for whatever God the Father does, Christ also does the same things because He and God the Father are the same yet two distinct persons.

So as the children of God, we do not follow some religious figure who himself is struggling to overcome his sins like every other sinner and who, along with every other human being, needs a savior to redeem him or her from their sin. The only person that the children of God are to follow is Christ the God, who is written about in the Bible. The Bible is the only accurate source of knowing who God is, and it is the only source from which we can know that He is the way and the life-giver to spiritually dead men and women.

Every human being will have to appear at the judgment seat of Christ. The children of God are not going to be judged for the things that they have done wrong for they were forgiven of every sin, and those things are forgotten by God. Wherefore, God will show in the judgment why He justified the redeemed.

The Lord Jesus is the only source of the new life in God. He is the only mediator between God and mankind, advocating the redemption on behalf of every sinner that is called by God. Any other way to find salvation outside of Christ is fruitless, and the pursuit of that fruitless way is unprofitable, for every hopeless pursuit will leave all its passionate followers thirsty and hungry for genuine and meaningful inner transformation.

When anyone is born of God, his or her sin nature is changed from one of disobedience and wickedness to a life that seeks to live right in the presence of God and is obedient to all what God says to do and not do, and these are they that no longer seek to do evil but live a life of obedience and victory in Jesus Christ; whereby, according to the Word of God, the children of God's minds are renewed by His transforming power through careful study and belief in His every Word, for the Bible also states in 2 Corinthians 1:10 that the children of God have been delivered from the penalty of sin, which is death, and is being delivered from the act of sin and who also shall be forever delivered from the presence of sin at Christ's second coming.

The new believers are they who follow Christ by doing all that He says they are to do in His written Word. Their helper is the Holy Spirit. He reveals His truth by helping them to understand what they are to do and how they are to live in this world. In 2 Timothy 2:15, it says,

> Study to shew thyself approved unto God, a workman that needeth not to be ashamed, rightly dividing the word of truth.

Daily study of God's Word will reveal what His will is for each one of us.

Getting the right understanding of the Word of God is received with the help of the Holy Spirit. It is He that teaches, and it is He that gives the reader the understanding of the revealed word. The renewed mind of the redeemed child of God does not think to commit sin, and it does not yield to the temptations of Satan. The mind of the true child of God is fixed on heavenly things, and we are to react to challenges the same way Christ did, for He is our pattern and example for godly living.

The Word of God says in Philippians 2:5,

> Let this mind be in you, which was also in Christ Jesus.

The children of God are to only think on the things that are holy, honest, and true. They are to think on the things that are lovely and that are pure and the things that are of a good report (Philippians 4:8). The new born-again spirit that we have received from God is what makes us who we have now become.

Some Christians at all levels and in all areas of leadership—in the home, in our communities, in our government, and in our churches— have committed grievous sins of indiscretions. These are people who should have known better and should have behaved wisely if they were in constant communion with God about their struggles with temptations. God will help anyone with any struggle to break bad habits and addictions if they would diligently seek and submit to Him every destructive power that is controlling their lives. Many of these same people who have had help from the Lord in times past, in other areas of their lives, when they had given those problems over to Him, now find it difficult, for whatever reason, to submit the other problems to the Lord, and why do we hold back from God those areas of weakness that only He can help us destroy? Why would we not talk to God and seek His Word for guidance and allow His Spirit to teach and to lead us into truth?

Those of us who overcame strongholds of sin and have resisted the devil with the help of God need to be in constant prayer that we do not give any opportunity for the deceptions of the devil to overrun us into sin for we had the sentence of death upon ourselves, that we should not trust ourselves but trust only in God, who raised us from spiritual death (2 Corinthians 1:9), and so the Bible says that God wants us to be in constant prayer about our walk with Him and to be the intercessory prayer warriors for the spiritual weaknesses of others. We know what the Scriptures says—submit yourselves to God; resist the devil, and he will flee from you—but like David, some of us have become careless with Satan, and we have wondered out of fellowship with God, and that door of opportunity allows Satan the opening he needs to lead the spiritually weak into sin.

Satan will always tempt us to sin in any area he thinks we might be weak in, and if we are not in one accord with God in our spiritual walk with Him, because we may not have allowed Him to transform us, Satan capitalizes continually and thoroughly on our weak spiritual condition and relentlessly seeks to steal, kill, and destroy his target. Some of us refuse to fully commit living the Word of God by faithfully doing what it says, and if the Word of God is not impressed into our heart and into our minds because we have slackened off in our study of the Bible and our fellowship with God is weakened, then we have no Word sword and armor protecting us from the tricks and temptations of the enemy; and if we allow other things, no matter what they are, to become more important in our lives than God, then Satan will always be the authority over our lives.

But that should not be our end if we have consented to Satan's temptation, for God is He who is merciful to give mankind space to repent and time to recover from the injuries that sin causes. God will help us heal from the wounds we received when we strayed from the presence of the Good Shepherd so that we can start living life His way with His help. There is plenty, an inexhaustible amount, of forgiveness from God for He is not only merciful, but He is also gracious to cleanse away all our sins that we did confess and repented to Him.

Christ the righteous, when we sincerely repent, will stand in as our representative and point out in the courts of accusations and condemnation that His blood is sufficient to cleanse us from all sin. We just need to allow God to completely heal and change us from living as sinful people to people as becoming saints.

We are to be watchful and stay soberminded.

Some married Christians have defiled the marriage bed in moments of temptations, which has damaged the covenantal relationship and the vow they have made between them and God and between them and their spouse. If any of us is considering the temptation of adultery because things are not going that well in our marriages, please do not do foolishly and fall for Satan's temptation. God can see what is done in secret, and He can see our thoughts.

Such unfortunate tragedies have, in many cases, severely bruised the trust between husband and wife and have led to many divorces among Christians in the church of God. If we have been hurt by the sin of our spouse, then we are to pray and ask God for the strength to forgive the other person and not we, ourselves, in turn, commit the same sin so that we destroy what God had made to be——one flesh. The wrongdoer must diligently seek God to repent and ask Him for His forgiveness of his or her sin. That person must understand the hurt that they may have caused members of the family, but as God has forgiven us of our sins, so are we to forgive others of their sins against us (Matthew 6 and Luke 11).

Being sinned against is hard, but living with unforgiveness is more difficult and destructive. Having sinned is hard, but living with the guilt of the sin that you have committed and believing that God will never forgive you is more difficult and is destructive. We are to behold the wholesome behavior that is from God by harkening unto His every Word.

We, the people of God, cannot for one moment become slack in our sobriety and watchfulness of how we ought to live—morally and ethically—before God and before others. Never test the edges of temptation and the edges of sin, whatever sin that may be. This is not just for married people, but it is for everyone, including those who are living together as though they are married. Know that God forbids such relationships, and He calls it the sin of fornication. God will always trouble us in our spirits of any sin that we are doing; those things that God forbids us from practicing, we must turn away from immediately and go and confess and sincerely repent of that or those sins to God.

God has said in His Word that we are to flee fornication. His Word also tells us what sin is and what evil looks like, and so any person who commits fornication and/or adultery has defiled their body and has sinned against God. Our bodies are to be the temple of the Holy Spirit, and it is not our own to do whatever pleases us; it belongs to God (1 Corinthians 7:18–19). This admonition is for all of us who may be struggling with any type of sin. We are not to kid ourselves regarding the power of temptation. When we disarm ourselves from the spiritual armor of God, our flesh will lead us into polluting ourselves with sin by breaking the commandments of God.

Anyone who practice fornication and those who commit adultery, together with every other practicing sinner, unless we receive the forgiveness of our sins from God after we have confessed and repented everything to Him, shall not enter the kingdom of God (1 Corinthians 6:9–10).

We are completely unprotected and unguarded in the enemy's territory when we flirt with temptations and when we yield to sin, for the flames of sin are hot, and we may be burned beyond recognition. Temptations are enticing to our flesh for they appeal to our senses and to our carnal reasoning, but their consequences are lethal. The Bible says that we are to flee the very appearance of evil. We must always be careful of the types of friendships we forge with other people and who we form alliances with. Many times, our behaviors match the patterns of those we follow. It's okay if married people have single friends, but we have to remember that many times they are in the arena of matchmaking, and we are not.

Married people are already matched by God, and many of us have birthed our own children, and they watch all that we do, so we ought to always regard God and do His Word. If we do not sleep spiritually, then it is more likely we will always be careful not to become careless and sin.

Parents, we are our children's earthly object teachers. We may not realize it, but we are our children's instructors on how we treat each other in the classroom of the marriage relationship. Do not allow Satan to tempt you with the grass that may appear greener on the other side of the marriage fence. It might just be artificial turf. Remember, we are not to covet what belongs to other people. We must avoid temptations at all costs so that we do not sin against God and sow seeds of corruption and destruction into our body and our lives; and if we were to take the time to water and nourish the garden of marriage that God has given us with love, forgiveness, and understanding, our relationship as husbands and wives will grow, and it will become greener with godliness.

Just because we may have moments of disagreements with our spouse does not mean we should find comfort in the arms of another, nor should we allow our minds to wander elsewhere where it does not belong. It's moments of deliberate vulnerabilities that cause damages that are difficult to rebuild. We may be forgiven by our spouse, but that's not always a guarantee that that person will choose to forgive.

Choosing not to forgive someone puts us in serious jeopardy of not being forgiven by God when we sin, but God will always forgive the sins of anyone whom He has led to repent. However, they may have to endure the consequences of their actions, not bear the reminder from others of what they have done wrong. Remember Brother David with the wife of Uriah the Hittite. His children did foolishly before the Lord, and so sometimes our sin also affects our children with generational curses that are not easy to break..

I know all too well of generational curses that plagued my family for decades. These strongholds can be destroyed with the weapons of God's Word. Everyone in your home has to turn away from sinful activities in their lives. The entire family has commit themselves to a season of fasting and praying. Everyone in the home has to be on board with this very serious matter, You have approach this matter with the utmost seriousness. You cannot bow to demons running your home . You have to take full control of the situation. And when you do these things you will be successful in making your home demon free. Satan is not going to leave quietly . He and his cohorts are going to put up fierce resistance, but you cannot give up on rooting out this devil and his imps out of your home because they are resisting your efforts. You have to keep on praying and seeking God for His help.

After you are successful in getting this prince of darkness out of your home, every portal has to be guarded. You have, with the help of God, guard your home from Satan's attempts to return. You have watch the things that come out of your mouth, Your words can be the opportunity opening that Satan needs to forcefully return into your home with demons much more wicked than the last set. No one in your home can be engaged in any sinful activities.

The entire family has to immerse themselves in the Word of God as a way of life. You have to be careful about the things you watch on television, the books you read, and the songs you listen to. Everyone in the home needs to be very careful of the people that come into your home and you must be vigilant of keeping your home free of any opportunity for Satan to return.

Almost all of David's children did evil In the sight of God . You must be vigilant in keeping your home free of any opportunity for Satan to return. David's Sons desecrated the temple of God as kings when they ruled Israel. They were engaged in animal and human sacrifices. They also turned the house of God into brothels where they were engaged in sexual orgies. The brought the gods of the surrounding nations which were Israel's enemies and built high places in the temple to worship their idols.

Sometimes we create our own storms; wherefore, we are unable to predict what the catastrophic aftermath would look like. If you are a single parent, then God is your coparent. He is your head of household. Let Him guide you through all the decisions you need to make. A matter of fact, Christ should be the head of every home regardless of our marital status. If God is leading the way, how can we go wrong?

The new spirit that a person receives from God is always at enmity with his or her fleshly nature. It is our feelings that get us in trouble. Trusting our own feelings in any situation makes us vulnerable to the deceptions and seductions of Satan. If any of us are having thoughts and feelings that are not pure and holy, we must immediately rebuke them; and after we have done that, we must pray to our heavenly Father about our struggles with sinful thoughts and habits and allow Him to guide us in His Word so that we may break the stronghold that those weaknesses have on our lives (2 Corinthians 10:3–5).

If every Christian is to give themselves continually to the careful study and meditation of the Word of God, then it will be very unlikely that we would stray from the presence of God. The Bible says in 1 Peter 1:23,

> Being born again, not of corruptible seed, but of incorruptible,
> by the Word of God, which liveth and abideth for ever.

That's the Word of God. Yes, it lives and abides forever because its author is He who is from everlasting to everlasting, and He and His Word are the same. God cannot change, and neither does His Word change.

It is God who gives sinners rest from a life of sin, and when the redeemed of God water their spirit man daily with His Word, they will become that peculiar and holy people that He wants them to be. When any of us stops watering our spirit with the water of the Word, that's when we stop growing, and we wither and eventually become disconnected from God. The Bible states, however, that God will always do everything in His holiness to keep us from falling away from His presence.

When God redeems sinners, it is the Holy Spirit who leads them to obey the Word of God. If your conscience troubles you—a nagging feeling in your spirit about an issue in your life—it is the Spirit of God who is speaking to you. God will always let you know in your spirit not to do that which is wrong. He does not want any of His children to be hurt or even be destroyed by sin. God wants us to have and live His abundant life in our living.

The Bible says that God is the one that lets us know, and it is He who confirms in our hearts that we are His children, and so the Bible says,

> The Spirit himself bears witness with our spirit that we are the children of God: And if children, then heirs; heirs of God, and joint-heirs with Christ; if so we suffer with him, that we may be also glorified together. (Romans 8:16–17)

Whosoever calls upon the name of the Lord, the same shall be saved (Romans 10:13); and in verses 14 and 15, the Word of God says,

> How then shall they call on him in whom they have not believed? And how shall they believe in him whom they have not heard? And how shall they hear without a preacher? And how shall they preach, except they are sent? As it is written, how beautiful are the feet of them that the gospel of peace and bring glad tidings of good things!

The gospel of peace is the gospel of grace, and the gospel of grace is the gospel of salvation, which is the good news of eternal life made available, through Christ, to every person that is led by the Spirit of God to confess and repent of all their sins for the Blood of Jesus to cleanse them away. Every true believer in Jesus is made a witness to others of the goodness of God in his or her life. The Bible should be such that it is explained to the unsaved by how we (the children of God) live the Word of God. In other words, our lives must be lived as an open Bible to others for them to read and know who God is so that they too can receive new life from Jesus Christ.

If God has called you to be His chosen vessel in the earth—and you will know in your heart, deep down inside of who you are, if He is indeed calling you—He will not forsake you, for the Bible says in Philippians 1:6,

> Being confident of this very thing, that he which begun a good work in you will see it until the day of Jesus.

Salvation is free, and when we receive it, it covers you with the righteousness of God's overflowing presence in your life, and the person that seeks anything from the Lord shall also find it, by faith; and so if you are looking for a better life in God, different from the one that you now have in bondage to sin, you shall find it in Jesus Christ today.

It is God's will for all whom He has called to continue reading the Scriptures and pray for the understanding that what is read is correctly understood. Allow the Spirit of God to speak to your heart about salvation and your need for the gift of God so that you may escape the second death in the judgment, which shall be the reward to every soul that refuses to repent of their sins. Do not put off from today to tomorrow the invitation for salvation for it can only be done today. Tomorrow means any other time from the present, and so no other time except the present is guaranteed to anyone.

Seek God now by asking the Lord Jesus to have mercy on you. . The Bible says in Matthew 7:7, "Seek, and ye shall find"; for everyone that asks anything of God, in faith, in Jesus's name, the Bible says He will give it to them (John 14:13–14), so that desire that God has placed in your spirit to know who He is, diligently seek Him in His Word and in prayer.

9

WE ARE BAPTIZED INTO CHRIST

In Matthew 28:19–20, Christ commands those whom He has redeemed and are baptized into the truth that is of God to go and teach all people everywhere on this earth (those with religion and those without religion), baptizing them in the name of the Father and of the Son and of the Holy Spirit, teaching them to observe all things whatsoever God has commanded them to preach. This is what Christ has commanded all those who believe the gospel and are made His disciples to be the evidence for others to see what true godly transformation looks like. God's children are His pillars and monuments of inspiration that He uses with the help of the Holy Spirit to lead other people to Himself from spiritual death to spiritual life. The scriptures says in Matthew 5:13 the children of God are made the salt of the earth, and as the disciples of Jesus Christ, we are equipped by God to preach the good news to any and every person without regard to their station and position in life.

That is the main purpose of this book. It is to point you to the source of eternal life, which is Jesus Christ. This book's only purpose is to steer its readers into the Bible, where the real truth is found, not the claims others make of what their definition or their religion say truth is, so please allow the God of redemption and the giver of salvation to give you true rest that is only found in Jesus Christ. The book is not about the religious or doctrinal view of any person or any particular church or any particular denomination, but rather, it is about what God has said in the Bible and the relationship between Jesus Christ (who is the Grace of God) and every sinner.

Water baptism is the symbol that God uses to indicate the actual washing away of our sins that Christ's blood alone is able to do. We are cleansed from all our unrighteousness by the blood of Jesus Christ, and we are washed from the memory of sin and are sanctified by His Word that He speaks to us: His Word is truth. Thus, water baptism symbolizes an outward sign of an inward change. This change is the total born-again experience of your spirit nature that is given to you only by God.

Water baptism, as it is demonstrated and taught in the Bible, is by full immersion into a body of water, symbolizing the total cleansing of the redeemed from all their iniquities and the washing away of all their sins. This symbolism also illustrates the burial of the sin nature of mankind and the bodily resurrection of the new person in Christ, made possible by a new spirit, given to that person by God.

Anyone who has been led by the Spirit of God and has accepted Jesus Christ as their Savior and Lord is buried with Him using the symbol of water baptism, and that person is also raised with Him, through faith, to a new life, in a new direction on the road of life.

God is He that gives new life to every repenting sinner. Only God can give life, and Jesus Christ is the maker of the new life that comes with salvation. He is the only Mediator between God and mankind whose atonement was sufficient to cleanse away every sin. There is supernatural working power in the blood of the Lamb of God, and so God's presence, in the person of the Holy Spirit, is in every new blood-bought, blood-washed person. His Spirit lives and abides on the inside of the redeemed, and we are told in the Bible that this is the operation of God the Father who had also raised Christ from the dead (Colossians 2:12). We also read in the Word of God that as many as are baptized into Christ have put on Christ (Galatians 3:27).

As our example, Jesus was water baptized (Matthew 3:16). Not that He had any sin in Him, but He was baptized as the one who bore the sins of the whole world in His body. This was particularly for all those who would believe in their heart and confess with their mouth that Jesus is Lord. His water baptism was a symbol to us of what takes place spiritually. God did this so that Christ would identify Himself with sinners in their death and burial of their sin nature.

The Bible declares that Jesus is He who spiritually baptizes us with the Holy Ghost and with fire (Matthew 3:11). The Holy Ghost (Holy Spirit) is the Spirit of God that teaches and guides the believer into all truth, and it is Christ that baptizes believers of the gospel by fire, for He is like a refiner's fire, and He is like the fullers' soap (Malachi 3:2–3).

The purifying fire of God are the trials and tribulations of life that He uses to refine the character of every true child of His, and we know that all things work together for good to them that love the Lord and are called according to His purpose (Romans 8:28). It was for this reason that the Israelites were led into a place called the wilderness of Sin (Exodus 16:1–2). This God did so that He can decontaminate their lives from the ungodly ways of the Egyptians that they had adopted. The behaviors and habits that they had learned and practiced for over four hundred years in slavery had contaminated their worship to and fellowship with God.

As we read the entire chapter of Exodus 16, we see the Israelites murmuring and complaining against God about what they did not have. They were so carnal in their thinking that they lusted for everything that God did not intend for them to have. Yet God's called-out people whom He had made a covenant with desired to rather satisfy the lust of their flesh, the lust of their eyes, and the pride of life. The Bible says in 1 Timothy 6:6–8,

> But godliness with contentment is great gain. For we brought nothing into this world, and it is certain we can carry nothing out, and having food and raiment, let us be therewith content.

We are no different today than the Israelites were back then. God is not punishing us when tribulations come into our lives, but rather, He is using the trials to decontaminate us from sinful behaviors and bad habits that had infected our very being when we lived according to our sinful fleshly nature and according to the systems of this world. We are not to confuse the consequences of our sin with the trials that God allows to help shape us into the image and character of Jesus ,;.Christ.

It may be uncomfortable for our flesh to bear the purging, but in the end, we become as pure gold, polished out of the furnace of affliction. It grieves God when we go through tribulation. He does not punish His people because they have sinned, nor does He abandon us to Satan when we have broken any of His commandments. God is always seeking the lost, and He pleads the cause of the guilty. He cannot bear to see His people afflicted even though it is necessary for them to be purified this way from the contaminations of a sinful life. He is with His people always just as He was always with the Israelites throughout their journey when they left the gates of Egypt to the crossing of the Red Sea and into Canaan.

God was with His people as they were led out from the wilderness to the entering into the Promised Land, for the Bible says in Deuteronomy 31:6 regarding the Israelites during their time of affliction and persecution,

> Be strong and of a good courage, fear not, nor be afraid of them: for the Lord thy God, he it is that doth go with thee; he will not fail thee, nor forsake thee.

The challenges that we will go through in this life are but for a moment. They don't last forever. The Bible says in 2 Corinthians 4:17,

> For our light affliction, which is but for a moment, worketh for us a far more exceeding and eternal weight of glory.

What you are going through or that which you will go through is temporary but necessary, for the Bible says that whoever the Lord loves, it is he or she whom He also chastens (Hebrews 12). This is what God has said in His Word. If we understand through divine revelation what God is doing in and through us, we need not be in despair, and we need not worry because God is always in control of every situation we're in from beginning to end.

When we are spiritually baptized, we are renouncing our sin nature by confessing all our sins unto God, repenting, and forsaking all our unrighteousness to Him. As stated previously, everyone who comes to God must first believe that Jesus is the only atonement for their sins. They who are led by the Holy Spirit to hear the gospel must also know that all spiritual roads and all religions do not lead to the God of the holy Scriptures. There is only one way to God, and that way is the Lord Jesus.

As discussed before in a previous chapter, every sinner who is being drawn to God by His Spirit must believe that Jesus died and shed His blood for their sins and that He rose from the dead on the third day as a symbol of that sinner's death, burial, and resurrection from spiritual death unto a new spiritual life. The redeemed deliverance (spiritually) is total and complete at the time when they are born again. Because Christ rose from the grave on the third day, the redeemed of God are also resurrected with Him; and if any die in the hope of the physical resurrection that is to come at Jesus's return, they will behold Him face-to-face on the last day.

Everyone who is truly baptized into Christ is baptized into one body, one truth, and one church. Christ is not divided, and denominationalism is man-made. There is one God, and there is one truth. The redeemed, whether Jew or Gentile, rich or poor—it does not matter, for we are all made free in Christ, and every redeemed person drinks from the Spirit of truth, which is the Spirit of God (1 Corinthians 12:13). They that keep the commandments of God through Christ and have the testimony of Jesus Christ are the remnant people of God, and thus, they are God's true people.

The dragon, which is the devil, is always seeking to make war with the people of God (Revelation 12:17). However, Satan can never penetrate the hedge that seals God's people from being deceived. He will wage a useless war against God's elect but to no avail. There is no spot of sin nor is there any wrinkle of unrighteousness in the garments that were made clean by the blood of Christ of them which follow the Lamb wherever He goes. That's why Jesus said in Matthew 16:24,

> If any man will come after me, let him deny himself, and take
> up his cross, and follow me.

We must deny self, wherein we must humble ourselves before God and allow Christ to exalt us in due time. As a redeemed child of God, Satan is now at war with you; but do not faint, do not be dismayed. If you are in God and He is in you, then He will protect you from the powers and forces of hell as is taught in His Word, and know that His blood covers you, and thus, Satan or his messengers cannot do you any harm or lay anything to the charge of any of God's elect. He may afflict you in the flesh only with the permission from God, but he cannot touch your soul. Count it all joy when Satan is attacking you, for God is with you all the way through to the very end. It is God that justifies all His blood-bought, blood-covered, sanctified children. If you are troubled about anything, seek God in prayer and seek Him in His Word and He will answer you.

Every convert to Christ needs to know that we who are called by God and that are chosen to be His people have been granted on behalf of Christ the peace of God, and if the chosen of God faint not because of the light afflictions that He allowed to happen to them, they shall not only reign with Christ in heavenly places but shall also suffer persecution in this life for the cause of the gospel.

Philippians 1:28–29 says,

> And in nothing terrified by your adversaries: which is to them
> an evident token of perdition, but to you of salvation, and that of
> God. For unto you it is given in the behalf of Christ, not only to
> believe on him, but also to suffer for his sake.

For the cause of Christ, God's children are hated by other people who are ignorant of who He is and are ignorant of His Word; but we do, with the love of Christ and the Word that makes for peace, pray for them that persecute the children of God. Matthew 10:22 says,

> And ye shall be hated of all men for my name's sake: but he that endureth to the end shall be saved.

There is no letting up of the attacks from Satan, for he will never give up his fight against you, and so staying connected to Christ is very important. As ambassadors of Jesus Christ and as messengers of His gospel, we must always pray for those who persecute and spitefully use us, even the people that threaten our lives with death. God will take care of all who hate His people without any reason. Those who persecute Christians may not know it, but they too need salvation. They, like we were, are some of the sheep who are lost in sin, and Jesus, the Good Shepherd, wants to redeem them also.

God does not lose any of His sheep who are the redeemed; it is the sheep that go astray from following after its Shepherd and stubbornly wanders into the arms of the enemy. According to the Bible, when Adam sinned and left God and hid himself, all humanity sinned and left God and hid themselves also. The lost are in the wilderness of sin and confusion. God has made His redeemed children to be fishers of men, and having said that, we are never to forget that we were as they are—sinners—but it was because of the grace and mercy of God that He sought us out from the graveyard of sin and delivered and made us alive unto Himself.

Every Christian needs to know that discipleship is a purposeful vocation, and it will cost us something, for we must endure persecution and maybe even death. Jesus warns us in Matthew 24:9–10 about the imminent perils from without and from within the church, for we read,

> Then shall they deliver you up to be afflicted, and shall kill you: and ye shall be hated of all nations for my name's sake, and then shall many be offended, and shall betray one another, and shall hate one another.

Throughout the Bible, God warns His people of what shall befall them in latter times; but God has never forsaken His people, and He will not forsake them during the time of great tribulations; for the true believers of God shall be sealed with the blood of Christ, their Savior. The Bible also says in Matthew 24:13, "But he that shall endure unto the end, the same shall be saved." The cost of wearing Christ is enormous but not as expensive as not having Him as Lord over our lives; and if it is Him whom we profess to follow, then we cannot allow our light of godliness to be hidden under the bushels of being ashamed of who you and I are to God because we are unable to endure the scorn and persecution of carnal-minded people. We cannot want the crown of glory only without experiencing the shame and pain of the cross. Every true believer must run with patience the race that is set before him or her, looking unto Jesus, the author and finisher of his or her faith (Hebrews 12:1–2).

God commands us to pick up and carry our own cross and follow Him, and if we do follow Him, it is through the rough and smooth places of the journey, drinking bitter and sweet waters along the way, but we must refuse to drink the gall that Satan may set before us to bring us into enmity against Jesus Christ. As our Shepherd, Jesus comforts His people with His rod and His staff in the face of evil and in the valley of the shadow of death. It is God's Word that will teach us to trust Him in every situation, and it is His Spirit who will comfort and lead us into the paths of living a pure and godly life. It is God's goodness and His mercy that shall follow us all the days of our lives, whereby we will dwell in the house of the Lord, our God, forever (Psalm 23).

Worshiping God together in fellowship with like-minded believers is necessary for our spiritual growth. If any of you are concerned about where you should worship and you are troubled about being in the right church that teaches the truth of the Bible and that is faithful to the Word of God so that you grow in the truth, earnestly pray and ask God to guide you where you are to worship. The assembly together of God's people in a church that teaches the truth of the Bible is extremely important to Him, and if we have the same mind of Christ, then the teachings we receive must also be important to us.

There are a lot of errors that are intentionally mixed with the Word of God that is being taught by some teachers of the Bible whose purpose is to deceive and mislead the hearers of God's Word, for the Bible says in Matthew 24:11, "And many false prophets shall rise, and shall deceive many." I cannot emphasize it enough that the people of God must always and seriously compare what they have heard preached with what the Word of God, the Bible, says. We must always pray for the Holy Spirit's guidance into the truth of what the Bible is saying to us. Never leave the worship hour with what the preacher or teacher said as the end-all truth. Check out what they said about the Bible in the Bible itself to be sure that the conclusion that they came to is the same conclusion that God is pointing you to.

Eternal life is too important for any person to be lost without it. God has invested too much, and the lives of His people are too important, and they are too precious to allow the forces of darkness to hijack the gospel. Thank God He has not left us without His Word, which must be hidden in our hearts, and He has not left us without a teacher, who is the Holy Spirit. Christ has given us His Spirit, who alone is able to instruct us thoroughly and is able to make us well equipped to do the works of God.

10

THE HOLY SPIRIT AND YOU

The Bible is a spiritual book, and it must be understood spiritually. No human being can understand the Bible without any revelation from God. Human reasoning is unable to comprehend the infinite wisdom of God. Understanding the Word of God is only possible by the teachings of the Holy Spirit. He reveals truth to the diligent Bible reader. The Holy Spirit is the Spirit of God. He is the third person of the Godhead, as noted earlier. He is God in every aspect of who God is. He is not a separate God. The Holy Spirit is not any less or any more than God the Father and God the Son, for He is the same yesterday, today, and forever. He is Alpha and Omega, the beginning and the end. The Holy Spirit has a will, and He has a personality. His nature is such that He is everywhere, omniscient, all-knowing and self-existent, for He is of the Godhead nature of God.

The Word of God is like a treasure hidden from the carnally minded reader, and such cannot understand the Bible unless he or she is given by God faith to believe in Him (Proverbs 25:2). The Holy Spirit uncovers the mystery of the Word of God and reveals its truth to the reader who diligently studies the Bible. He is more than just power; He is the all-intelligent Spirit of God. He is also caring and compassionate. The Holy Spirit is called the Comforter because He comforts all who are in Christ with divine counsel. The counsel that the Holy Spirit gives is that which testifies of Jesus Christ as the Savior of all whom God has called and those whom He has redeemed to Himself. The Holy Spirit is given to them that Christ did make to be that chosen generation, that royal priesthood, that holy nation, and that peculiar people (1 Peter 2:9).

The Holy Spirit is sent to reprove the world of sin and of righteousness and of judgment (John 16:8). The Holy Spirit is the Spirit of truth. He will guide every obedient and faithful believer in Christ into all truth—not some truth but all truth that is of God. He speaks not of Himself, but He speaks to you and me about whatever He hears that is spoken by Christ. No person of the Godhead speaks of Himself or speaks anything different from each other. God is one, and the Godhead message is the same within itself. The Holy Spirit will also show all of God's people things that must come to pass, the perilous and the glorious (John 16:13). If what you hear is not consistent with what you read in the Word of God, rebuke it, for it may be from Satan; and thus, it becomes all the more important for all of us to diligently and consistently study and meditate on God's Word, for it is of a surety that if what was said and taught as though it was the Word of God, whatever is taught that is not written in nor is it supported by the Bible, the words spoken are from the minds of men and from Satan, who is behind such teachings of deception. These false teachers say God had said when He did not say, and for sure, the words that these false teachers speak into the ears of the unsuspecting listener are not of God.

The Holy Spirit will only talk to us and will give us the understanding that is consistent with all that is written in the Bible, and so if the message is inconsistent, then its author is the father of confusion, who wants to deceive you with his lies about God and His Word. Again, the Holy Spirit is the Spirit of truth and not the spirit of lies and confusion. Therefore, if we see confusion and trouble in any church, it may be evident that the spirit of confusion that is operating in that congregation is the spirit of Satan.

How do we try the spirits to see whether they are of God? To answer this question for us, we must look into the Word of God and read where God has given His people guidance to test the spirits to see whether they are from Him or if they are from some other source, and so we read where God says in 1 John 4:1–3,

> Beloved, believe not every spirit, but try the spirits whether they are of God: because many false prophets are gone out into the word. Hereby know ye the Spirit of God: Every spirit that confesseth that Jesus Christ is come in the flesh is of God: And every spirit that confesseth not that Jesus Christ is come is come in the flesh is not of God: and this is that spirit of antichrist, whereof ye have heard that it should come; and even now already is it in the world.

The Spirit that confessed that Christ came in the flesh will also reveal to you the Word of truth in stages as you diligently study what has been written in the Bible by God (John 14:26).

Faithfully continue in fervent prayer, asking God to show, guide, and declare to you the truth of His Word. My friend, as you consistently continue in the Word of God, faith will come, and it will become stronger as you begin to trust God with and in every area of your life. No one should ever regard any of Satan's enticing words sweetened with the sugary phrases of deception. His deceptions are only intended to lead mankind away from knowing who God is when they read the Bible and consider the promises of salvation and eternal life. He wants to destroy anyone who lends their ear and their mind to consider his lies.

Satan is nothing but a serial killer out to destroy every human being by taking their life, using any means necessary to do so. His method of your destruction is such that he first raises doubt in your heart about who God is and raises doubt about the truthfulness of His Word. He will also try to let you believe that you are not forgiven of your sins. This he does in his attempts to have you deny and then reject the Holy Spirit speaking to you so that you may serve sin. He will then try to draw you away to consider other spiritual beliefs and vain philosophies that may appear to make sense but are immeasurable light years apart from the truth which is found only in the holy Scriptures.

Satan knows quite well that the Word of God can and will profoundly change your life for the better. Of course, he does not understand why God would bother to draw you to Himself, for Satan is a spiritual corpse. He has no knowledge of the truth, and it is not in him. Satan is a liar, and he is the father of it. The fact of the matter is that Satan would try to use any and every trick at his disposal to lure you away from God and then enslave you back into sin, but he cannot do so unless you and I give him the opportunity and the consent to enslave us again under his dominion.

Some people claim they speak for God, and they kill those who do not believe what they believe. Regardless of Satan's methods, his devices are meant to eliminate you out of existence. He wants to claim victory over your life. The enemy of your soul is after your mind to rob you of the peace of God that He has given you. It's the peace of God, which passes all understanding, that shall keep your heart and mind through Christ Jesus (Philippians 4:7).

That devil will unsettle your mind and keep it spinning with worry, fear, doubt, anxiety, and discouragement. Things that should not bother you is keeping you up at night in consuming worry—to the brink of losing your mind. Let those things go. Give them all to Jesus. The enemy's devices are also intended to discourage you and others from knowing Christ through the reading, studying, and the meditation of the Scriptures. The devil is a liar.

Every child of God is called to be witnesses of the gospel of Jesus Christ and what He did in their lives. These disciples of Christ are equipped by God with the Holy Spirit to disciple the message of salvation to wherever He commands them to go, and thus, we read,

> And being assembled together with them, commanded them that they should not depart from Jerusalem, but to wait for the Promise of the Father, which, saith he, ye have heard of me. For John truly baptized with water; but you shall be baptized with the Holy Ghost (Holy Spirit) not many days hence. When they therefore, had come together, they asked of him, saying, Lord, will thou at this time restore again the kingdom to Israel?' And he said unto them, It is not for you to know the times or the seasons which the Father hath put in his own power. But ye shall receive power after that the Holy Ghost is come upon you: and ye shall be witnesses to me both in Jerusalem, and in all Judea and Samaria, and to the uttermost part of the earth. (Acts 1:4–8)

So the Holy Spirit is given to empower the people of God with wisdom and understanding so that they may be able to live through this life, resisting every temptation of the devil.

In 1 Corinthians 12, the Bible talks about the different manifestations of the Spirit that are given to every child of God to profit the church. To some is given by God the word of wisdom, to another the word of knowledge, to others faith—very great faith—to others the gift of healing, to others the working of miracles, yet to others the gift of prophecy, to others God gives the gift of the discerning of spirits, to others He gives the gift of speaking in different tongues, and to others God gives the gift of the interpretation of tongues. All these gifts are given to the church by the Spirit of God so that all of God's people can operate in their gifts to grow in Christ as members of His body. We should not try to covet the gifts that God has given to others. We must operate in our gifts to the honor and glory of God.

Each of us must know from God what our spiritual gift is and function in that gift with contentment. We all have our unique spiritual gifts given to us by God so that we may complete the purposes He has made for us to live out in this life. Satan will tempt you, as a child of God, to misuse your spiritual gift or gifts to shame and confuse the church and dishonor God. Prayerfully ask God for the spirit of contentment to be content with the spiritual gifts you have been given and be thankful for what God has blessed you with.

There exists among some Christians a lack of understanding with regard to the use of our spiritual gifts. Some Christians, a minority number, have allowed the spirit of covetousness and the spirit of envy to contaminate the true use of spiritual gifts and their purpose in the church. They have selfishly and greedily merchandised and have used what God has given to benefit the church to profit themselves and not others. It's not about us; it's about the church's benefit even though we receive a blessing with the proper use of the gifts. Whatever gifts God has entrusted to us must be utilized in a way that glorifies Him. The caution to us is this: we must never worship the gift nor the gifted. All praise and worship must only go to God. We cannot be genuine and faithful witnesses of Christ, and we cannot be effective disciples of His gospel if we are weak in faith and we are easily overcome by the temptations of envy. We need to study the Word of God and have the help of the Holy Spirit so that we may understand how we are to live in this world.

The Holy Spirit is He who dwells in the heart of those who have received salvation from God. He is also the gift of God, given to guide you and me into all truth. He resides in the believer forever and never leaves him as long as that person does not turn from following after God and backslide into sin. Even then, the Holy Spirit does not leave anyone who turns back into sin unless we grieve and quench His presence from being in us. It is we who leave the presence of God to go and live in sin again.

We read in Hebrews 6:4–6,

> For it is impossible for those who were once enlightened, and have tasted of the heavenly gift, and were made partakers of the Holy Ghost, And have tasted the good Word of God, and the powers of the world to come, If they shall fall away, to renew them again unto repentance; seeing they crucify the Son of God afresh, and put him to an open shame.

If we reject the Holy Spirit, we are rejecting God. The Holy Spirit is He who convicts us of our sin, and He convicts us about our need to sincerely repent to God from every sin that we have done in His presence;

and so if we reject the Holy Spirit, we are left powerless and open to every attack of Satan.

The Bible says in 2 Corinthians 12:3, "And that no man can say Jesus is Lord, but by the Holy Ghost." The Bible clearly teaches that if a person turns away from the gospel that he has been exposed to through the teaching of the Holy Spirit, wherein he was enlightened about what he must do to be saved—that is, what his response should be to the gift of eternal life from God but has chosen to disregard the truth of God's Word that he has known and decided in his heart he wants to remain an unbeliever—that person has fallen away unto unbelief.

For that person to fall away from the knowledge of what the gospel is and knowing what God has done to redeem mankind from sin may mean that such one has allowed Satan to deceive him or her into unbelief. Also, if a person has been called to God by the Holy Spirit and he or she rejects the Holy Spirit's pleadings to repent of his or her sins and he or she refuses to heed the commands of God, he or she has denied his or herself salvation from Him, through Jesus Christ, and in effect, refuse eternal life with Him. I do believe, from the teachings in the Word of God, that He will do and has done for many all that is in His power to redeem every sinner from the jaws of Satan. Please read Matthew 13 for clarity of Hebrews 6:4–8.

According to the Bible, a person who is converted by God from a spirit of unbelief to know the Lord Jesus as his Lord and personal Savior and then live as a follower of Jesus Christ in all his ways, that person's soul shall be saved from the lake of fire. This born-again believer in Christ walk with God is as a result of the faith that he or she had received from Him. Faith from God is the key that unlocks the message of the gospel so that people may know what they must do to be saved. Without salvation from God, no one can have eternal life. God is not going to force His will on anyone if he or she refuses to receive it. The new spirit that the believer receives from God desires to know and do His Word. When we talk and walk with God, we will begin to speak like Him and walk like Him, speaking life and healing to difficult and dead situations. We usually imitate those we associate ourselves with, and if the Lord Jesus is our friend, then let us be imitators of the character of God in Him, for the redeemed are joined to Him spirit to Holy Spirit.

The people who are transformed by Christ into His image are always convicted in their spirit by the Spirit of God to live a life of right doing as they diligently read and study the Word of God. They believe that God came in the flesh, born into the world by way of a virgin woman. These Christians believe that Christ lived as the example of obedience to the commandments of God and was crucified as the atonement for the sins of all those whom God has quickened and is quickening to Himself, for Jesus Christ is made a quickening Spirit (1 Corinthians 15:45). They believe that Christ rose from the dead on the third day and is in heaven, seated at the right hand of God the Father. This conviction is given to all people who hear the voice of the Holy Spirit given to them by God to validate all that they have heard preached and all that they have read in the Bible are indeed truths from the Word of God.

The Holy Spirit cannot be caught by anyone. No one can give you the Holy Spirit, for He is a gift given directly by God the Father at the time of your born-again experience. He is given to teach and to guide you and me into all truth of the Bible, and thus, we become what God had recreated us to be, and that is to be the image bearer of Himself in our lives.

The Spirit of God is not received by the laying on of hands as is believed by some Christians. That would mean that God uses men as mediums to give someone His Spirit. That is not what the Word of God teaches, and neither is there any such thing found anywhere in the Bible. Every true child of God should stay away from those who teach and practice this untruth. The Holy Spirit is Almighty God. No one can give the power of God to others. He is not some magic potion that is in the possession of some special and privileged persons. The Holy Spirit is the source of the power of God, who is sent by God the Father to be every born-again person's comforter and teacher, helping them to resist Satan.

The Bible clearly teaches in Acts 8:16,

> For as yet he was not fallen upon none of them: only they were baptized in the name of the Lord Jesus.

Some preachers preach and teach the wrong understanding of this scripture. The baptized persons described in the passage were not baptized in the name of the Father and of the Son and of the Holy Ghost as is taught by Jesus in Matthew 28:19,

> Go ye therefore, and teach all nations, baptizing them in the name of the Father, and of the Son, and of the Holy Ghost.

These individuals were only baptized in the name of Jesus, and so in order for them to receive the power of God to live holy lives and to receive understanding from the Word of God, it was a necessary one-time act given to the apostles by God to baptize these new believers in the name of the Holy Ghost by the laying on of hands; and unless Jesus Christ be glorified in any person and they believe in Him, such have not received the Holy Spirit. God nowhere else in the Bible commands the church to baptize after another manner than that of the Matthew chapter 28 commandment. When one is baptized by the instruction Jesus gave to those appointed to perform the baptismal ceremony, the baptized is given the Godhead presence at that moment.

At Jesus's baptism, the Holy Spirit, in the form of a dove, rested upon Him, and God the Father spoke from heaven as the witness in a declaration to us of what had occurred in His baptism. All three eternal persons in the Godhead operate in the redemption of every soul, and so there is no more need for the laying on of hands for the baptizing of the Holy Ghost into that person's life after they have already been baptized, and no one can receive the Holy Spirit in baptism without receiving God the Father and God the Son, for God is one. All three persons of the Godhead are received at the same time when we baptize after the manner Christ has commanded the church to do. The Word of God says that the redeemed are baptized by water and the Spirit.

God is not confused, and neither does He confuse anyone. The Holy Spirit comes and lives on the inside of every true born-again child of God. Just as God the Son was sent by God the Father to die in your place, so also is the Holy Spirit, as mentioned before, sent to us by God the Father in Jesus's name to teach and to guide all of God's faithful children into His truth. It is a mystery how the Godhead exists this way, but it does, and that mystery is not for us to unravel. No human being nor the angels in heaven nor any created thing have the mental capacity to understand the nature of God. Read Isaiah 40:12–18.

Every child of God receives measured amounts of truth from God into his or her life as he or she grows from faith to faith, from milk to meat, and from less understanding to more understanding. God will not give us more than we are able to handle at any point, and no one will see the full power of God operate in his or her life until he or she is in one accord with Him and with his or her fellow brethren. We read in Acts 2:1–4,

> And when the day of Pentecost was fully come, they were all with one accord in one place, and suddenly there came a rushing mighty wind, and it filled all the house where they were sitting, and there appeared unto them cloven tongues like as fire, and it sat upon each of them, and they were all filled with the Holy Ghost, and began to speak with other tongues, as the Spirit gave them utterance.

Here we see the Spirit of God supernaturally and directly empowering the disciples. No one laid hands on them. Christ did tell the disciples that the Father would send the Holy Ghost to do the work of growing and nurturing the believer after He had gone back to into heaven. The Holy Spirit is the presence of God in our lives. We don't catch the Holy Spirit. He is not a thing to be caught. We have to seek Him in the Word of God, but it is God who first has to birth that interest into us. The other tongues spoken of in the passage are other languages of the different ethnic groups of people that were present on the Day of Pentecost. The Holy Spirit gave the disciples supernatural abilities to preach the gospel of Christ to every person in his and her own language. The outpouring of the Spirit of God into the life of the disciples on the Day of Pentecost is an accurate picture that many Christians believe will happen—again, in greater measure in the last days—when God shall pour out His Spirit upon all flesh. The "all flesh" are the true disciples of God. They are the sons and daughters of the faithful people of God who shall prophesy, and the old godly men shall dream dreams, and the godly young men they shall see visions (Joel 2:28).

All that we know and what we understand about our salvation comes to us through the teachings of the Holy Spirit, for He is all-knowing. When He is in us, we know what He wants us to know. Because we are blind spiritually, and our understanding is limited to the things of God, the Holy Spirit gives us wisdom to know, and He opens the eyes of our understanding through revelation to see that God is good and that He desires to save us from destruction. The Holy Spirit helps us to understand that all the ways of God are good and just. He lets us know that God is merciful and that He is gracious, and since the Holy Spirit of God is all-seeing, He knows the secret areas in our lives where we may still be practicing sin, and He knows our struggles, and so He reveals those ungodly habits that need to be cleansed away by the power of God. When we do not know what to do, the Holy Spirit helps us make the complicated fixes after we have confessed and repented of our sins to Christ, whereby we are made whole. The Holy Spirit helps us to hear the voice of God in our spirit so that we may understand what significance the Word of God has for our lives when we read the Bible.

When we are unable to accurately make our request known unto God in prayer because we don't know what we should ask for, the Holy Spirit makes our supplications crystal clear in the throne room of heaven with groanings that cannot be uttered. He intercedes on our behalf with the sincere prayers God impresses us to make, and if we ask for things in lust or with greed in our hearts, God will not give us those things He knows will destroy our relationship and fellowship with Him. Since the Holy Spirit is the Spirit of wisdom, He knows that we would do foolishly with those things we do not know how to effectively manage.

Many of us should be thankful that God did not give into our cries of greed as if they were the cries of need. We may deceive ourselves, but no human being can fool God. He knows the thoughts that are produced in our minds are meant to deceive Him. He knows about those evil thoughts before they get to us, and when the Holy Spirit sees that the intentions of our prayers are deceptive and manipulative, He troubles us in our spirit about what we've done wrong.

God is a discerner of the thoughts and the intents of the heart (Hebrews 4:12). He understands our thoughts from far off, meaning our thoughts before they are conceived in our minds, God knows and understands them. That revelation alone should sober us to think what we need to do as far as humbling ourselves before the Almighty and how we are to behave before Him. God knows exactly what things we have need of, and He gives us only those things that will glorify Him and really bless our lives and the lives of others. Sometimes He has to first teach us lessons on managing bigger blessings so that those things do not manage us. We are never going to receive anything from God without first being polished in the furnace of affliction so that God proves us to be worthy vessels for His precious blessings. God does not want the things he gives us to be the objects of our worship.

God's people are always the recipients of every good and precious thing from Him. Some of us have already received from God what we need, but we are so busy looking, with eyes of envy and with eyes of lust, at the glittery things that others have that we do not appreciate the blessings that He has given us. Ask God to help you see that what you have already received from Him is sufficient for your life at the level of need you're at. Don't worry, God knew you and I before the world was, and so He has our lives perfectly planned out for the entire length of our days. He has measured it and has determined the level of stress you and I are able to handle. You and I are uniquely created by God to handle the stresses of life by having the peace of God and being focused on knowing that He is in control, as the Scriptures have said, of everything that is happening in and around us. The events of our lives (all that will happen and when they will occur) are marked on the eternal calendar of God. There isn't a thing that God does not know about that happens in the universe and beyond.

None of us is ever alone in situations and matters that occur in our lives, for God is actively always with us in the person of the Holy Spirit. You and I must stay connected to Him by listening to His voice and doing everything His way. Do His Word (every detail), and He'll do the rest. We must trust God by letting Him lead the entire way in our lives. He will only give you and me enough light to take the next step. Step by step, the Spirit of God guides you and me along the journey of life. His Word is a lamp unto the feet and a light in the paths He has made for His true children to walk in (Psalm 119:105), and the Scriptures says in Matthew 6 we are not to worry about the needs of tomorrow because God said in His Word He has that taken care of also. Let God know, with a heart of contentment, that you are thankful for what you have. A thankful and contented heart is great gain to us, and such is that which glorifies God and stretches Him to make more deposits of His goodness into our lives.

Ask God to help you to use, in a God-glorifying way, the blessings He has given you. It will surprise you to know that what you have, which is His presence in your life, is worth more than any precious thing found on earth. God wants you to appreciate, with thankfulness, the things He has done for you. We all need to allow God to open our eyes to see the things we have are indeed gifts from Him that matches our uniqueness, designed by the Creator Himself. Just as we all are made differently by God, so also are we given our own gifts by Him to be executed differently from others. It is the Holy Spirit that teaches us how to use our gifts, and we must listen to Him.

No one who receives the understanding of the Word of God and comes to know its truth does so by academic intellectualism. The unsaved person cannot understand the Word of God unless God is operating in their spirit to quicken him or her to make them spiritually alive. Without faith, it is impossible to please God, and all unsaved men and women have no faith to trust God because they are dead in trespasses and sin (Ephesians 2:1) and are not spiritually aware of who Jesus is in that He is the only way to receive salvation from God. No one can redeem himself or herself from a sinful life except Christ the Redeemer does it.

Every soul God quickens is by Jesus Christ. He was made a quickening (life-giving) spirit (1 Corinthians 15:45). All spiritual things are spiritually discerned. The Bible says in 1 Corinthians 2:13–14,

> Which things also we speak, not in the words which man's wisdom teacheth, but which the Holy Ghost teacheth; comparing spiritual things with spiritual. But the natural man receiveth not the things of the Spirit of God: for they are foolishness unto him: neither can he know them, because they are spiritually discerned.

God does not speak through spiritually dead people, for such must first be born again by God to spiritual life, and so the Word of God is foolishness to every unbeliever. Without the Holy Spirit, no man can understand God and know Him in His Word.

Doubt is a spirit, and it is a spirit of the devil. Satan uses doubt to create in the minds of people ambivalences about God and the Bible, and when anyone receives the Word of God, Satan tries to choke it out of them with the spirits of doubt and unbelief. If he can get you to doubt the Word of God so that you may not know Christ, then he has succeeded in discouraging you from receiving salvation; but God commands us to rebuke that spirit immediately and continue in the study and the meditation of His Word with much prayer. Friend, do not lend your mind to evaluate the lies of Satan. Let your mind stay on God and God alone so that you do not defile yourself with thoughts to commit sin.

The Bible says in John 8:31–32, 36,

> Then said Jesus to those Jews which believed on him, If ye continue in my word, then are ye my disciples; indeed, And ye shall know the truth, and the truth shall make you free. If the Son therefore shall make you free, ye shall be free indeed.

You shall be free from all fear, free from doubt, and free from the cares of this world if you would trust in the Lord with all that is within you and magnify His name and exalt His presence in your life. Let your lips praise Him, and let your heart worship and magnify who He is to you. Let your life be an instrument of praise to God. Do not focus on the problems that you are in, for if you give attention to the cares of this world and to the challenges that you are facing, they will control you.

When our focus is on anything else besides God, then His power cannot operate in our lives to bring us to victory. You and I must release our control of everything to Him. So let the praise of God continually be in our mouth, for out of the abundance of a heart that is filled with praise to God, the mouth will only speak of such in worship to Him. Keep your heart with all diligence in studying the Word of God, for out of it are the issues of life manifested (Proverbs 4). Even though we are not insulated from tribulations, God is with us when our faith is tested by the trials of life.

The Word of God says in 2 Timothy 1:7,

> For God has not given us the spirit of fear; but of power, and of love and of a sound mind.

If any of us lack the wisdom to know God's truth and to differentiate His truth from the enemy's bible of errors, let us ask the Lord, and He will give it to us liberally (James 1:5).

The things that God has for us—love, peace, joy, patience, kindness, and the like—are more of value than anything that are of this world, and they are more precious than any of earth's contents. Having the opportunity to know Jesus and to be given the gift of eternal life are more precious than any earthly thing. That's why God commands us to come out of the world system (Revelation 18:4). He is not saying that we go and isolate ourselves in some desolate place, but what God is saying to us is that we are not to do and think like the world does because the world systems do not regard God nor the Bible. Its concept of who God is and its disobedience to His commandments are not consistent with the teachings of the Bible. The world is the environment where lawlessness and sin are practiced and God is disregarded. The world puts God last in everything—if they acknowledge Him at all.

The world is offended when God is mentioned in any setting. The world labels Christians as being judgmental of what it does. Some Christians may be that way, but that I'm sure this is a small minority. However, no Christian should ever be ashamed of the gospel of Jesus Christ in any setting, for it is the power of God unto salvation to everyone that believes (Romans 1:16).

The mindset of some people is such that earthly pursuits are more important than knowing Jesus Christ as Savior and Lord. Oh yes, some people who do not acknowledge God nor believe anything the Bible says to do—feed the poor, take care of the sick, and take care of their families—and they may observe the law of the land, but is that good enough? Are our good deeds and good works enough to take the place of what God says we are to do?

I have found from my experience of living in the world that mankind, in general, is always looking beyond themselves to some higher power, besides the God of the Bible, for guidance and for answers to life's complex questions. If mankind believes that they are in control of their lives, then they do what is right in their eyes, but that is precisely what God has said in the Bible about people who deny that there is a God (Romans 1). God knows infinitely more about us and our nature than we could ever know and understand anything about ourselves. He is the one that made us, and even though we may think or believe otherwise, we were created by God to serve Him. It is the Holy Spirit that breathes into our spirit the knowledge of God.

If we are God's true children, then we did not come out from ungodly living on our own. It was God, through His Spirit, who got hold of us and wrestled us from the hands of Satan. God separated us from the attachment that we had to sin. That's why God asks us to pray for others whose ways of living are contrary to what His Word teaches because they too need God to extract them from the prison of sin. Some Christians live with family members who are still not saved, and as the disciples of God and messengers of His gospel, we should have a burden to win them as well to Christ, and so we have the work of discipleship to do in our home and to be Christ's faithful witnesses to members of our own families. That does not mean that we have to only preach to them with words, but rather, we can also preach to them with the power of the Holy Spirit by being the example of Christlikeness in action.

Some people who should know better have knowingly condoned and/or knowingly participated in deviant practices so that they can have what others have, but such gain will not last, and if any of us are guilty of such behavior, then we too will be judged by God for our evil actions unless we repent. At times, some people, including Christians, believe that to make it in this world, they have to do whatever it takes to get what they want or to get ahead in life, and that includes doing the things that they know are wrong, but that is not what God wants His people to do. God wants His people to be the example of godliness to others. If we indeed have put on Christ and we indeed have the Spirit of God operating in us, then we ought to let our lives be the shining example of right doing so others can see the light of God in us. God never made living His way complicated. We, the church, did. Christians aren't God's help, but rather, He is ours according to Psalm 33 and 46. The church need to do the work it's been assigned to do and let God do His. We all need to trust God and let go of whatever we think is important and let the Spirit of God do His work of transforming us into His image.

The Holy Spirit is called many names in the Word of God because of who He is. In 1 Corinthians 12:7–11, the Bible says that the Holy Spirit is the source of spiritual gifts. He is referred to as the Spirit of Wisdom (Isaiah 11:2). He is the Spirit of Understanding (Isaiah 11:2). He is the Spirit of Counsel, for He counsels us when we are distressed about the things God has under His control, and it is God who shows us how to live a godly and sanctified life in this world (Isaiah 11:2). He is the Spirit of Might (power). He makes us bold and courageous when we are afraid and confused (Isaiah 11:2 and 2 Timothy 1:7). He is the Spirit of Knowledge (Isaiah 11:2). He is the Spirit of the Fear of the Lord (Isaiah 11:2). He is the Spirit of Judgment, for He judges all things righteously (Isaiah 28:6).

The Holy Spirit is the Spirit of the Lord (Micah 2:7), and He is the Spirit of Grace that gives us the spirit that hears God (Zechariah 12:10). He is the Spirit of prayers and appeals to God (Zechariah 12:10). He is the Spirit of God (Matthew 3:16). He is the Spirit of your Father who is in heaven (Matthew 10:20). He is the Spirit of Truth, for He will guide us into all truth and bring all things to our remembrance (John 14:17, 25). He is the Spirit of Jesus Christ, who is in His disciples, for we are made new by way of a born-again spirit by the Spirit of God (Romans 8:9). He is the Spirit of Holiness. I believe the verse is referring to the Holy Spirit of God (Romans 1:4).

He is the Spirit of Life (Romans 8:2). He is the Spirit that gives us utterance to preach (Acts 16:6). He is the Spirit of Adoption, and He is our witness (Romans 8:15). He is the Spirit of the Living God (2 Corinthians 3:3). He is the Spirit of the Son of God (Galatians 4:6). He is the Spirit of Promise (Ephesians 1:13). He is the Spirit of Wisdom (Ephesians 1:17). He is the Spirit of Revelation (Ephesians 1:17). He is the Spirit of Love (2 Timothy 1:7). He is the Spirit of Grace (Hebrews 10:29). He is the Spirit of Glory (1 Peter 4:14), and He is the Spirit of Prophecy, the Spirit of God that knows the beginning and the end, who gives to many of the saints in the church the spirit of prophecy to prophesy the truth from God. It is the Holy Spirit that gives some of the saints the utterance to speak of heavenly things (Revelation 19:10, Joel 2:28, and Acts 2:16–18).

Friend, the Holy Spirit may be speaking right now about the life you are living. God cares about your spiritual condition. He does not want you to perish in the lake of fire. God wants you to have a relationship with Him. Would you stop running from Him? He wants you to cleanse you from all unrighteousness and give you His righteousness. God wants you to be with Him forever.

About the Author

Garfield Cambridge has been a registered nurse for twenty-seven years. He was raised in Brooklyn, New York, but moved to the Baltimore area with his wife and their young children in 1998 after accepting a position as a pediatric intensive care unit nurse at a top hospital in Baltimore, Maryland. He is an elder in his church, which is in Reisterstown, Maryland. He is husband to his wife, Natanya, and together, they are parents to four children. He loves to read books that are of a biblical nature and books on world history. He enjoys sharing his knowledge on a variety of topics with others, but most important of all, he enjoys sharing the gospel of salvation, which is of Jesus Christ, with whomever God would lead into his life. He firmly believes that Jesus Christ is the only source of salvation and eternal life with the God of the Bible—He is the place and the source where all mankind can have peace here on earth with God.

Printed in the USA
CPSIA information can be obtained
at www.ICGtesting.com
CBHW021310020824
12554CB00001B/11